Latinos in American Society and Culture
Mario T. García, Editor

BORDER
CORRESPONDENT

RUBEN SALAZAR

Early 1960s.
Courtesy of Special Collections, University of California, Los Angeles.

BORDER CORRESPONDENT

Selected Writings, 1955-1970

RUBEN SALAZAR

Edited and with an Introduction by
MARIO T. GARCÍA

University of California Press

Berkeley   Los Angeles   London

University of California Press
Berkeley and Los Angeles, California

University of California Press, Ltd.
London, England

First Paperback Printing 1998

Library of Congress Cataloging-in-Publication Data

Salazar, Ruben, 1928–
    Border correspondent : selected writings, 1955–1970 / Ruben
Salazar ; edited and with an introduction by Mario T. García.
        p.   cm. – (Latinos in American society and culture ; 6)
    Includes index.
    ISBN 0-520-21385-8 (pbk : alk. paper)
    1. Mexican-American Border Region.   2. Mexican Americans –
Southwest, New.   3. United States – Relations – Mexico.   4. Mexico –
Relations – United States.   I. García, Mario T.   II. Title.
III. Series.
F787.S18   1995
972'.1–dc20   94-40809
                                                                   CIP

Printed in the United States of America
9   8   7   6   5   4   3   2   1

The paper used in this publication meets the minimum requirements of
American National Standard for Information Sciences—Permanence of Paper
for Printed Library Materials, ANSI Z39.48-1984. ♾

*To two special teachers and role models in El Paso
who taught me about commitment and high standards,
Julius Lowenberg and Brother Amedy Long,
and to my finest role model,
my mother,
Alma García Araiza*

M. T. G.

Corrido De Ruben Salazar

Con infinita tristeza
Mis versos voy a cantar
Y perpetuar la memoria
De Don Ruben Salazar.

Al componer estos versos
Yo les quiero demonstrar
El odio pa los sherifes
Y respeto a Salazar.

El 29 de Agosto
Fecha tan particular
La policia asesino
A Don Ruben Salazar.

La policia y los sherifes
Comiensan a disparar
Pa, dentro del Silver Dollar
Donde estaba Salazar.

Tambien Guillermo Restrepo
Estaba con Salazar
Cuando de fuerza comiensan
Los Chotas a disparar.

Vamos para otro sitio
Dice Guillermo a Ruben
Que nos estan tiroteando
Y yo no se ni por que.

Una granada de gas
De ese que es para llorar
en la cabeza le dio
A Don Ruben Salazar.

Marcha de la moratoria
Que en realidad fue ordenada
Pero los cobardes chotas
La hicieron desordenada.

Los del Canal 34
Todos con mucho pesar
Porque se ha muerto un amigo
Que era Ruben Salazar.

Ya nos vamos al panteon
Ya termine de cantar
Versos que le dedique
A Don Ruben Salazar.

Jesús Sánchez
La Raza, 1970

Contents

List of Articles

III: Foreign Correspondent, 1965–1968

IV: The Chicano Movement, 1969–1970

Acknowledgments

I wish to thank first of all the *Los Angeles Times* for assisting me in this project by providing its file on Ruben Salazar, which included most of his printed articles. For permission to reprint the Salazar articles, I want to thank Judy Colbert and Lupe Salazar at the *Times*. I am grateful to Tom King, the editor of the *Herald-Post*, for permission to reprint Salazar's articles in the *El Paso Herald-Post*, and to Raul Ruiz, publisher of *La Raza*, for permission to reprint the "Corrido de Ruben Salazar" by Jesús Sánchez.

I particularly wish to thank Rupert Garciá for permission to use his memorial poster of Ruben Salazar for the book cover. I also wish to acknowledge Special Collections at the University of California, Los Angeles, Lisa Salazar Johnson, Raul Ruiz, and Miguel Juárez for permission to use the photographs in this book.

Funding support for the initial phases of the project came from the Faculty Research Fund of the University of California, Santa Barbara, Academic Senate. Additional support came from the Center for Chicano Studies at UC Santa Barbara.

For assisting me in organizing the material as well as typing the drafts of the manuscript, I want to thank Sylvia L. López and Jim Viegh of the Department of Chicano Studies at UC Santa Barbara and my research assistants Jeff Garcilazo and Alicia Rodríguez.

I also wish to thank Jim Clark, Edward Dimendberg, Eileen McWilliam, Lynne Withey, Nina D'Andrade, Sheila Berg, and Erika Büky at the University of California Press.

Special thanks go to Lisa Salazar Johnson, the eldest daughter of Ruben Salazar, who graciously allowed me to examine and use her father's personal collection, and to Professor Bill Drummond at the University of California, Berkeley, and Félix Gutíerrez of the Gannett Foundation, who read the manuscript and offered important suggestions concerning my perspectives on Ruben Salazar and on additional Salazar material.

Particular acknowledgments go to Bill Drummond, Bob Gibson, Frank del Olmo, Bill Thomas, Earl Shorris, and Danny Villanueva, who graciously consented to be interviewed about their associations with Ruben Salazar.

As usual, my love and appreciation to Ellen and to my children, Giuliana and Carlo.

Mario T. García
July, 1994
Santa Barbara, California

Introduction

Requiem 29

On August 29, 1970, in East Los Angeles, Chicanos staged the largest antiwar demonstration ever organized in the United States by people of Mexican descent. More than twenty thousand marched in a spirited Chicano moratorium against the Vietnam War. Demonstrators came from all over southern California as well as from other parts of the state and from the Southwest. Although predominantly young, the demonstrators included older Mexican Americans. They protested, like Americans across the country, a war that many of them had initially supported. After years of seeing their young men killing and being killed, Chicanos began to question the reasons for the bloodshed and the U.S. role in the conflict. It was an especially relevant issue for Chicanos since they, like African Americans, were being drafted in numbers disproportionate to their percentage of the total population. And once in the military, they were again being killed in numbers disproportionate to their representation in the armed forces.[1] Hundreds of Chicanos were returning in body bags or seriously maimed, both physically and psychologically. For young Chicanos now further engaged at home in a militant social movement for self-determination and self-identity — the Chicano movement — the Vietnam War represented one more example of the ongoing exploitation of Mexicans in the United States, beginning

---

1. See Ralph Guzmán, "Mexican American Casualties in Vietnam," *La Raza* (1970), Vol. I, no. 1, 12–15.

with the U.S. seizure of half of Mexico's territory—virtually the entire Southwest—in the mid-nineteenth century.

And so they marched and protested that fateful day in August, down Brooklyn and Whittier avenues until they converged on Laguna Park. They arrived by the thousands and were greeted with Mexican music and a festive atmosphere on a filtered sunny/smoggy L.A. day. As the first to arrive sat on the grass, watching the rest of the marchers streaming in, they listened to the entertainment and to the speakers. But apprehension soon began to set in among the crowd, and then intermittent police sirens were heard. Rumors began to spread about a disturbance on Whittier Boulevard: police were roughing up and arresting some of the demonstrators. As the crowd turned to look, they saw the ominous arrival of hundreds of helmeted police—Los Angeles County Sheriff's deputies—who were assembling at one end of the park, some wearing gas masks. Without warning (the Sheriff's Department would later claim provocation on the part of the demonstrators) they moved on the crowd. Pandemonium broke out as the deputies fired tear gas cannisters into the dispersing assembly of men, women, and children. Some of the Chicanos fought back. They pelted the deputies with their own tear gas cannisters and whatever else they could find. The deputies charged into the crowd. Flaying nightsticks found their marks. A young Chicana was struck on the back of her head and fell to the ground. Tears from the gas mingled with blood and streamed down the faces of the demonstrators. Moratorium leaflets were dropped and scattered on the streets.[2]

Out of the park, many Chicanos began to vent their anger and frustration at having their peaceful moratorium violently repressed by the police—another example of the oppression of La Raza. Windows were broken, cars were set on fire, and rocks were thrown. Reinforcement deputies arrived and joined in the beatings. That afternoon, East L.A. became a battleground.[3]

Ruben Salazar, a columnist for the *Los Angeles Times* and the news director of KMEX, the Spanish-language TV station in Los Angeles, covered the moratorium that day. He and his TV crew witnessed much of the disturbance. Later that afternoon, they retired to the Silver Dollar

---

2. On the Chicano moratorium, see special issue of *La Raza* (1970), Vol. I, no. 3. Also see Rodolfo Acuña, *Occupied America: A History of Chicanos*, 3d ed. (New York: Harper-Collins, 1988), 345–350; Oscar Zeta Acosta, *The Revolt of the Cockroach People* (New York: Bantam, 1974; orig. pub. 1973); and the film documentary *Requiem 29* (1970; produced by Moctesuma Esparza and directed by David García).
3. Ibid.

Cafe on Whittier Boulevard to relax and have a beer. According to cameraman Guillermo Restrepo, Salazar believed that he and his crew were being followed after the breakup of the moratorium.[4] Shortly after arriving, they heard a police radio outside the café. Through the window they saw armed deputies in riot gear. The deputies ordered everyone outside back into the café, and without warning, a tear gas projectile blasted through the door. Another cannister — a ten-inch missile — smashed into the café. Two others followed. The deputies would later claim that they had been told that an armed individual was inside the café, but no weapon ever turned up. Behind the café, Salazar's colleagues realized that Salazar was still inside. Their attempts to go back to find him were rebuffed by the deputies. Despite his friends' insistence that Salazar remained in the café, the deputies refused to check inside or to allow anyone to enter. When the deputies finally entered several hours later, Salazar's body was found. One of the projectiles, an inquest later determined, had torn through his head.[5]

Raul Ruiz and Joe Razo of *La Raza* magazine, a Chicano movement publication, happened to find themselves across from the Silver Dollar at the time. At the first signs of a disturbance, both began to photograph the actions of the Sheriff's deputies. Their photographs, later published in both *La Raza* and the *Los Angeles Times,* revealed that one of the deputies fired directly into the café. Ruben Salazar was forty-two at the time of his death. He left a wife and three children.[6]

Two other people died at the moratorium, and sixty-one were injured. More than two hundred were arrested, and property damage reached over $1 million.[7] When news of Salazar's death reached the Chicano community, its anger and hatred toward the police were mixed with great sorrow over the death of a journalist whom many in the community knew and respected. The inquest into his death was televised and lasted sixteen days. According to Los Angeles County Coroner Thomas T. Noguchi, whose office conducted an autopsy of Salazar's body, Salazar had died almost instantly from a "through-and-through

4. Interview with Danny Villanueva, February 8, 1994, by Mario T. García. Also see Edward J. Escobar, "The Dialectics of Repression: The Los Angeles Police Department and the Chicano Movement, 1968–1971," *Journal of American History* 79, no. 4 (March 1993): p. 1503.

5. See *La Raza* (1970), Vol. I, no. 3, and Acuna, *Occupied America*, 345–350.

6. Ibid.; Raul Ruiz, "August 29th & the Death of Ruben Salazar," in program for production of "August 29" produced by the Los Angeles Theatre Center Latino Theatre Lab and directed by José Luis Valenzuela in 1990 on the 20th anniversary of Salazar's death.

7. Ibid.

projectile wound of the left temple area causing massive injury to the brain."[8]

The police, including Deputy Thomas Wilson, who fired the missile, were questioned, as were some of the Chicanos who were at the moratorium. One of the key issues was whether Wilson was acting in accordance with proper procedures when he fired the projectiles. This question, however, was never examined because the Sheriff's Department refused to turn over its training manual, which covered the use of tear gas equipment, and the manual was never subpoenaed by the inquest officer, Norman Pittluck. According to Sheriff Peter Pitchess, "There was absolutely no misconduct on the part of the deputies involved or in the procedures they followed."[9]

Instead the questioning turned into an indictment of the moratorium. The District Attorney's office, which was supposed to remain neutral so as to determine the facts of the case, in fact functioned as defense attorneys for the Sheriff's Department. The moratorium, it was suggested by Pittluck, was an unruly mob determined to do violence. And the Sheriff's deputies, furthermore, were there only to protect the community and restore law and order. The demonstrators were also portrayed as subversives: "Is that Castro's man?" Raul Ruiz was asked about a photograph that showed some of the demonstrators holding a picture of Che Guevara. "Che Guevara," Ruiz responded, "was a great hero to the people of Latin America. He struggled against oppression and injustice." The Chicanos in the court cheered, and the jury ruled by a 4 to 3 vote that Salazar had met death "at the hands of another."[10]

However, District Attorney Evelle Younger concluded that the facts from the inquest did not justify criminal charges against Deputy Wilson or the Sheriff's Department. According to Younger, no criminal intent on the part of Wilson or the other Sheriff's deputies could be determined. Younger further concluded that the split decision by the jury suggested that it would be difficult to convince a trial jury that a crime had been committed. The Department of Justice added insult to injury when it also refused to investigate Salazar's death after requested to do so by twenty-two California state legislators.[11]

The case was closed for the police and the investigating officials but

8. See José Angel de la Vera, "1970 Chicano Moratorium and the Death of Ruben Salazar," in Manuel P. Servin, ed., *An Awakened Minority: Mexican-Americans* (Beverly Hills: Glencoe Press, 1974), 274.

9. Ibid., 281.

10. See *Requiem 29;* de la Vera, "Chicano Moratorium."

11. See de la Vera, "Chicano Moratorium," 279, 281.

not for Chicanos, who held the police guilty of murder. A well-known Chicano attorney and subsequent celebrity, Oscar Zeta Acosta — aka the "Brown Buffalo" — accused authorities of criminal conspiracy to commit political assassination, another vicious example of police state tactics in America with precedents not confined to the Chicano community.[12] Acosta was twice forcibly ejected from the hearing room for protesting the injustice of the hearing. The ejections in turn provoked scuffles in the courtroom between Chicanos and courtroom deputies.[13] Danny Villanueva, who was then station manager of KMEX and Salazar's boss, is perplexed to this day by the lack of prosecution of the officers involved in the Silver Dollar incident. "If there wasn't a conspiracy," he concludes, "it is an incredible set of circumstances."[14]

The protests continued, and the Chicano movement had another martyr. Yet, ironically, and despite the many dangerous assignments he undertook throughout his career, Salazar would never have conceived of himself in this way. Salazar was neither a martyr nor a politico but a hardworking reporter whose career and work needs to be appreciated beyond his tragic death.

Salazar can be seen as a "border correspondent," not only because he himself was literally a product of the U.S.–Mexican border or because he covered the U.S.–Mexican border as a reporter at one point in his career but symbolically as well. Salazar's career was marked by crossing new borders or frontiers. Although there exists a long history of Mexican American journalism in the United States primarily catering to a Mexican American or *mexicano* immigrant population, Salazar was the first journalist of Mexican American background to cross over into mainstream English-language journalism.[15] He was the first Mexican American journalist to work as a reporter for the *Los Angeles Times*. He was the first Mexican American journalist to become an important foreign correspondent. And he was the first Mexican American journalist to have a column in a major American English-language newspaper.

12. See Acosta, *Cockroach People*. For transcripts of the Salazar inquest, see Oscar Zeta Acosta Collection in the California Ethnic and Multicultural Archives (CEMA) in Special Collections at the University of California, Santa Barbara, Library.

13. See de la Vera, "Chicano Moratorium," 278.

14. Villanueva interview.

15. Examples of such nineteenth- and twentieth-century newspapers exist in microfilm. These include *La Prensa* (San Antonio) and *La Opinión* (Los Angeles). Also see my chapter on the Mexican-American journalist Ignacio López, publisher of *El Espectator* in the Pomona Valley of southern California from the 1930s through the 1950s, "Mexican-American Muckraker: Ignacio L. López and *El Espectator*," in Mario T. García, *Mexican Americans: Leadership, Ideology, and Identity, 1930–1960* (New Haven: Yale University Press, 1989), 84–112.

In his short career, ended too soon, Salazar crossed a variety of borders, certainly professional ones and undoubtedly personal ones as well. This work is dedicated to examining Salazar as a professional border crosser — a border correspondent.

Who Was Ruben Salazar?

While little is known about Salazar's early life, we do know some general facts. He was born on March 3, 1928, in Ciudad Juárez — "Juaritos," as the Chicanos on the other side of the border in El Paso called this notorious Mexican border town. When Ruben was eight months old his parents moved across the shallow Rio Grande and settled in El Paso, or "El Chuco," as it was known by the Chicanos and pachucos of the 1940s and 1950s. There Ruben became a naturalized citizen. His father worked at a downtown jewelry store, where he was in charge of the silver department. This job paid well, and apparently the Salazar family enjoyed a middle-class life in El Paso. After graduating from El Paso High School, Salazar served in the U.S. Army in Germany from 1950 to 1952. In the early fifties, as a result of his own ambition and the encouragement of his parents, Salazar became one of the few Mexican Americans to attend college. He chose Texas Western College, later to become the University of Texas at El Paso, where he majored in journalism and wrote a few pieces for *El Burro,* the campus paper. After graduation, he joined the *El Paso Herald-Post,* the first Mexican American reporter for that paper. The editor, Ed Pooley, had been a longtime champion of Mexican Americans, who, because they lacked education and a political voice (even though they represented the majority in El Paso), had few employment opportunities and most often lived in poverty.[16]

Cub Reporter

Salazar's work during his apprenticeship at the *El Paso Herald-Post* is obscured by the lack of byline articles carrying his name. Nevertheless, according to Earl Shorris, who began his career at the *Herald-Post* while Salazar was there, Pooley thought Salazar could do no wrong and considered him to be his best reporter.[17] What can be identified as Salazar's

---

16. See Ruben Salazar résumé in Ruben Salazar File with the *Los Angeles Times.* Interview with Earl Shorris, February 28, 1994, by Mario T. García. On Pooley and the *El Paso Herald-Post,* see García, *Mexican Americans,* 113–141.

17. Shorris interview.

own work confirms his talent as a reporter and provides some fascinating reading, especially a short series of investigative pieces. Assigned to the police and Juárez beats and aware of the poverty and accompanying alienation of many Chicanos in this border city, Salazar volunteered to investigate the Chicano underworld. For one story, "25 Hours in Jail — I Lived in a Chamber of Horrors" (May 9, 1955), Salazar had himself booked on a phony drunk charge in order to experience conditions in the city jail. He was locked in Tank 6 along with several other Chicanos. Salazar reported on the filthy and repulsive conditions of the jail, where the prisoners had easy access to drugs. Under the influence of drugs and alcohol and almost totally unsupervised, the inmates committed violent acts against each other. After one night, Salazar had had enough. "I left the jail," he wrote, "knowing how it feels to live in a hophead Chamber of Horrors."

Shorris recalls that Arturo Islas, who was on the detective staff of the El Paso Police Department, remarked after the story broke that he had seen Salazar in jail but had assumed that Salazar had indeed been arrested for being drunk and therefore had done nothing to secure his release. Shorris further notes that the jail story quickly became the journalistic coup of the decade in El Paso. Before that story the local newspapers had carried very little investigative reporting. According to Shorris, Salazar's story and similar pieces helped change the nature of journalism in El Paso.[18]

In another investigative story (August 17, 1955), on La Nacha, the dope queen of the border, Salazar posed as a drug user. He hired a drug addict known as "Hypo" for $15 to demonstrate a purchase from La Nacha. Accompanying Hypo, Salazar visited La Nacha's home in the barrio and revealed to his readers how easy and open the trade in drugs, including heroin, was in El Paso.

It was just as easy for poor down-and-outs to purchase homemade liquor from one of the several speakeasies in South El Paso, the main barrio. On this story (July 3, 1956), Salazar met Chencha, the queen of the speakeasies, who was famous for her ten-cent shot of the potentially lethal "alky." "It rasped my throat like sandpaper," Salazar wrote. While these early Salazar pieces contain some stereotyping of Chicanos, they are also poignant expressions of the plight of the inhabitants of this Chicano underworld. They achieve an intense social realism, a kind of muckraking social reformism, and they reveal Salazar's willingness to

18. Ibid.

investigate a story even under the most difficult conditions. According to Shorris, these stories made Salazar into something of a hero in El Paso. "Ruben was the best reporter El Paso had ever seen," Shorris concludes.[19]

Like many of the other reporters at the *Herald-Post,* Salazar, according to Shorris, possessed the ambition and the dream of eventually moving on to California, specifically, to the Los Angeles papers.[20] Consequently, sometime in 1956 or 1957, Salazar moved to California, where he first worked for the *Santa Rosa Press Democrat* and a short time later moved on to the *San Francisco News.* After moving to southern California in the late 1950s, Salazar found a position with the *Los Angeles Herald-Express.* In 1959, Salazar got his big break and joined the *Los Angeles Times.* It was with the *Times* that Salazar would mature as a journalist.[21]

The *Los Angeles Times* and Ruben Salazar

While Salazar's death covering the Chicano moratorium led to his appropriation as a martyr by the movement, in fact Salazar was not in any sense a movement follower, much less a leader. He reported the movement and articulated some of its aspirations and frustrations, but he was not a movement activist. Above all Salazar was a reporter, a journalist. He can be understood better not through the Chicano movement or ethnic politics per se but in particular through his association with the *Los Angeles Times* and the dramatic changes that characterized the *Times* during the 1960s.

Since its origins in 1881 as the *Los Angeles Daily Times,* founded by Harrison Gray Otis, the *Los Angeles Times* had been a mediocre, highly partisan Republican newspaper. During its early years, it was noted for its antilabor views. It helped to organize the Merchants and Manufacturers Association, whose goal was to keep Los Angeles a nonunion city. When Otis died in 1917, his son-in-law, Harry Chandler, along with his wife, assumed control of the *Times.* Chandler had worked as both circulation manager and business manager. This first member of what was to become the Chandler dynasty did not make significant changes at the *Times,* which remained a right-wing Republican organ.[22] One critic dismissed the *Times* as "reactionary, self-serving and provincial."[23]

---

19. Ibid.   20. Ibid.   21. Salazar résumé.

22. See Marshall Berges, *The Life and Times of Los Angeles: A Newspaper, a Family, and a City* (New York: Atheneum, 1984), 3–34.

23. Jack R. Hart, *The Information Empire: The Rise of the Los Angeles Times and the Times Mirror Corporation* (Washington, D.C.: University Press of America, 1981), 2.

When Harry Chandler died in 1944, his son, Norman, became publisher. It was Norman Chandler who in the late 1950s began to recognize that the *Times* needed to change and to improve. One historian of the *Times* describes the malaise at the newspaper in these words:

> Measured against the best newspapers of the East and Midwest, it [the *Los Angeles Times*] was arguably a narrow, parochial, self-serving paper, boosting its friends and denouncing its enemies. Narrow in viewpoint and erratic in coverage, its reporting and editing had a distinct smalltown quality.[24]

One of Chandler's first improvements was to appoint Nick Williams managing editor in 1958. Williams also wished to make the *Times* more than a local institution. Chandler instructed Williams to "push." "I want some investigative reporting," he told Williams. "I want reporters to go out there and dig. And above all I want the paper to be fair."[25]

One of Williams's charges was to reconstruct the *Times* into a regional newspaper. "A metropolitan paper could survive," Jack R. Hart observes, "only with a regional identity that followed the readers to the suburbs."[26] To achieve this broader coverage, Williams diminished the role of "beat" coverage, what he called "protective coverage," which involved assigning individual reporters to cover city hall, the police department, the courts, and so on. Television, it was argued, could better cover fast-breaking stories. Instead, Williams assigned reporters to cover stories of greater regional importance, which included Salazar's reports on the U.S.–Mexico border and on the Bracero program in California.[27]

Yet the most significant decision to change the *Times* came when Norman Chandler decided to retire in 1960 and to appoint his son, Otis, who was only thirty-two, publisher. Building on his own sense of competition, developed as a skilled athlete in college, Otis Chandler, Jr., understood that in order for the *Times* to become competitive into the 1960s, it had to recognize significant new developments. First, Los Angeles was no longer just a western town but a huge metropolis in the most populous state in the nation. This demographic shift had created what some observers referred to as a "continental tilt" to the West, in terms of both population and political and cultural influence. Second, Otis recognized that in the age of television, newspapers had to change

24. Berges, *Life and Times*, 73–74.
25. Ibid., 98.
26. Hart, *Information Empire*, 124.
27. Ibid., 124–125.

to compete. Television could more easily report highlights of the news as the *Times* had been doing. "Perceiving the broad outlines of this threat," Berges notes, "Otis reasoned that newspapers of the future would have to provide much more, giving their readers interpretive and analytical stories, plus practical service-type, consumer-oriented features that would prove useful in coping with the increasingly complex challenge of daily life."[28] Otis recognized also that by improving the *Times,* he would be tapping and retaining a ready market of better-educated and more affluent men and women, which in turn would attract advertisers. As Hart says of this strategy, "The whole *Times* revamping was guided by a decision to keep the paper's circulation concentrated in the households of relatively wealthy college grads, nearly 90 percent of whom already subscribed."[29]

A shrewd businessman, Otis Chandler first moved to secure the morning newspaper market. He understood that afternoon newspapers would find it more difficult to compete with the evening TV news. He canceled the *Mirror,* the afternoon suburban newspaper owned by the *Times,* and struck a deal with the rival Hearst paper, the *Herald-Express,* in which the Hearsts agreed to close their morning paper, the *Examiner,* in return for control of the afternoon market. What the Hearsts did not realize was that Chandler had outmaneuvered them to gain control over what would become the more lucrative morning newspaper market.[30]

Bill Thomas, who began his career with the *Mirror* and would become city editor at the *Times* under Otis Chandler, recalls that the cancellation of the *Mirror* allowed the *Times* to merge some of the better reporters and editors of the *Mirror* with the *Times* staff. This merger gave the *Times* the opportunity to reorganize and revitalize its reporting. Besides getting the best people from the *Mirror,* the *Times* got rid of its worst people. "I always felt that the emergence of the *Times* as a serious newspaper on the national scene got its start from two things," Thomas notes. "One was Otis who as a publisher was determined he didn't want to be known as the publisher of one of the worst ten newspapers in the United States. And the other was the merger of the *Times* and the *Mirror.*"[31]

Having eliminated his morning competition, Chandler set out to attract new and more educated and affluent readers and advertisers by

28. Berges, *Life and Times,* 101.
29. Hart, *Information Empire,* 144.
30. Berges, *Life and Times,* 99.
31. Interview with Bill Thomas, October 1, 1993, by Mario T. García.

redefining the *Times*. Instead of being a provincial, limited, Republican newspaper, it was to be a first-class, nonpartisan national and international newspaper. Chandler told Williams, "I want it [the *Times*] to be the number-one newspaper in America."[32]

Chandler instructed Williams to recruit and develop top-flight editors, writers, correspondents, critics, and columnists. He did this by paying salaries and benefits comparable to the largest Eastern-based newspapers and news magazines. Reporters were now recruited not only for their general reporting abilities and for their writing but also for their expertise in particular areas. The *Times* began to emphasize specialized and interpretive reporting in such areas as education and science. In addition, the *Times* expanded its news bureau in Washington, D.C., and its foreign bureaus. Bob Gibson, who was recruited from *Business Week* and became the *Times*'s foreign editor in 1964, observes that the *Times* increased its foreign bureaus from three to fifteen by 1966. Moreover, from 1958 to 1965, the news and editorial budgets of the paper doubled.[33]

Within the span of a few years, the *Times,* through Otis Chandler's commitment to change, had been almost completely transformed. No longer a joke in the world of print journalism, the *Times* had achieved Chandler's goal of prominence based on high-quality reporting and writing. In 1963, *Time* magazine for the first time included the *Los Angeles Times* in its list of the nation's ten best newspapers. And two years later, the *Wall Street Journal* reported, "The [L.A.] *Times* has been converted from a newspaper of dubious reputation to one of the more respected and complete papers in the country. . . . Otis has also beefed up news coverage, both in quality and quantity, and, largely, under his aegis, the paper has shucked its traditional image as a spokesman for archconservatism."[34]

Bill Thomas recalls some of these changes when he became city editor in the mid-1960s. First was the inclusion of new talent, seasoned reporters and editors from other news publications or young, well-educated college graduates who in the 1960s began to see journalism as an exciting profession. This infusion of college graduates into the ranks of working journalists, Thomas notes, was unprecedented. Besides their brightness and energy, they brought new perspectives. Thomas also witnessed and encouraged more aggressiveness in covering the news. Finally, he re-

32. Berges, *Life and Times,* 108.
33. Ibid., 101; Hart, *Information Empire,* 146, 149, 269; interview with Bob Gibson, September 17, 1993, by Mario T. García.
34. Berges, *Life and Times,* 112.

members that the *Times* was profoundly influenced in its news coverage by the significant social changes and tensions of the 1960s.[35]

Among the social changes was a growing awareness by the *Times* of the complex and diversified population of Los Angeles. Thomas claims that even before the Watts riots in 1965, in which African Americans violently reacted to years of poverty and police harassment, the *Times* was beginning to cover the African American community, but clearly the riots forced the *Times* to become more aware of this community. Thomas recalls his attempt to recruit African American journalists, which proved to be no easy task as their numbers were few at that time.[36] In like manner, while the *Times* had paid some attention to the even larger Mexican American community, it was not until the 1968 school "blowouts," when thousands of Chicano students in East Los Angeles walked out of their high schools and junior high schools to protest inferior education, that the *Times* began to do more reporting on the conditions affecting the Chicano community.[37]

All of these significant changes in the *Times* during the 1960s created a space—a border area—for the development of Ruben Salazar as a journalist. His arrival at the *Times* in 1959 coincided with far-reaching changes at the *Times*. Salazar's rise at the newspaper is explained not only by his considerable talent and the political events of the 1960s but also, and perhaps more important, by the transformations inaugurated by Otis Chandler. Salazar was a product of these changes and he, in turn, helped to change the *Times*.

Politics, the Border, and Braceros, 1959–1965

Ironically, Salazar seems not to have been very keen on being assigned to cover Mexican American issues when he first began at the *Times*. City editor Bill Thomas recalls that Salazar's concern was that he would be typed only as a "Mexican" reporter. Thomas believes that Salazar's reaction also involved a certain snobbishness. Nevertheless, as a good reporter, Salazar accepted his assignments and in time became quite committed to the Mexican American community.[38]

During his first period of reporting for the *Times*, between 1959 and 1965, Salazar focused on the concerns of, and protests by, Mexican

35. Thomas interview.
36. Ibid.
37. On the "blowouts," see Carlos Muñoz, Jr., *Youth, Identity, Power: The Chicano Movement* (London: Verso Press, 1989), 64–68.
38. Thomas interview.

Americans in the pre–Chicano movement years. Although these protests were not framed in the militant terms of the later *movimiento*, they revealed the origins of both the problems and the issues to be taken up by the Chicano generation. In writing about these more moderate efforts at social reform by Mexican Americans in the early 1960s, Salazar reflected and influenced the moderate objectives of Mexican American leaders and their faith that the system could work for them. The Chicano generation, by contrast, despaired of the system, for the most part rejected it, and instead looked to alternative political strategies to obtain justice.[39]

Salazar's reporting in the early sixties reveals a growing sense of frustration among Mexican American leaders. Having worked to elect John F. Kennedy to the presidency in 1960 through their organization and participation in the Viva Kennedy Clubs, Mexican Americans expected important concessions, patronage, and programs designed specifically for them. Instead they received only token appointments and meaningless efforts on the part of the Kennedy administration.[40] By 1963, before Kennedy's assassination, Mexican American leaders in Los Angeles were openly criticizing the administration for its poor record concerning Mexican Americans. Salazar reported these complaints in his coverage of a meeting between Mexican American leaders and Vice President Lyndon Johnson during the summer of 1963 (July 29, 1963). The grievances brought to Johnson's attention were varied. They included Mexican American opposition to the bracero program, which since World War II had brought thousands of Mexican contract laborers to work in the fields of California and the Southwest. The program resulted in the dislocation and alienation of many domestic Mexican American farmworkers, while the braceros met with hardship and exploitation.[41]

Other issues taken up with Johnson were the continued segregation of Mexican Americans in low-wage jobs, the lack of educational mobility, extremely low median family incomes, the insensitivity of the schools to the language and cultural backgrounds of Mexican American students, and the pressing problems of newly arrived immigrants from Mexico. The inability to obtain relief and attention from the Kennedy

39. See García, *Mexican Americans*, and Muñoz, *Youth, Identity, Power*.
40. See Mario T. García, *Memories of Chicano History: The Life and Narrative of Bert Corona* (Berkeley, Los Angeles, and London: University of California Press, 1994), 193–231.
41. On the bracero program, see Ernesto Galarza, *Merchants of Labor: The Mexican Bracero Story* (Charlotte and Santa Barbara: McNally & Loftin, 1964).

administration disillusioned many Mexican American leaders with the
Democratic party. As Salazar noted in "Papacitos [bosses] Era Seen on
Way Out" (June 13, 1964), new aggressive Mexican American leadership,
characterized by groups such as the Mexican American Political Association (MAPA), was less willing to tolerate Mexican American Democratic
"papacitos" who only worked to ensure Mexican American support for
the Democratic party. Instead, MAPA and other groups moved toward
a more independent political position.

Besides writing on other aspects of Mexican American politics of the
early 1960s in Los Angeles, such as urban problems and growing tensions between Mexican Americans and African Americans over the division of the meager allotments of federal programs, Salazar devoted considerable attention to the issue of education and its relationship to
Mexican Americans. Education, of course, had always been central to
Mexican American political and community concerns; it was viewed as
the key vehicle for social and economic mobility.[42] However, Mexican
Americans had historically been denied access to greater educational opportunities. Teachers, school administrators, employers, and others believed education was wasted on Mexican American children because of
their "cultural deficiencies" and "intellectual underdevelopment." They
saw the primary value of Mexican Americans as cheap manual labor. As
a result, segregated and inferior "Mexican schools" came to character-
ize the public school system's relationship with the Mexican American
population.[43]

Earlier efforts to deal with these and other problems led Mexican
American leaders to struggle on two fronts: to improve the conditions
of the segregated schools by obtaining more resources for them and to
litigate actively for desegregation of the schools. Some of these struggles
created improvements and legal breakthroughs (for example, the West-
minster case in Orange County in 1946) that threw the weight of federal
law behind the Mexican American contention that segregation on the
basis of race and culture was unconstitutional.[44] By the early 1960s, as
Salazar's reports indicate, Mexican American leaders were becoming
convinced that educational reforms had to take into account the lan-

42. See García, *Mexican Americans*, and Guadalupe San Miguel, Jr., *Let All of Them
Take Heed: Mexican Americans and the Quest for Educational Equality in Texas, 1918–1981*
(Austin: University of Texas Press, 1987).
43. See Mario T. García, *Desert Immigrants: The Mexicans of El Paso, 1880–1920* (New
Haven: Yale University Press, 1981), 110–126, and Gilbert G. González, *Chicano Education
in the Era of Segregation* (Philadelphia: Balch Institute, 1990).
44. See García, *Mexican Americans*, 53–59.

guage and cultural backgrounds of Mexican American children. The inability of the schools to address these issues effectively and positively led to the high dropout or "kick-out" rates of Mexican Americans.

Salazar's articles on the educational concerns of Mexican Americans not only brought attention to this issue but, by his positioning of arguments and quotes, favored a Mexican American perspective. In a piece on dropouts (October 22, 1962), Salazar quoted the educational scholar George R. Borrell, who astutely observed that what was lacking in the earlier debates on the issue of education and Mexican Americans was the Mexican American perspective. "What we need," Salazar quoted Borrell, "is the inclusion of that basic element that has been conspicuously absent in the discussions, the Mexican American himself." And in writing about the plight of Pablo Mendez, a dropout, Salazar noted, "Though he looks like a Mexican, Pablo is not. He's an American, but doesn't think of himself as one, and in many respects is not looked upon as one by non-Mexican-Americans."

In covering important conferences in the Southwest during the early 1960s on the educational needs of Mexican Americans, Salazar reinforced the key theme of educational alienation. This involved frustration over the efforts by the schools to force acculturation on Mexican American children without any sensitivity to Mexican culture and the Spanish language as spoken by Mexican Americans. The answer, as Salazar reported, was effective bilingual and bicultural education, which would include a curriculum that focused on the cultural heritage of Mexican Americans. On September 16, 1963 (Mexican Independence Day), Salazar reported on a Mexican American ad hoc education committee that attacked the Los Angeles Board of Education for ignoring Mexican American problems. "We recognize that an educational philosophy based primarily on the principle of assimilation has proven historically inadequate," the committee asserted. Instead, it suggested an acculturating process that is "basically the acceptance of the plurality of culture as a functional principle. This entails the implementation of both cultures (Mexican and Anglo) to the greatest advantage possible in creating a personality who will find dignity in both."

Specifically, the committee called for the teaching of Spanish at all levels of education, the introduction of Mexican and Latin American literature into the curriculum, and the hiring of bilingual teachers, counselors, and administrators, as well as other reforms that would assist in supporting the retention of Mexican American children in the schools. The failure of the Los Angeles school system, and other school systems in the Southwest, to implement these recommendations led to intense confrontation later in the decade and to the polarization of the issues — as occurred, for example, in the 1968 blowouts in East Los Angeles.

In early 1963, Salazar brought attention to some of the conditions affecting Mexican Americans in Los Angeles in an award-winning six-part series, "Spanish-speaking Angelenos." In this series Salazar focused on the unique history and identity of Mexican Americans. Anticipating the later Chicano movement's search for historical and cultural roots, Salazar recognized that Mexican Americans could not be understood as simply another immigrant ethnic group. Instead, Mexican American identity and culture were rooted in the earlier, pre–U.S. history of California. "Los Angeles has one of the largest Spanish-speaking urban populations in the Western Hemisphere," Salazar wrote (February 24, 1963).

> Most are "Mexicans," but historians tell us this does not accurately describe these people because in many respects they are "indigenous" to Southern California and the Southwest. Though they also help make up what generally is known as California's "Spanish heritage," Spain is not their "mother country." They are so highly heterogeneous they can not be adequately understood by studying the cultures of Spain or Mexico. This [the series] is an attempt to trace where they came from, what they are and where they are going.

It was this history that was responsible for the unique biculturalism of Mexican Americans. As would later Chicano activists and intellectuals, Salazar insisted that Mexican American culture was guaranteed its existence by the Treaty of Guadalupe Hidalgo of 1848, which had ended the U.S.–Mexican War (1846–1848) and had led to the U.S. annexation of the Southwest. American society, according to Salazar, had to understand and appreciate this biculturalism and its value for Mexican Americans. It was the failure to do so, especially by the schools, that had led to the continued marginalization of Mexican Americans. At the same time, Salazar stressed that Mexican Americans themselves had to appreciate their own bicultural backgrounds. Faced with hostility and discrimination, Mexican Americans too often turned their backs on their own cultural legacy. This was wrong, Salazar contended, and until Mexican Americans could be proud of their own identity, little social progress could be achieved.

Other issues that Salazar addressed in this series were Mexican American residential segregation in Los Angeles, what Salazar referred to as the creation of a "Serape Belt," and the lack of political unity among

Mexican American leaders. Challenging the stereotype that all Mexican Americans are marginalized, Salazar called attention to the presence of successful middle-class Mexican Americans who had "made it" and who were committed to uplifting less fortunate Mexican Americans.

Readers responded both positively and negatively to Salazar's series. In a letter to the editor (March 2, 1963), one reader, Manuel Lopez of Los Angeles, wrote that Salazar had done more damage than good and specifically criticized Salazar for employing "barroom dialogue." Other readers believed differently. "This is the first letter I've written to a newspaper," wrote Mrs. Julia Cereceda of Montebello, "but I feel I have to thank Ruben Salazar for the articles he has written. I am glad he works for a newspaper such as *The Times* that allows him to write blunt truth." Salazar was awarded a California State Fair Gold Medal for the best local story to have appeared in California newspapers with a circulation of over one hundred thousand in 1963.

Besides writing on specific Mexican American political and social issues of the early 1960s, Salazar reported on border conditions between the United States and Mexico. The border, of course, has been a factor not only in relations between the two countries but also in relations between the peoples on both sides. Rather than divide people, the border in some instances has brought people together as communities have become intertwined economically and culturally. Unfortunately, since its creation following the U.S.–Mexican War, the border has likewise been a source of political and racial tensions as, for example, during the Mexican Revolution of 1910 and during periods of increased alarm over mass immigration from Mexico. This has resulted in efforts to restrict and/or deport Mexican immigrant workers during the Great Depression of the 1930s, during "Operation Wetback" in 1954, since the 1970s, and more recently in 1994.

In his writings on the border and particularly in a series on Mexican border towns written in 1962, Salazar tended to see border conditions in an optimistic light. Obviously influenced by the Kennedy administration's efforts to improve U.S.–Latin American relations in the wake of the Cuban Revolution of 1959 through the Alliance for Progress, Salazar suggested that life in the Mexican border towns had significantly improved. He applauded, for example, the development of the Border Industrialization Program, which sponsored the relocation of U.S. industrial plants (referred to as *maquiladoras*) to the Mexican side, in order to take advantage of cheaper Mexican labor. In his report on the Ciudad Juárez–El Paso communities (January 10, 1962), Salazar idealistically proposed that El Paso represented a "model of democratic living" for its lack of overt racism toward Mexicans and for the earlier election of Raymond Telles as mayor of El Paso in 1957.[45] In the piece, Salazar expressed a hope for even more improved race relations and revealed his own border background when he wrote,

> The southwest is the area in which the American and Mexican cultures can blend most successfully because the Mexican side and the American side of the southwest are geographically really one. The only thing that divides the nations physically is an easily crossed bridge or a border line.

This rather uncritical view, often belied by inequities between U.S. and Mexican border towns and the disparity of wealth and power between Anglos and Mexican Americans in the United States, reveals Salazar's generally liberal temperament in the early 1960s. Such liberalism, which Salazar never fully moved away from even during the Chicano movement years, was linked to accomplishing reforms through established channels. In the area of foreign policy, this translated into support for international reform programs such as the Alliance for Progress, which by the mid-1960s had been greatly reduced in scope and was replaced by the Johnson administration's counterinsurgency programs to combat popular revolutionary movements, some of which Salazar would later cover as a foreign correspondent for the *Los Angeles Times*. Salazar did report on the particular problems of the Mexican border communities: unplanned growth, burgeoning populations as a result of migration to the border from the interior of Mexico, the lack of water, the widespread availability of drugs, and so on. In an article that appeared on December 9, 1962 (not included here), Salazar noted that precisely because of these problems, a viable radical movement had surfaced in northern Mexico. However, he cast doubt on the movement and suggested that it represented an "anti-American peasant movement."

Another news issue on which Salazar concentrated during his initial assignment with the *Times* was the controversial bracero program. According to Thomas, the *Times*'s focus on this program was indicative of the newspaper's growing social awareness.[46] The bracero program was initiated as an emergency measure during World War II to provide Mexican contract labor for U.S. agriculture and was continued into the 1950s. With the election of Kennedy in 1960, antibracero groups such as the

45. On the election of Telles, see García, *Mexican Americans,* 113–141.
46. Thomas interview.

AFL-CIO, the Catholic church, and Mexican American organizations exerted sufficient pressure to terminate the program by the end of 1964. Opposition focused not on the exploitation of the braceros but on the unfair labor competition that allowed agribusiness to keep wages low for domestic farmworkers (mostly Mexican Americans in the Southwest) and to obstruct unionizing efforts of farmworkers by using braceros as scabs (strikebreakers).

The bracero program also was blamed for the continued poverty of Mexican American farmworkers. Salazar wrote extensively on the ways in which the program helped maintain what Michael Harrington called at the time "the Other America," consisting of the poor, the aged, and the displaced.[47] In his reports, Salazar highlighted the terrible living and working conditions of domestic farmworkers. While he conveyed the arguments of the growers that the lack of domestic workers made it imperative for them to rely on braceros, Salazar at the same time provided a forum for antibracero opponents such as Dr. Ben Yellen of Brawley in the Imperial Valley (November 27, 1962), who for years had waged a one-man crusade against the growers. Salazar quoted Yellen's denunciation of the bracero program:

> This amounts to a government handout to the big farmers, the handout being Mexican labor. You do not see the government importing Mexicans to factories so that the manufacturers can have low labor costs. If the lettuce growers need farm workers, let them pay decent wages and they will get farm workers. But they do not want to pay American wages. They want the cheap labor from Mexico.

During the 1963 fall harvest, Salazar visited a number of bracero camps in the San Joaquin Valley and wrote a series of articles on labor conditions affecting both braceros and domestic farmworkers. These stories resemble the classic accounts of the plight of migrant workers in California during the Great Depression by John Steinbeck and Carey McWilliams.[48] Reporting from Stockton (October 21, 1963), Salazar observed the despair and squalid living conditions of domestic workers trying to find jobs. They rose early in the morning in the hope that they would be selected by the labor contractor and put on a bus for an op-

---

47. Michael Harrington, *The Other America: Poverty in the United States* (Baltimore: Penguin Books, 1963).

48. See John Steinbeck, *The Grapes of Wrath* (New York: Viking Press, 1939), and Carey McWilliams, *Factories in the Fields: The Story of Migratory Farm Labor in California* (Santa Barbara: Peregrine Smith, 1935).

portunity to earn a day's wage. "It's like a mechanized slave market," one labor organizer told Salazar. In Firebaugh the next day, Salazar reported on the apathy he perceived among domestic farmworkers concerning the possibility of a union for farm labor. Here Salazar interviewed a young César Chávez who agreed that there was apathy but was able to put it into perspective. "Let's face it: Most agricultural workers are in the lowest educational level and don't even understand what unionization means. Many are Mexican immigrants who think joining a union could get them in trouble."

While Mexican Americans, including many farmworkers, opposed the bracero program because of its detrimental effects on domestic labor, many felt a pang of guilt as it involved mexicanos like them who had no other recourse for survival than to enter the United States as braceros. "I suppose it's wrong in a way to want the bracero program to end," Juan Contreras told Salazar in Tracy (October 23, 1963). "It means the end of jobs they probably need very much. . . . After all many of us and our parents came from Mexico not too long ago." On January 1, 1965, Salazar wrote about the last braceros to leave California.

While a clear image of Salazar the journalist emerges from his writings of the early 1960s, we know little about his personal life during these first years at the *Times*. By all accounts he maintained his privacy and tried to separate his professional from his family life. In 1959, he met and married Sally Robare, who was from Alhambra, east of Los Angeles. Sally had worked in classifieds at the *Times* but was employed as a department store clerk when she was introduced to Salazar by a mutual friend. After their marriage in 1960, the Salazars lived first in Alhambra and then in Whittier. Three children were born during the 1960s: Lisa Marie, Stephanie Ann, and John Kenneth.[49]

Foreign Correspondent, 1965–1968

After six years of covering predominantly Mexican American issues, Salazar was unexpectedly approached about becoming a foreign correspondent. While the *Times* was implementing its new policies by recruiting veteran foreign correspondents from other newspapers, it was also recruiting from the existing staff. This was necessary, according to the foreign editor, Bob Gibson, to avoid morale problems. Gibson's survey of the city staff reporters to assess potential recruits to the foreign staff brought Salazar to his attention. Gibson did not know Salazar person-

---

49. Salazar résumé; interview with Lisa Salazar Johnson, March 12, 1994, by Mario T. García; and note by Lisa Salazar Johnson to Mario T. García, July 15, 1994.

ally, but he had been impressed by Salazar's balanced reporting on the bracero program. He believed that Salazar possessed the characteristics of a good foreign correspondent: he was a good reporter; he was stable and reliable; and he demonstrated good judgment. Moreover, Gibson saw in Salazar a reporter he could use to expand the *Times*'s coverage of Latin America. At the time, the only *Times* Latin American bureau was in Mexico City. In addition to establishing bureaus in Rio de Janeiro and Buenos Aires, Gibson hoped to increase the *Times*'s coverage of Mexico, and it was there that Gibson expected to use Salazar. However, Gibson did not want to be accused of sending Salazar to Mexico only because he was Mexican American. Gibson's idea was first to allow Salazar to gain experience — to "cut his teeth," in Gibson's words — somewhere else. His plan was to expand the *Times*'s coverage of the growing American military involvement in Vietnam by sending Salazar there as the paper's second reporter.[50]

Before Gibson could carry out his plan, the U.S. military intervention in the Dominican Republic occurred in April 1965, and on short notice he borrowed Salazar from the city bureau to cover this conflict before formally bringing him into the foreign bureau. City editor Bill Thomas recalls that Salazar was quite enthusiastic about this new opportunity. According to Thomas, this was natural for reporters, who hated the idea of becoming stagnant. "Ruben was ambitious," Thomas notes, "so that becoming a foreign correspondent satisfied some of his ambitiousness."[51]

With his Mexican American background and his ability to speak and understand Spanish, Salazar was a good choice to cover the Dominican Republic. Unwilling to tolerate what the Johnson administration considered to be a Marxist-supported military rebellion that threatened, in the administration's view, to lead to another Cuban-style revolution, the United States all but destroyed the Alliance for Progress by resorting to an earlier traditional policy toward Latin America centered on military intervention. Over twenty thousand Marines and other military personnel were sent into the Dominican Republic to install a government more acceptable to the United States. Salazar's reports from the island regrettably echoed the convenient arguments of the State Department that the United States had no choice but to intervene to protect American lives and to protect "democracy" on the Caribbean island. Salazar, like most other mainstream American reporters, subscribed to the government's rationale despite no real evidence to justify the allegation of the threat to

50. Gibson interview.
51. Thomas interview.

American lives or a Marxist uprising. Ironically, it was the conservative faction of the Dominican military, supported by the U.S. invasion, that had curtailed and indeed destroyed what little democracy existed in the Dominican Republic.[52]

Salazar's uncritical reporting of the U.S. invasion, however, was balanced somewhat by an activist approach that at least provided a voice for the so-called rebels in his articles. Rather than wait around with his colleagues in the bar of an American-owned luxury hotel for official U.S. briefings, Salazar got into the streets in the capital, Santo Domingo, and into the provinces. He was thus able to humanize the insurgents whose cause other journalists dismissed by simply referring to them as "Communists."

In covering a rally by supporters of deposed President Juan Bosch (who had been overthrown by the military in 1963) in the town of San Francisco de Macoris (May 31, 1965), Salazar stepped over the journalistic line by becoming a part of the story he was reporting. Prevented from holding the rally, the "constitutionalists" or "rebels" swarmed around Salazar once it became known that he was an American journalist. Unable to speak elsewhere, the people voiced their complaints to Salazar, and when one young woman was arrested by the police, Salazar and his driver followed in their car, only to be pursued in turn by hundreds of protesters who now looked on Salazar as one of them or at least a mediator in the conflict. "By the time we got to Caren St.," Salazar wrote, "six or seven blocks from the plaza, the crowd was growing. . . . I looked back and realized that about 1,000 angry, emotional, hysterical, men, women and children were following us, as we inched our way toward the *fortaleza* [police headquarters]." Prevented from entering the fortaleza, Salazar instructed the people to go back to their homes, and they did.

In his report on the incident, Salazar remained leery of the "rebels," but his article expressed genuine sympathy with their plight and the frustrations of the people whose freedom had been curtailed by a military junta propped up by the United States.

Following his coverage of Santo Domingo, Salazar was approached by Gibson about going to Vietnam. Gibson recalls that Salazar was quite positive about this new assignment. He told Salazar that if he did well there, he might be put in charge of one of the other foreign bureaus. However, Gibson did not specifically mention Mexico City so as not to

---

52. See Piero Gleijeses, *The Dominican Crisis: The 1965 Constitutional Revolt and American Intervention* (Baltimore and London: Johns Hopkins University Press, 1978).

raise Salazar's expectations or cause a morale problem with his current bureau chief in Mexico.[53]

Salazar arrived in South Vietnam in the fall of 1965, as American military intervention in that country accelerated. Salazar spent almost a year covering the military and political aspects of the war. Although many of his stories from Vietnam were on-the-scene accounts of particular military operations or political developments, again Salazar occasionally allowed himself to participate in the events he was covering. While it appears that Salazar, like many other American journalists at this juncture of the war, supported U.S. involvement, in time he expressed in some of his dispatches the misgivings as well as the excitement he felt in covering the war. In perhaps his most poignant story (May 31, 1966), he wrote about the death of PFC Jimmy L. Williams, age nineteen, a young African American soldier. When Williams's body was returned to his family in Wetumpka, Alabama, they were not permitted to bury him in the local all-white cemetery. "He deserved to be buried any place — even in the White House grounds," one of Williams's friends told Salazar. "That he was not permitted to be buried where his parents wanted him to be is going to bother me for a long time." Salazar concluded his piece on the politics of race in the Vietnam War by writing,

> Operation Hardihood, which started May 16, continued Monday. Jimmy Williams' platoon has suffered heavy casualties. All of Williams' buddies killed with him were resting this Memorial Day where their survivors wanted them to be. All but Williams.

According to Gibson, Salazar grew to oppose the war not necessarily for political reasons but because of the tragedy and destruction of war itself. He became more of a pacifist. Salazar's changing views about Vietnam paralleled those of the *Times,* which went from wholehearted support of U.S. involvement to critical support and finally to complete opposition to it.[54] In a 1970 interview, Salazar said of the war, "It was a mistake that we were there."[55]

In the fall of 1966, Salazar left Vietnam and the tragedy that was unfolding there to become the *Times*'s Mexico City bureau chief. This time the entire Salazar family relocated to Mexico City. Salazar liked this assignment because he could be more independent and enjoy the perks of

---

53. Gibson interview.
54. Gibson interview.
55. See videotaped interview with Ruben Salazar by Bob Navarro, May 13, 1970, "The Siesta Is Over," KNXT-TV, Los Angeles. Courtesy of Lisa Salazar Johnson.

being a foreign correspondent. It was also undoubtedly a welcome relief from the jungle war. The assignment put Salazar back in a familiar environment, where he covered events not only in Mexico but also in Central America and the Caribbean, including Cuba. He wrote on the strains within the ruling Partido Institucional Revolucionario (PRI) in Mexico and on the extreme poverty of Honduras, referring to that small country as a "child of another century."[56] He reported on the political discontent within Nicaragua that arose from the authoritarian nature of the ruling Somoza family and the lack of democracy. He interviewed members of the oligarchy in El Salvador but portrayed its members inaccurately—as favorable toward liberal political and economic reforms. In Mexico, Salazar called attention to the continued poverty and marginalization of the various Indian groups—conditions still prevalent in the 1990s. He commented on the problems that the Mexican American actor Anthony Quinn had encountered in his efforts to film *The Children of Sanchez*, the controversial book by the anthropologist Oscar Lewis.

Before Salazar's departure from Mexico at the end of 1968, he witnessed the Mexican government's brutal repression of the student movement in what came to be known as the massacre at Tlatelolco in early October. Since the spring of 1968, Salazar had been keeping the *Times*'s readers informed about the growing and serious student protests in Mexico City against what was widely acknowledged to be an undemocratic and corrupt political system imposed by the PRI. On October 3 Salazar filed his report on the incident, in which the military opened fire on the protesting students. Hundreds died, and many more were arrested and imprisoned. Although informal accounts of the killings recorded hundreds of deaths, Salazar reported the much lower figure announced by the government.[57]

Two weeks after its suppression of the students, the Mexican government hosted the Olympic Games, proudly displaying its attendant symbols of peace and harmony among nations. Salazar was not oblivious to this bitter irony.

Everywhere the visitor goes he is sure to see the symbolic white peace dove. It is on banners, painted on windows and placed on car stickers. A close look shows that on some of the snow-white doves a bleeding heart has been painted in red.   *(October 13, 1968)*

56. On Honduras, see Salazar report, "Honduras Still 'Child of Another Century,'" *Los Angeles Times*, December 22, 1966.

57. On the Tlatelolco massacre, see Elena Poniatowska, *Massacre in Mexico* (Columbia and London: University of Missouri Press, 1993); originally published in Spanish as *La Noche de Tlatelolco* (Mexico City: Ediciones Era, 1971).

After almost four years of covering wars, poverty, and social unrest in the Third World, Salazar prepared to come home. He had been asked to return to Los Angeles, and this time his beat would be a more personal one, on his own turf involving his own people.

Covering the Chicano Movement, 1969–1970

Salazar was recalled to Los Angeles to cover the accelerating tensions in the Chicano communities in Los Angeles and throughout the Southwest. According to Bob Gibson, the city staff was under intense pressure to expand its coverage of Chicano issues following the 1968 East Los Angeles school blowouts. The blowouts had represented the clarion call for the commencement of the Chicano movement in Los Angeles. For two weeks in early March 1968, several thousand Mexican American high school and junior high school students had walked out of their schools to protest what they believed to be inferior education and discriminatory treatment of Mexican Americans in the Los Angeles public school system. The schools affected, in predominantly Mexican American East Los Angeles, included Wilson, Belmont, Garfield, Roosevelt, and Lincoln. The blowouts had appeared to be spontaneous but in fact had been discussed and planned for weeks. The students were supported and encouraged by members of growing Chicano student groups such as the United Mexican American Students (UMAS) of California State College, Los Angeles, as well as new and militant community organizations such as the Brown Berets. Some teachers, most notably Sal Castro at Lincoln High School, also aided the students. A lengthy list of demands issued by the striking students included implementation of bilingual and bicultural education programs; a revised curriculum to reflect the history and contributions of Mexican Americans; a student free speech area in each school; increased numbers of Mexican American teachers and counselors; and the requirement that teachers and administrators who staff the schools of East Los Angeles initially live in that area. Negotiations between student representatives and the Los Angeles School Board resulted in some reforms but not enough to allay tensions. The crisis atmosphere was not helped when thirteen people were arrested on conspiracy charges associated with the blowouts.[58]

---

58. See Muñoz, *Youth, Identity, Power,* 64–68. Thirteen Chicano college and community leaders who had supported the walkouts were arrested on conspiracy charges. Bail was set exceedingly high for the defendants, who came to be known as the "East L.A. 13." The charges were eventually dropped.

The *Times* needed to do something dramatic with respect to its coverage of these events and the Chicano community, in particular the spreading political activism of the Chicano movement. Gibson recalls being asked how he would feel about Salazar returning to the city bureau. Gibson was not happy but recognized that the paper was in trouble. It was Gibson's suspicion that the decision to bring Salazar back came from the top — from Otis Chandler himself.[59] Salazar apparently was not pleased with this turn of events either but accepted his new assignment — his new border crossing — like a good soldier.

City editor Bill Thomas was delighted to have Salazar back. After Salazar's departure in 1965, no other Mexican American reporters had been added to the staff. According to Thomas, there were even fewer Mexican American than African American reporters. Consequently, Thomas had found himself at a disadvantage in covering the developing Chicano movement. Thomas recalls that Salazar exhibited, as he had done earlier, a reluctance to be pegged as a "Chicano reporter," but recognized the importance of covering the movement.[60] Bill Drummond, a journalist of African American background who had joined the city staff in 1967, recalls that Salazar underwent a tough transition on returning to the city desk. "He had to find his niche again," Drummond notes. Nevertheless, according to Drummond, Salazar quickly became the most popular reporter on the city staff because of his cheerfulness and tolerant nature.[61]

Despite the abrupt transition, Salazar once again concentrated his full attention on Mexican Americans. At this juncture, however, the struggle was no longer a moderate effort by middle-class Mexican Americans to achieve social reforms. This time it was the Chicano movement, that constellation of youth protest, countercultural assertions, and separatist tendencies, combined with a struggle on the traditional issues affecting Mexican Americans in the United States: racism, poverty, educational discrimination, and police oppression. Added to these was a new phenomenon — the emergence of a significant anti–Vietnam War movement.[62]

The Chicano generation of the late 1960s and early 1970s spearheaded the most vocal and widespread social protest movement among Mexi-

59. Gibson interview.
60. Thomas interview.
61. Interview with Bill Drummond, August 30, 1993, by Mario T. García.
62. See Muñoz, *Youth, Identity, Power;* and García, *Memories of Chicano History,* 245–285.

cans in the United States since the conquest of the Southwest. While maintaining the legacy of struggle of previous Mexican American protests, the Chicano generation put its unique stamp on a historical period. For the first time, and on a considerable scale, a new generation of Chicanos openly and politically rejected the mythical "American Dream." Instead, Chicanos sought their own political and cultural alternatives to achieve justice and liberation. *Chicano Power, Viva La Raza, Brown Is Beautiful, La Causa,* and other slogans symbolized a new and more profound militant consciousness. Such a culture of opposition was dramatically expressed in pronouncements such as the Plan de Aztlán written at the 1969 Chicano Youth Liberation Conference in Denver, Colorado. The plan set out a nationalistic strategy for the eventual recovery of Aztlán (the mythical original homeland of the Aztecs, which the movement equated with the Southwest), if not in an actual physical sense, then at least in a cultural sense that would serve as a foundation for the renewed struggle by Chicanos to achieve freedom.

How this freedom would actually be achieved and what exactly it would mean, the Chicano movement never spelled out. Yet if an armed revolution was not the raison d'être of the movement, it was at least a call to Chicanos to revolutionize their consciousness and way of life by sweeping away the illusion and false ideology of the American Dream and replacing it with the power of La Raza and of Chicano culture. Only by the substitution of La Raza for the self could true freedom, at least freedom of the soul, be attained.

These changes in consciousness and the direct assault by the Chicano movement on particular issues affecting Chicanos in Los Angeles and elsewhere provided the unifying theme for Salazar's writings between 1969 and 1970. Throughout 1969, for example, Salazar reported on a variety of movement issues and in so doing provided a history of the movement, especially in Los Angeles, in the pages of an institution many Chicanos regarded as the standard of their adversary. Yet while Chicano activists regarded the *Times* as a potential opponent, some recognized Salazar as a reporter who could provide access to it. Salazar wrote on the continued struggles of Chicanos in education. He reported on the efforts to promote Spanish as a language of instruction in the schools rather than to prohibit it as though it were an alien and dangerous intrusion. "Mexicans are indigenous to the Southwest," Salazar wrote in early 1969 (January 14, 1969), and "the Spanish language is part of their culture which should not be tampered with. Having colonized the Southwest, Spanish-speaking people refuse to abandon their traditions because of the advent of Anglo-American culture." Salazar also commented on the efforts of Alicia Escalante and the L.A. Welfare Rights Organization as exemplifying the renewed grassroots efforts of Chicanos to achieve changes and greater control over the institutions that affected their lives (February 11, 1969).

Salazar also wrote on the militant youth such as the Brown Berets, a pseudomilitary contingent in Los Angeles and other communities. Such groups were patterned after the Black Panthers and committed themselves to rectifying specific social problems, including police abuse. Although the police and others regarded the Brown Berets as violent and dangerous, Salazar described them as constructive young activists with a cause. In an article on David Sánchez, head of the Brown Berets (June 16, 1969), Salazar wrote, "Indicted himself for his part in the East Los Angeles High School walkouts last year, Sánchez, 20, looks like a clean-cut Mexican-American boy." Of the efforts by the Brown Berets to politicize the *batos locos,* the throwbacks to the alienated pachucos and zoot-suiters of the 1940s and 1950s, Salazar quotes Sánchez as saying: "The Brown Berets recruit from the rebels without a cause and make them rebels with a cause." In covering the 1969 Chicano Youth Liberation Conference in Denver, Salazar (March 30, 1969) referred to Rodolfo "Corky" Gonzales, head of the Crusade for Justice in Denver and host of the conference, as the "guru" of Chicano youth, stressing Gonzales's independence from the Establishment. Salazar likewise covered the growing Chicano student movement on the campuses of southern California (March 30, 1969). Besides reporting on the new social protest movement and giving it a voice in the pages of the *Times,* Salazar helped to introduce a new discourse and consciousness by his employment of the terms of identity utilized by this new political generation, such as *Chicano* and *La Raza.*

In reporting on the Chicano movement, Salazar came to empathize with the movement's critique of the establishment. In a May 13, 1970, interview with correspondent Bob Navarro on KNXT-TV, Salazar noted that Chicanos no longer were accepting authority blindly. Observing that the United States was historically a revolutionary country, Salazar asserted that the Chicano movement represented a revolution, although a peaceful one, aimed at transforming society. When Navarro asked if Salazar had now become an advocate for the movement, he responded that he was advocating the Chicano community in the same way that the general media advocated the Anglo power structure. "Someone must advocate a community that has been forgotten," he added. Did this advocacy affect his "objectivity"? Salazar responded that there was not a single reporter who believed in "objectivity."[63]

Salazar's return to Los Angeles had obviously filled a gap for the *Times.* Yet, according to fellow reporter Drummond, Salazar's stories did not get the play accorded those of other reporters. Drummond notes that even with Salazar's return, the *Times* still did not express particular interest in Mexican American issues. Despite the larger Mexican American population in Los Angeles, the *Times* provided greater coverage to the smaller African American community. But even this coverage was limited. Part of this lack of attention to minority issues, Drummond concludes, was due to the *Times*'s perception that Los Angeles really consisted of the outlying suburbs populated mostly by whites and that no one lived in the central city, which in fact was home to most Mexican Americans and African Americans.[64]

Perhaps because he felt this lack of attention, in April 1970 Salazar informed Thomas that he had decided to leave the *Times* and to accept an offer from KMEX, the Spanish-language television station in Los Angeles. According to Danny Villanueva, who was then the news director of KMEX, Joe Rank, vice president and general manager of the station, had decided to promote Villanueva to station manager and offered Salazar the opportunity to come to KMEX as Villanueva's replacement. Villanueva, a former professional football player, had instituted a "participatory" type of news reporting since his arrival at KMEX in 1968; it included investigative reporting and advocacy of Mexican American community issues. Rank believed that Salazar would complement and add to what Villanueva had started.[65]

At the time Villanueva could not understand why Salazar would want to leave a secure position at a mainstream news institution such as the *Times,* but he recalls that Salazar mentioned to him that he saw working at KMEX as an opportunity not only to inform Anglos about what was happening in the Chicano community but also to inform Chicanos themselves through Spanish-language media.[66] In his May 13, 1970, interview with Bob Navarro, Salazar told Navarro that the reason he had decided to leave the *Times* was that he had become frustrated and

63. Navarro interview.
64. Drummond interview.
65. Villanueva interview; Sally Salazar, "Reporter Salazar."
66. Ibid.

felt his career had come full circle at the paper. Perhaps more important, the position at KMEX gave him new opportunities as a journalist. "I really wanted to communicate in their language with the people I had written about so much," Salazar said, and noted that most of the Spanish-speaking people in Los Angeles received their news not through the print media but through television and radio.[67] "In his mind," Earl Shorris suggests, concerning what he believes to have been Salazar's media philosophy, "the press was a political instrument, and it was to be used to bring about a better life for his people."[68] In his interview with Navarro, Salazar corroborated Shorris's analysis when he informed Navarro that "the press's obligation is to rock the boat."[69] Drummond was not surprised at Salazar's resignation. "He had outgrown the *Times*," Drummond concludes.[70]

Bill Thomas recalls thinking that the KMEX offer was a good opportunity for Salazar because it would give him high visibility. Thomas advised Salazar on the terms of his KMEX contract. According to Villanueva, Salazar "negotiated a very good deal." However, reluctant to lose Salazar completely, Thomas came up with the idea of having Salazar write a weekly column on Chicano issues for the *Times*. Salazar would be paid for these columns, but he would no longer be on the *Times* staff. According to Thomas, Salazar enthusiastically welcomed the idea of maintaining connections to the *Times*.[71]

Salazar used the column as an opportunity to express his thoughts and opinions regarding "el movimiento" more directly. *Newsweek* magazine commented (June 27, 1970) that the *Times* had provided Salazar with his own column to "close an information gap" on Chicano life in Los Angeles. This arrangement was an answer from the *Times* to the charge of being insensitive to the Chicano community. For their part, the *Times* editors continued to regard Salazar as a *Times* man. Salazar represented a responsible and professional voice or "translator" that the *Times* could accommodate, and at the same time his voice could be utilized as a way for the Chicano movement to communicate with and to challenge the establishment, a paradoxical role not uncommon for minority professionals.

67. Navarro interview.
68. Earl Shorris, *Latinos: A Biography of the People* (New York: W. W. Norton, 1992), 232.
69. Navarro interview.
70. Drummond interview.
71. Thomas interview; Villanueva interview.

The column worked out well and received a great deal of attention. As *Newsweek* pointed out,

Instead of writing blank descriptions of Mexican-American family life, Salazar regularly turns in hard-hitting weekly columns attacking "Anglo" racism and voicing serious Mexican-American grievances. "In the last two or three months, Ruben has actually come out and stated his own feelings," says one *Times* reporter. "Previously, he was restrained. Now he's been fired."

Enrique "Hank" López, a close friend of Salazar's, who was both a writer and a lawyer, observed the relish and commitment Salazar displayed in his column. López wrote of Salazar,

In his weekly column for the *Times* he somehow managed the amazing feat of "bugging the establishment" while still giving his fellow Chicanos some shred of hope that the system might possibly work. There was great soul in his writing, a gentle irony that could chide the *gabacho* [Anglo] and *Chicano* with equal and unfailing affection. Thus, even the most angry militant Brown Beret could trust him, because he knew where Ruben's heart was—that it was always beating at the very core of *la raza*.[72]

As news director of KMEX, Salazar also produced reports on police abuse in the Chicano community. These, along with his criticisms of the police in his newspaper column, did not endear him to authorities, who regarded him as a "rabble-rouser." At the time of his death, according to Villanueva, Salazar was writing a book on police abuse.[73] It was to be based on information, apparently including confidential documents, that Salazar had received or was receiving from Manuel Ruiz, a longtime Mexican American attorney and community leader in Los Angeles. At the time Ruiz was also a member of the U.S. Civil Rights Commission. A heavily censored FBI file on Salazar reveals that Salazar was being investigated by federal authorities as well as by the Los Angeles Police Department, who considered him to be a "slanted, left-wing oriented, reporter."[74] According to another longtime community leader, Bert

72. See Enrique Hank López, "Ruben Salazar Death Silences a Leading Voice of Reason," *Los Angeles Times,* September 6, 1970, C-7.
73. Villanueva interview.
74. Ibid. FBI documents on Salazar in possession of Salazar's daughter, Lisa Salazar Johnson. Also see Escobar, "Dialectics of Repression," 1499–1501.

Corona, Salazar suspected that he was being followed by the police.[75] Villanueva also recalls Salazar expressing the same suspicion to him.[76] Bill Thomas downplays police scrutiny of Salazar but does recall that Police Chief Ed Davis once called on Thomas to fire Salazar and abolish his column.[77]

Police reaction to Salazar also manifested itself at KMEX. Villanueva observes that on one occasion, shortly before the Chicano moratorium, a representative from one of the police agencies came to see him at the station about Salazar. "Ruben was getting under their skins," Villanueva concludes.[78] Earl Shorris confirms this tension and recalls that Salazar told him that the sheriff had threatened him directly by telling him, "You had better stop stirring up the Mexicans."[79] Shorris also remembers that Salazar was frightened by the threat but not immobilized by it.

"What are you going to do?" Shorris asked Salazar.

"Keep writing," Salazar responded.[80]

In his columns, Salazar dealt with a variety of issues. But the question of Chicano identity was one that particularly intrigued him. In one column entitled "Who Is a Chicano? And What Is It the Chicanos Want?" (February 6, 1970), Salazar noted that the term *Chicano* was as difficult to define as, for example, the term *soul* in African American discourse. He proposed, however, that *Chicano* be defined more broadly than its linguistic content. "Such explanations," he stressed, "tend to miss the whole point as to why Mexican-American activists call themselves Chicanos." Salazar felt the term should be defined in a social context to reflect the historical exploitation of Chicanos. Because Chicanos had been taught for generations that to be a Mexican was to be inferior, asserting their identity as Chicanos was, according to Salazar, an "act of defiance and a badge of honor." Yet, Salazar did not accept the strong separatist tendencies within the movement. He still clung to some of the pluralistic concepts favored by those who preferred to call themselves Mexican Americans. He concluded, "Chicanos, then, are merely fighting to become 'American.' Yes, but with a Chicano outlook."

The search for identity was of crucial importance to him in dealing with years of prejudice and discrimination that had made Chicanos insecure about their culture and identity. Salazar's ambivalence toward

75. See García, *Memories of Chicano History*, 277–279.
76. Villanueva interview.
77. Thomas interview.
78. Villanueva interview.
79. Shorris interview.
80. Shorris, *Latinos*, 8.

Chicano identity informed his more moderate approach to the tensions surfacing in the Chicano communities. "If you read those columns," Bill Drummond observes,

> you get a sense that Ruben was very much under control. He had a centrist approach. He was not someone throwing firebombs. It was a very rational approach. The column couldn't have happened otherwise, at least not in the *Times*.[81]

In a column entitled "A Mexican-American Hyphen" (February 13, 1970), Salazar wrote that being a Mexican American and feeling the pull of two cultures and identities "can leave you with only the hyphen." The identity crisis in some respects was more acute for Chicanos, not only because of the racism they encountered, which made them feel like "foreigners in their own land," but also because of the proximity of Mexico, which made it impossible for Chicanos to think of the place abstractly, as, for example, Irish Americans might think of Ireland. It was the urgent need to overcome a sense of inferiority that gave the Chicano movement its force. For Salazar, the movement, in its militant and strident defense of Chicano culture and Chicano worth, created a political approach for dealing with earlier feelings of ambivalence and even self-hatred. In the process, the Chicano movement not only combated the identity crisis and provided a foundation for a new identity but also counteracted racist attacks on Chicanos. Salazar, for example, in "Reason in Washington, Passion in Denver — What Will Work?" (April 10, 1970), contrasted the futility of formal meetings in Washington that tried to convince the establishment of the errors of its ways with the surpassing anger and sense of power expressed by Chicano youth at the Denver conference.

In these and other columns during the first eight months of 1970, Salazar informed the *Times* readership of the Chicano movement. But he did more than inform; he provided a voice for the millions of Chicanos who had been denied a public forum for years by institutions such as the *Times*. At the same time, it would be a misreading to label Salazar a "Chicano journalist." Raul Ruiz recalls that while activists were aware of Salazar's work, he does not believe that Salazar's journalism affected the politics of the movement.[82] "Ruben was watching and observing the movement," Drummond insists, "but the movement was not Ruben."[83]

81. Drummond interview.
82. Interview with Raul Ruiz, April 2, 1993, by Mario T. García.
83. Drummond interview.

Villanueva agrees and recalls how furious Salazar once became when someone referred to him as a "Chicano newsman." Salazar angrily responded, "I'm a newsman. I'm a journalist who happens to be a Chicano. Don't you ever call me a Chicano newsman." Villanueva remembers, in addition, that in time Salazar had serious reservations about the direction of the movement and expressed frustration over what he considered to be the chaotic circumstances surrounding it.[84] According to his colleagues, Salazar looked forward every day to returning to his suburban Orange County home where he could escape from the tumult of covering the movement.[85]

Salazar's last column appeared on August 28, one day before his death. Just a few weeks before he had almost prophesied the clash that he sensed was coming between the movement and the police. The police, Salazar believed, were out to crush the movement, and, he wrote, the "mood is not being helped by our political and law-and-order leaders who are trying to discredit militants in the barrios as subversive or criminal" (June 19, 1970).

The Friday before the moratorium proved to be a hectic one at KMEX. Salazar had mobilized all the station's news resources to cover what he expected to be a big event, even though he appears to have had forebodings of the tragedy that awaited. Danny Villanueva recalls what he considered to be Salazar's strange behavior that Friday. After lunch, Salazar, who was not known to be a tidy person, cleared off his desk. He took everything off his office walls and packed many of his belongings. He was preoccupied with whether Laguna Park, the site of the moratorium, was in the city or in the county of Los Angeles. When Salazar left later that day, Villanueva wished him goodnight: "I'll see you Monday." Salazar responded, "Yeah, if I survive, you'll see me." These were his last words to Villanueva. The next time Villanueva saw Salazar was when he identified his body on Saturday evening.[86]

Years later Sally Salazar also remembered her husband's strange behavior before the moratorium. "Ruben had changed in those last few weeks," she noted.

Whenever he left the house, he made a special point of telling me exactly where he was going to be—something he'd never done before. He started coming straight home from work every evening. That week [the

---

84. Villanueva interview.
85. Interviews with Drummond and Thomas.
86. Villanueva interview.

week of the moratorium] he had taken all of the pictures off his walls at the office. He cleaned out his wallet.[87]

Conclusion

After his death on August 29, 1970, Ruben Salazar became a martyr for the Chicano movement, which now eulogized him as their hero. Laguna Park, the site of the antiwar moratorium, was renamed Ruben Salazar Park. Murals and paintings by Chicano artists commemorate Salazar as a hero of the people. Parks, libraries, university buildings, scholarships, and housing projects have also been named after him. *Corridos,* the genre of Mexican folk songs popularized during the Mexican Revolution of 1910, added a new hero to a pantheon that included Pancho Villa and Emiliano Zapata, among others. The corrido by Jesús Sánchez entitled *Corrido de Ruben Salazar* opens with these lines:

> Con intima tristeza
> Mis versos voy a cantar
> Y perpetuar la memoria
> De Don Ruben Salazar.[88]

Yet Salazar's death did more than create a martyr. It silenced an expression of hope that American society would keep its promises. Salazar had still believed that broad social reforms might be possible without pursuing the separatist route urged by some Chicano militants. Committed to his profession, although sympathetic to the movement, Salazar supported more moderate political strategies to achieve basic reforms. "Ruben was a moderate," Thomas concludes. "He would have laughed at being martyrized."[89] Villanueva concurs. According to him, Salazar would have responded to the efforts to canonize him as a movement saint with one of his favorite phrases: "This is ridiculous!"[90]

Sally Salazar also found it curious that the movement transformed her husband into a movement leader when she, like his colleagues, recognized his true identity as a professional journalist. On the tenth anniversary of his death, she wrote, "My memories are confused by the murals and memorials and a creation built in the public mind — someone other

87. Sally Salazar, "Reporter Salazar the Man, Not the Myth," *Los Angeles Times,* August 31, 1980.
88. *La Raza* (1970), Vol. I, no. 3, 32.
89. Thomas interview.
90. Villanueva interview.

people call Ruben Salazar, but someone to this day I don't fully recognize." Sally Salazar believed that the Ruben Salazar whom the movement converted into a martyr "was someone he himself may have just been in the process of discovering." More important for Sally Salazar and her young children, August 29, 1970, meant the tragic loss of a husband and a father. "I don't claim that we were the only persons who knew Ruben," she recalled.

> But we knew him very well. He was what a husband and father should be. There's an age children reach when their fathers share more of their time and their selves with them. Our children had reached that age and Ruben had responded.[91]

For Salazar's children, of course, would grow up with only faint memories, if any, of their father. Twenty years after Salazar's death, Lisa Salazar Johnson, his eldest child, who was nine at the time of his death, wrote,

> Because I was so young at the time of his death, I fantasized that it was all a mistake and that one day he would be back. In the very short time that I did have my Dad, I remember a happy, funny man who always told us he loved us and had special nicknames for us. He took good care of us, and we shared special times together as a family. It hurts, but I often like to look back at family photos because there on his face it is very clear to see the love he had for us.[92]

Salazar's death removed from the scene the most significant Mexican American journalist of his time. "He was not the first Latino reporter or even the first Latino columnist," his friend and fellow journalist Earl Shorris recalls of Salazar, "but he was the best and the bravest. . . . For one corruscating moment Ruben Salazar gave political and social purpose to Latino media."[93] Salazar was a professional who held to principles of truth and fairness. Bill Drummond noted these qualities in his eulogy to Salazar.

---

91. Sally Salazar, "Reporter Salazar." Sally Salazar died on March 11, 1993, of a sudden illness. She had returned to work for the *Times* as a copy clerk in classifieds in the *Times* Orange County bureau.

92. See note by Lisa Salazar Johnson in "August 29." The ages of Salazar's other children at the time of his death were Stephanie Anne, seven, and John Kenneth, five.

93. Shorris, *Latinos*, 9, 232. In recognition for his contributions to the Mexican American community through his columns in the *Times*, in 1971 Salazar was awarded posthumously a special Robert F. Kennedy Journalism Award.

But without a doubt, this man's death had meaning, for he had struggled all these years to stand erect against the pressures of compelling allegiances. And in the end he was true to himself. He made no stale compromise with an authority in which he did not believe. He was neither a pimp for the revolution nor a shill for the Establishment.   *(Esquire, April 1972)*

Perhaps his friend Hank López put it best when he wrote of Salazar's death,

So when the fatal bullet-like missile struck him down in the searing violence of the East Los Angeles riot, instantly killing him as he was covering the story where the action was, we Chicanos suffered a terrible loss — an irreparable loss. He was our only establishment newspaper columnist, the most experienced and articulate Chicano writer in this whole country. Such a loss no community can afford.   *(Los Angeles Times, September 6, 1970)*

Regrettably, Salazar's death did not have an immmediate impact on the *Los Angeles Times*. It would be some ten years, according to Drummond, before the *Times* realized it needed to cover the Latino communities in Los Angeles with more than one reporter.[94] Frank del Olmo, the sole Chicano reporter for the *Times* during the 1970s, notes that because of the efforts of both Bill Thomas, who was then the editor, and Mark Murphy, the new metro editor, additional Latino reporters were hired at the *Times* by 1980. These reporters represented the best talent the *Times* could recruit. That talent paid off when the new team of reporters wrote a twenty-seven-part series on southern California's Latino communities that won a Pulitzer Prize Gold Medal for Public Service in 1984. Although they were a new generation of Chicano reporters, they, according to del Olmo, still looked back to Salazar as a role model. That model was attractive because it "showed you could believe strongly in wanting to help the Chicano community and even be a bit of an advocate for it and still maintain your journalistic integrity."[95]

A full biography of Ruben Salazar will no doubt be written some day. For now, it is my hope that these selections of some of the best of his

94. Drummond interview.
95. Interview with Frank del Olmo, December 14, 1993, by Mario T. García. By the 1980s, not only had the *Los Angeles Times* expanded its staff of Latino correspondents but so too had many other newspapers in the United States, including those in parts of the country where various other Latino groups such as Puerto Ricans, Cuban Americans, Central Americans, and South Americans resided.

journalism will serve to remind those of us who knew his work how important it was and to introduce him to a new generation for whom he has both historical and current relevance. That relevance stems less from his death than from his work as a journalist. This is the finest tribute Ruben Salazar could receive.

1. Immigrant Identification card of Ruben Salazar, February 15, 1929.
Salazar at 11 months of age.

Courtesy of Lisa Salazar Johnson.

2. *Los Angeles Times* prize-winning reporters, early 1960s. Front row:
Harry Nelson, Charles Hillinger, Art Berman. Second row: Ray Hebert
and Bill Thomas. At rear: Ruben Salazar.

Courtesy of Special Collections, University of California, Los Angeles.

3. Salazar interviewing former president Dwight D. Eisenhower, early 1960s.
Courtesy of Lisa Salazar Johnson.

4. Salazar with Robert F. Kennedy, early 1960s. Frank Sinatra
in the background.

Courtesy of Lisa Salazar Johnson.

5. Salazar interviewing junta troops in the Dominican Republic,
August 6, 1965.
Courtesy of Special Collections, University of California, Los Angeles.

6. Salazar interviewing civilians in Santo Domingo, Dominican Republic,
August 8, 1965.
Courtesy of Special Collections, University of California, Los Angeles.

7. Salazar with his children: Lisa, age 4 (right), Stephanie, age 3 (left), and Johnny, 6–7 months (center), 1965.

Courtesy of Lisa Salazar Johnson.

8. Salazar in Vietnam, 1965.
Courtesy of Lisa Salazar Johnson.

9. Salazar in Mexico City, 1967 or 1968.
Courtesy of Lisa Salazar Johnson.

10. Salazar greeting *Los Angeles Times* publisher Otis Chandler Jr. and Mrs. Chandler at Mexico City airport, 1967 or 1968.

Courtesy of Lisa Salazar Johnson.

11. Salazar with his wife, Sally Salazar,
Mexico City, Christmas, 1967.

Courtesy of Lisa Salazar Johnson.

12. Salazar at KMEX, Los Angeles, 1970.
Courtesy of Lisa Salazar Johnson.

13. Chicano Anti-War Moratorium, Los Angeles, August 29, 1970.
Courtesy of Special Collections, University of California, Los Angeles.

14. Los Angeles County sheriffs break up Chicano Anti-War Moratorium,
August 29, 1970.
Courtesy of Special Collections, University of California, Los Angeles.

15. Sheriffs outside of the Silver Dollar Cafe, August 29, 1970.
Courtesy of Raul Ruiz.

16. Sheriffs ordering customers into Silver Dollar Cafe before shooting into it,
August 29, 1970.

Courtesy of Raul Ruiz.

17. Raul Ruiz, editor of *La Raza,* showing one of his photographs of sheriffs outside the Silver Dollar Cafe.

Courtesy of Special Collections, University of California, Los Angeles.

18. Salazar's body lying in state at an East Los Angeles mortuary, September 2, 1970. KMEX manager Danny Villanueva is standing at the head of the casket.

Courtesy of Special Collections, University of California, Los Angeles.

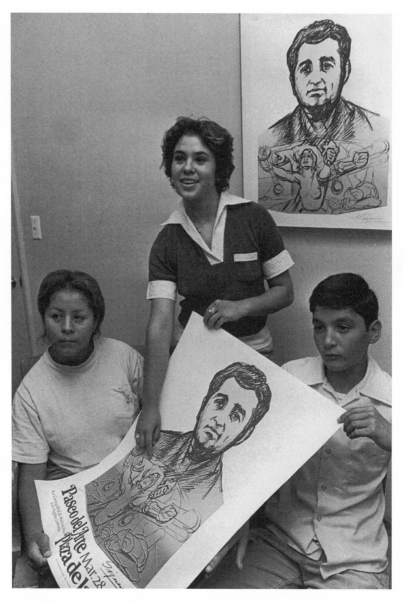

19. Chicano school children proudly display copies of a sketch of Salazar that was drawn by Mexican artist David Alfaro Siqueiros, early 1970's.

Courtesy of Special Collections, University of California, Los Angeles.

20. Memorial to Ruben Salazar, 1988. Salazar Housing Complex,
1000 Cypress Avenue, El Paso, Texas. Sponsored by the Private Industry
Council summer youth employment program under the supervision
of Carlos Callejo.

Photograph courtesy of Miguel Juárez.

ONE

EL PASO, 1955 - 1956

El Paso Herald-Post

25 Hours in Jail—"I Lived in a Chamber of Horrors"

May 9, 1955

EL PASO, Texas — I spent a night in a Chamber of Horrors.

I saw City Jail prisoners take dope inside Tank 6. I saw powder capsules swallowed and dissolved in hot water and men become crazy with dope.

I saw packages smuggled into the jail by prisoners who lived from day to day for dope parties that began at 5:30 p.m. and lasted until dawn.

On an assignment for the *Herald-Post* I had myself "arrested" on a drunk charge last Thursday. I was fined $15, but, acting like a broke drunk, I said I could not pay. I was sentenced to Tank 6. My acting became better when I entered. The stench was so repulsive I vomited twice.

That was at 8 a.m. Twenty-five hours later I had all I could take.

Tank 6 is a disgusting combination of live and inanimate filth. The men are systematically killing themselves: some with liquor, the rest with narcotics. The cells are like pigsties. There are two stinking toilets in the 22-foot-long tanks. At one end of the tank is a bathtub. The whole inside is one solid black bathtub ring. The "cots" are thin slabs of interwoven steel strips attached to the walls. One blanket is given each man.

When I was taken in about 10 men were in Tank 6. They were friendly, for most were drunks, not hopheads.

At 2:30 p.m. the chain gang came in from work. Their chains were removed and they charged into the tank with authority. They chased off the non-chain gang inmates using the toilets and the bathtub. The friendly group meekly retreated into their cells. The bosses had come in.

At 4:30 p.m. we lined up for chow. Next to me was a small red-headed individual with a ravaged face who appeared drunk. He looked down at my shoes and mumbled. "Like your shoes. Let's trade." I refused and he boomed obscenities.

We ate standing up crowded as in a 5 o'clock bus and we gobbled down the food fast with the help of the jailers yelling, "Hurry it up, you guys, hurry it up."

Red took out a small wad of tissue. Inside were two red capsules. He put them in his mouth and downed them with black coffee. Then a small brown paper bag was passed to him, coming quickly from the direction of the food servers, and he immediately took the bag and dropped it down a convenient hole to his cell downstairs. We marched down to our cells.

Red and a couple of his cronies were pretty "loco." Their speech was incoherent and their eyes blurry.

One of the friendly men warned me to stay in my bunk. "They got a big load today," he said.

It wasn't long before Red summoned me to his cell. He was sitting on a high bunk surrounded by his henchmen. Red took me by the collar and his vile breath hit me in the face. He said, "First-timer, ain't you?" I said "Yes." He let go my collar and showed me his yellow shaking hands.

"See these hands?" he asked. "They can beat you up or kill you and no one here will say anything about it."

I went back to my bunk and lay still while lice crawled all over me.

Red and his crowd starting heating water in a can over some burning newspapers. A half hour later all of Red's gang was goofier than Snake Pit. Some of them began wailing like maniacs. Once in a while one would shout horribly: "Pasame un calmante" ("Pass me a calmer").

Then they would "sing" at the top of their voices. It sounded more like the writhings of sinners in hell you read about. Minor fights broke out, but were stopped by other hopheads.

"You want to ruin everything?" one of them asked, meaning that the jailers would come up. Why the jailers didn't come, anyway, considering the loud noise, I'll never know.

The night wore on slowly. Nobody in the jail could have gotten a wink of sleep — except the hopheads when they passed out. The rest of us were kept awake by fear, the horrible noise and the ever-present lice.

One of the hopheads was sent to his bunk crying when he refused to go through an unnatural demand by a big hophead.

Finally the morning broke through and the hopheads became quiet.

"I hope we get a bigger load tomorrow," one of them said.

I decided to end my experiment in misery. I called the *Herald-Post* and asked to be freed. I had intended to stay longer. I couldn't.

I left the jail knowing how it feels to live in a hophead Chamber of Horrors.

La Nacha Sells Dirty Dope at $5 a "Papel"
Herald-Post Reporter Makes Purchase from Border "Queen"

August 17, 1955

EL PASO, Texas—La Nacha is the Dope Queen of the Border. She is big stuff. But she will sell you one "papel" (paper) of heroin just like any "pusher" on a street corner.

If you aren't too far gone, the dirty-looking stuff in the folded paper is good for two shots. But that's true only for those who are beginning.

A dope addict, whom I will call "Hypo," buys the $10 size. It has more than the two of the $5 papers, Hypo said. One lasts him a day—most days.

He Met the Queen

La Nacha—right name Ignacia Jasso—lives in a good house in a bad neighborhood. She's fat, dark, cynical and around 60. She deals out misery from her comfortable home.

She sells usually what is called a "dirty load," which is one that is not white as heroin should be, but a dirty, dusty color.

Her prices are in American money. She does business with many American addicts. She's as casual about it as if she were selling tortillas.

Hypo took me to La Nacha's home and introduced me to the dope queen.

I visited her twice. The first time Hypo and I bought a $5 paper of heroin. The second time we bought the large economy $10 size.

The papers contained dope all right. I saw Hypo, an El Paso married man of 24 whose 19-year-old wife has a three-month-old baby, inject himself with the "carga" (load).

He's Got to Have It

Hypo, who says he wants to be cured, cannot live without heroin. It costs him about $10 a day—or hours of excruciating pain. Hypo prefers heroin to pain and gets the $10 a day any way he can. He sold all his furniture for heroin. He was evicted from his apartment for not paying rent. He has stolen, borrowed and now has given me his story for $15 which he spent on heroin.

Hypo and I went to visit La Nacha in the afternoon. We parked the car a few blocks from her house. She lives in Bellavista district, which means "Beautiful View." It is far from beautiful. The streets are unpaved and most of the houses are adobe. Naked kids were running about the streets.

We turned on Mercuro alley and walked toward La Nacha's house, which is on the corner of the alley and Violetas (Violets) street. Hers is the only decent-looking house in the neighborhood. It is yellow and has fancy iron grillwork on the windows.

She Has a TV Set

Hypo and I walked through the nicely kept green patio.

Inside, the house has all the conveniences of a modern home: gas, stove, nice living room furniture, TV and a saint's statue on the wall.

I had been to Hypo's El Paso apartment and couldn't help thinking about his bare rooms after he had sold the furniture for heroin. The last time I had been at Hypo's apartment, I had seen the baby on the floor on a blanket and Hypo's wife sitting in a corner watching the baby. There was a sad, vacant look in her eyes.

Once inside the house, which Hypo knows so well that he doesn't even bother to knock, we met Nacha's daughter. She was sitting on a bed talking to another woman. Hypo told her he was going away and wanted to introduce me so I could buy the stuff myself.

"You'll have to ask Mother," Nacha's daughter said.

Then I was introduced to Nacha's son. He is heavyset, wears a mustache and had on an expensive watch.

I noticed a stool nearby which had white strips of paper neatly arranged on top.

She Looked Him Over

Then La Nacha came in. I remembered Hypo's advice that I should be polite to her. She gave me the once-over, I was introduced. She sat in front of the stool and started working the strips. They were the heroin papers.

Hypo told La Nacha that I was a musician working in a dance hall in El Paso and wanted to start buying "loads."

La Nacha glanced at my arms. Hypo explained that I wasn't a "mainliner." That I just liked to "jornear" — breathe the heroin. A "mainliner" is one who injects himself with a hypodermic needle.

La Nacha said, "All right, any time."

"At night we sell it across the street," La Nacha's daughter said.

Hypo asked La Nacha for "a nickel's worth." She handed me a paper of heroin. (She wanted to know if I would handle the stuff, Hypo told me later.) Hypo gave her $5 and we left.

Quicker and Better

After we bought the load we went to a cheap hotel in Juarez. There I saw Hypo, who is a "mainliner," inject himself with heroin.

"You feel better quicker that way," Hypo said.

"Mainliners" need a cup of water, a syringe with a needle, an eye dropper, a bottle cap and the expensive heroin to make them feel, in Hypo's word, "normal."

"A man who is hooked (that is, one who has the habit bad) never feels normal unless he's had at least two shots a day," Hypo said.

I watched Hypo go through the process of injecting himself with heroin. First he carefully placed half a paper of heroin in the bottle cap with a knife. Then with an eye dropper he placed a few drops of water in the cap. He took a match and placed it underneath the cap while holding it with the other hand. After it was heated Hypo dropped a tiny ball of cotton in the cap. "This is so the hypodermic can suck all the heroin out the cap," Hypo explained. The cotton works like a filter.

Wild Eyes Gleam

Hypo then placed the hypodermic syringe in the cap and the brownish substance could be seen running up into the syringe.

Hypo's wild eyes gleamed with excitement.

Hypo crouched on the floor balanced on the front of his shoes. He injected the heroin in his vein. His vein was swollen from so many punctures.

Almost as soon as the heroin had gone into his vein he started rocking back and forth. I asked him how he felt.

"Muy suave, ese," he said. "Real good."

Before long he passed out. His stomach sounded like a washing machine. He snored loudly and uncomfortably. I tried to wake him. I couldn't. So I went home.

Took an Overdose

Later he explained that he had taken an overdose.

"The load was real clean and I misjudged the amount I should have taken," Hypo said. "I could have died."

The second time I saw Hypo we must have bought a load not as clean or he judged the right amount. For the reaction was much different.

Before he injected himself he looked worse than I had ever seen him. His eyes looked like two huge buttons. He complained of pains all over his body. Hypo couldn't even hold a cigarette because of his shaking hands.

We went to La Nacha's and bought some heroin. We only stayed a minute. Hypo needed to be "cured" quick.

After he injected himself this time he actually looked better than before, talked better and acted better. He was only half dead — instead of three quarters.

He stopped shaking. He smoked almost calmly and was talkative. "I've got to quit this habit," he said. "For my little daughter's sake. I love her very much. God, I wish I could stop it."

I, too, hope he can.

Speakeasies Sell 'Atomic' Booze in South El Paso

July 3, 1956

EL PASO, Texas — The age of the speakeasy is not over in El Paso.

Just recently I sat in one of those alcohol joints at 1217 South Oregon street and had a glass of tequila. It was cut with something which made it smell like kerosene. The taste is terrible. The effect on my stomach was atomic.

The man who took me to the speakeasy had the specialty of the house: an "alky." That, simply, is a drink of rubbing alcohol cut down with boiled water.

It all started when a South El Paso woman called me to ask: "Why don't the police do something about all these places down here that sell alcohol to bums?

"My kids are growing up having to observe the parade of alcoholics staggering up and down our streets all day long on their way to the speakeasies."

Bum Buys Booze

I went to South El Paso and started a conversation with a bum who looked like he needed a drink. He did. He immediately asked me for a quarter for a "pisto," a drink.

I followed him to an apartment house in the 500 block of South Mesa avenue. The bum went in through the back and came out right away. He had a pint bottle of a smoky-looking liquid. He offered me a drink and I took a swig. It rasped my throat like sandpaper. A few minutes later I felt the results. I didn't get drunk—I was dazed.

I poured a sample from the bottle into a small container. Later I struck a match to the sample. It burned like gasoline.

The bum killed that bottle and announced he was going to "work"— that is, panhandle.

I went a little deeper into South El Paso and found another bum.

Queen of the Speakeasies

We went to three places where we were informed the supply hadn't arrived.

"Guess we'll have to go to Chencha's," the bum said. "It's the best place anyway."

Chencha is at 1217 South Oregon street. The speakeasy is in a basement apartment. Chencha, I am told, is the queen of the speakeasies.

A member of Alcoholics Anonymous told me later he used to drink there 18 years ago.

At Chencha's the alcoholic, if he has money, can satisfy his thirst with anything he desires: alky, tequila, mescal and beer. The specialty, though, is the 10-cent alky.

I had a tequila because I had had enough alky. The tequila cost me 25 cents. In Juarez you can get unadulterated tequila for a nickel.

Big Bruiser in Action

My bum friend had an alky. A woman poured the alcohol into his glass. Then she took a coffee pot from which she poured boiled water into the alcohol. We were told to pay when served.

A couple of men went in while we were at Chencha's and had an alky. They paid their dimes and left.

I left after a big bruiser, said to be a relative of Chencha, started asking me a lot of questions. He didn't like me; I didn't like the polluted tequila so I didn't mind leaving.

According to information I gathered there must be about 20 speakeasies in South El Paso. Most of them do not offer as much as at Chencha's, but all of them specialize in the dime alky.

The respectable people in South El Paso don't like it a bit.

He Likes It

"Why do they get away with it?" a woman asked. "Doesn't the police or the Liquor Control Board care what happens in South El Paso?"

"My husband likes to drink. We have a big family to support so he doesn't have much money to spend on drinking. A few months ago he discovered he could get a drink of alcohol diluted with water for a dime."

"Now he drinks it all the time. I'm sure it's affected his health and mind. When I found out I even tried to get him to start drinking good liquor. He didn't want to. He says he likes that poison."

Why Not Raids

An irate man, who said it is hard to rear a family in the midst of speak-easies, commented: "I read in the paper that several policemen raided a bingo game in which old respectable people were having bare innocent fun."

"Why don't these policemen raid these speakeasies? Just because we're poor down here does it mean we're not entitled to police protection?"

Yes sir, the speakeasy is not a thing of the past in El Paso.

TWO

MEXICAN AMERICANS, THE BORDER, AND BRACEROS, 1961-1965

Los Angeles Times

Mexican-Americans Move into New Era
of Political Awakening

January 8, 1961

LOS ANGELES — Lorenzo Marquez, a 30-year-old Mexican-American who lives on Brooklyn Ave. in East Los Angeles, is experiencing a political awakening.

Until recently, Marquez, a mechanic, thought a workingman's business was that of doing his job well and taking care of his wife and children. But on Dec. 1, at a hearing before the Board of Supervisors, Marquez carried a placard which read:

"Have a heart. Let East Los Angeles Incorporate."

Taking time off from a greasy transmission which he was repairing, Marquez recently mused:

"You know, my father lived in East Los Angeles for 45 years. He never became a citizen of the United States and never even learned to speak English. I remember once after I got back from the Army I asked him why he never learned English."

Things Are Different Now

He answered half seriously, "Who wants to speak to these gringos?"

"Well, my good father belonged to another generation. Things are different now and I very much want to talk to my neighbors, no matter what their national origin is."

"I'm working for the incorporation of East Los Angeles because I know that Mexican-Americans can progress only if they participate in civic affairs. Though my father worked here for almost a half a century, his heart was really in Mexico. I know nothing about Mexico, but I know something about East Los Angeles. It's my home and I want it to get better. If we make it into a city we Mexican-Americans will at last have a voice in our civic affairs."

Others Have Their Objections

At the meeting in which Marquez carried his incorporation placard, another man was there with different ideas about East Los Angeles. He was George Hansel, president of the East Los Angeles Improvement Assn., who told the lawmakers that he represents property owners on Atlantic Blvd. and that 85% of them are against the incorporation.

Hansel, who said East Los Angeles now enjoys a tax rate of 17th from the lowest among 80 communities in the county, told the hearing in part,

"(There) seems to be an awful lot of money spent for the incorporation of East Los Angeles, but we don't know where the money is coming from. . . ."

"We feel that with the revenue of a million to a million and a half dollars at stake that we should have better control and a better accounting of who is going to be city manager, the city government and what they have in mind."

(Charges have been made, though not by the official opponents, that if East Los Angeles is incorporated it will become another Gardena-type gambling town and that gangster elements will move in.)

East Los Angeles is a workingman's district with the reputation of being more wicked than it really is. It has the police problems characteristic of low income communities in large metropolitan areas.

Gang riots, dope peddling and shootings have marred its character in the eyes of people outside East Los Angeles.

Has Better, Less Spectacular Side

But the East Side has its better though less spectacular side. Mexicans love big families and like to raise their children without moving around. The many modest, but well-kept, homes attest to the Mexican-American's love for the "hogar" (family home). Most have been there for generations and intend to stay there, unlike their higher income brother who hopes sometime to buy a larger home in a "better neighborhood."

East Los Angeles' old business districts along Brooklyn Ave. and 1st St. could be something out of Chihuahua City or parts of Mexico. There is everything from chorizo (Mexican sausage) factories and tortilla factories to used clothing stores and cobbler shops where worn shoes are remade from top to soles.

Then there is the "new" East Los Angeles in the northwestern side.

There, West Bella Vista, with its new tract homes, and Atlantic and Whittier Blvds., with their supermarkets and car dealers, point to what all of East Los Angeles would like to be. New East Los Angeles is flanked by Monterey Park and Montebello, two communities which eye the territory as possible revenue-producing annexation land.

Decision Thursday

Next Thursday, the Board of Supervisors will decide whether an election should be called on the proposed incorporation of East Los Angeles and, if so, what the boundaries would be.

On the surface, the squabble centers on two basic issues:

The proponents of the new city, in which the 60,000 to 70,000 residents would be overwhelmingly Mexican-American, claim they seek a long-overdue community identity and that the run-down sections of their area would improve under home rule.

The opponents, business interests along Atlantic and Whittier Blvds. and some property owners in West Bella Vista, argue that a new city would only bring new taxes. This new burden, they contend, is unnecessary because they now receive excellent services from the county government.

The Citizens Committee for Incorporation of East Los Angeles knows that if it excluded West Bella Vista and Atlantic and Whittier Blvds. from its incorporation plans, there would be little trouble in forming the new city.

Integral Part

But the committee feels that these areas are an integral part of the proposed city and that businesses on Whittier and Atlantic Blvds. owe any economic success they might have to the support of the Mexican-American population in the East Side.

However, the hundreds of signatures on petitions filed with the supervisors which ask that East Los Angeles not be incorporated or that their section be excluded attest to the great concern many have over the proposed creation of the new city.

The Rev. William Hutson, a top Catholic Youth Organization official, who was influential in the recent incorporation of Pico Rivera, feels that opponents to the new city "suffer from vain fears."

"I know and have worked with East Los Angeles people for years,"

Father Hutson said. "I trust them without reservation. In no hands would democracy be safer. In a time when Fidelismo (Castroism) is making strides among Latin Americans, I see the reverse trend in East Los Angeles. In the future, East Los Angeles will be not only an economic asset, as it is now, but also a social and political asset in Los Angeles County. Besides, the incorporation of East Los Angeles would make the residents better Americans."

The map filed with the supervisors by the proponents of the city of East Los Angeles is of a 38-sq-mile area containing about 17,000 dwelling units. The 1959–60 assessed valuation of the area is approximately $27,661,570, according to the tax division of the auditor-controller of Los Angeles County.

The incorporation position, signed by at least 25% of the property owners representing at least 25% of the assessed property valuation, describes the proposed city as follows:

Bounded on the north by Floral Dr. and a line approximately one-half mile north of Brooklyn Ave., bounded on the west by the city of Los Angeles north of 3rd St. and by Eastern Ave. south of 3rd St., bounded on the south by 3rd St. west of Eastern Ave. and by Telegraph Rd. east of Eastern Ave. and bounded east by an irregular line along Goodrich Blvd. and in the general vicinity of Atlantic Blvd.

Proponents say that the city of East Los Angeles would not fall into the category of industrial cities that incorporated to keep out homes, so school taxes could be avoided, or dairy cities, which were created to protect milk farms from urban development.

"These are not true cities, as East Los Angeles would be," an incorporation tract reads. "These are nothing but incorporated tax loopholes. . . . The incorporation of East Los Angeles is a dramatic story of a people, who once controlled California, and now want to enjoy self-government."

Over the years several groups have attempted to incorporate East Los Angeles without success.

Speaking at a Public Relations Counsel Conference in 1956, councilman Edward Roybal observed:

"One of East Los Angeles' biggest failures is a lack of coordination among Eastside Organizations."

This does not hold true anymore. Twenty-three Mexican-American organizations have a co-ordinating group called the House of Delegates. The membership includes such organizations as the Council of Mexican-American Affairs, Catholic Youth Organization, Inter-American Club,

Inter-American Library Assn., Lulacs* and the Mexican Civic Patriotic Committee.

Not Directly Involved

The House of Delegates is not directly involved with the incorporation as some of its member groups lie outside the proposed boundaries. But it encourages all Mexican-Americans to exercise their civic rights and obligations.

It is estimated that there are from 600,000 to 750,000 Mexican-Americans in Los Angeles County and politicians drool when they dream of controlling this group as a bloc.

The East Side of late has been able to point with pride to one of its own, Judge Carlos Teran, who was appointed municipal judge by Republican Gov. [Goodwin] Knight and later superior judge by Democratic Gov. [Edmund G. "Pat"] Brown.

Political Victory

But East Los Angeles only recently tasted its first real political victory when attorney Leopold G. Sanchez, a novice politician, beat incumbent Judge Howard H. Walshok by a vote of 23,767 to 20,519 in the East Los Angeles Judicial District.

In part, it is this political consciousness on the part of the East Los Angeles Mexican-Americans that disturbs some anti-incorporation petitioners.

"It's not that I want to deny anyone the right to democratic process," a West Bella Vista resident said. "It's that I feel that they're forming a bloc and I wonder whether they have my interests in mind, too."

Complaints by anti-incorporation East Los Angeles residents might be summed up by a letter which appeared Dec. 23, in the *East Los Angeles Tribune:*

"I am opposed to East Los Angeles' incorporation," it read. "I have lived here many years. My folks moved out here in 1922. The majority of the people I talk to are satisfied the way we are now."

"I think a few aspiring young men are looking for a city job. Several of them aren't even property owners, so why should they be concerned. It's for a selfish reason."

* League of United Latin American Citizens.

Movement Leader

Leader of the incorporation movement is Joseph Galea, an attorney. Among the advantages listed by his committee are:

There would be no new property tax in the new city with income coming from gasoline tax returns, in lieu of tax returns, sales tax, county gasoline tax returns and liquor license fees. These would provide a surplus over expenditures. The "Lakewood Plan" would be used, with municipal services being furnished by the county on a lease plan.

Businessmen along 1st St. and Brooklyn Ave. are generally for the incorporation because they feel a closer affinity to the old "East Los Angeles." The businesses on Atlantic and Whittier Blvds. are generally bigger and have more modern facilities.

Alfred Paquette, who operates a sportswear factory at 3545 E. 1st St. which he says grosses about $2 million a year, puts his faith in the proposed new city.

"My business has been here for about 15 years and I am for the city of East Los Angeles because I'm interested in this area from a business standpoint."

John Siegwein, a property owner in West Bella Vista, thinks it's a mistake to think of East Los Angeles, especially his area, as strictly a Mexican-American section.

Cosmopolitan Group

"The falseness of this statement becomes readily apparent when Bella Vista is included in this area. Here we have a very cosmopolitan group of home owners and they are all Americans. There are people of various European, Latin and Oriental ancestries here and they embrace a large variety of religious beliefs and are living in harmony."

"We enjoy excellent county services and we want to continue to enjoy them. Should we become part of a new city, a city council could change all this. We feel that the city property tax is inevitable if the proposed area is incorporated, and we feel that this tax will be particularly oppressive on the 653 parcels in West Bella Vista."

But to Mrs. Elizabeth Porras, also of West Bella Vista, the fact that her area and the Atlantic and Whittier Blvds. business houses are the "nice parts of East Los Angeles and most prosperous proves why they belong to the proposed City of East Los Angeles."

The Board of Supervisors has a tough job cut out for it on Jan. 12. The supervisors must decide whether West Bella Vista and Whittier and

Atlantic Blvds. should be included in the proposed new city. If these areas are excluded, the proponents of the city of East Los Angeles will complain that they have been robbed of much of the tax base required for the city and of the added prestige which West Bella Vista would bring the new city.

If the supervisors approve the tentative boundaries, businessmen will protest that they are headed for higher taxes and a group of homeowners will complain that they are being forced into a community for which they feel no affinity.*

No Troops Line Border that Has Become Big Business; Changes Loom

January 7, 1962

LOS ANGELES — One hundred and forty miles south of Los Angeles and only 16 miles south of San Diego, although it is often difficult for Californians to remember, lies a foreign nation.

Its northern border snakes 1,800 miles from the Pacific to the Gulf of Mexico; yet, in that entire length, no troops stand guard on either side of the international line. A chain link fence is all that separates the two nations for about half that distance; the waters of the Rio Grande do the job for the rest of the way.

Across this friendly border, like neighbors everywhere, the United States and Mexico eye each other with equal mixtures of toleration, good will, mystification and cautiousness.

Such an atmosphere happily has minimized friction but has not eliminated important differences in race, culture, outlook and ways of life. For more than a century, this casual intermingling was taken for granted.

Now It's Big Business

But in recent years, the border has become big business. About 16 million Americans live in what we might call "borderland" on our side of the border, and 5 million Mexicans on their side. According to Mexican government figures, their border cities, towns, and villages have grown by more than 83% in population in the last 10 years as compared to 34% in the rest of Mexico.

So the border has become big enough to be vitally important not only to the adjacent communities but to the two nations themselves.

*The incorporation of East Los Angeles has never been approved.

In 1960, for instance, American "turistas" spent $520 million in the interior of Mexico.

In monetary terms, the people of Mexico's northern border strip — which includes nine cities facing American "sister" communities — had an annual income in 1959–60 of $652 per person, 135% higher than the average of $280 per person in the interior of Mexico.

Prosperity Can Be Deceiving

Statistical prosperity, however, can be deceiving. For those border Mexicans who are engaged in selling services and goods to the ever-increasing numbers of tourists, life is pretty good.

For many, including the peasants, the unskilled and the thousands of interior people who are flocking to the border looking for the Yankee dollar — and not finding it — life has an ugly side obvious to anyone who explores outside the "tourist zone."

Because the Mexican federal government is aware of this, it has initiated an ambitious project, "Programa Nacional Fronterizo" — the National Border Program.

Before getting into the details of that ambitious plan, a little more about the border itself:

The present international line was established following the Mexican-American war. Under the Treaty of Guadalupe [Hidalgo], signed Feb. 2, 1848, Mexico lost the land that now constitutes Texas, Arizona, New Mexico, Nevada, California, and parts of adjacent states — an area of 851,598 square miles, or about half of Mexico's territory. Later, the United States bought from Mexico for $10 million, through negotiations with Gen. Santa Ana, 54,532 square miles between the Gila River and the Rio Grande — now part of New Mexico and Arizona.

The loss of these territories to the Americans still rankles many Mexicans. Even today they argue that they were "robbed." Mexicans, like many diehard Dixieites, often view the United States as a nation which took advantage of them through an unjust war. And this perhaps has warped their view of the "colossus of the north."

Line Follows Devious Course

The international line itself starts from a point just west of Tijuana. From there the border runs straight east to Yuma, where the line starts sloping southward at about a 30-deg. angle between Arizona and Sonora, Mex., until it reaches the twin cities of Nogales, Ariz., and Nogales, Mex.

The international line, all a chain link fence so far, runs straight easterly again from Nogales until it reaches New Mexico and Chihuahua states, where it shoots out in a northerly direction for about 30 miles. It then becomes easterly for 100 miles to El Paso, Tex., and Juarez, Mex.

From El Paso on eastward to Brownsville, on the Gulf of Mexico, the border is the winding Rio Grande — called the Rio Bravo del Norte on the Mexican side.

Bordering States

On the American side of the border lie California, Arizona, New Mexico and Texas. On the Mexican side are the states of Baja California, Sonora, Chihuahua, Coahuila, a tiny section of Nuevo Leon and Tamaulipas.

Topographically speaking, the border wends its way through the arid deserts and mountains of California, Arizona and New Mexico, the rugged, uptilted terrain extending from El Paso almost to Laredo, and, from there to the Gulf of Mexico, the lush lower Rio Grande Valley.

Of the National Border Program, the face-lifting project, President Adolfo Lopez Mateos has said: "Due attention must be given to the anxious desires of the border population to improve and develop their communities, and to increase and modernize the public services at the border cities."

Leader Heads Program

Chosen to head the program was Antonio Bermudez, ex-head of Pemex, Mexico's nationalized oil industry, and former mayor of Juarez, the largest of the border cities.

Bermudez, whose good name gives the program both respectability and strength, sees the border as a "great show window, 1,800 miles long, facing the country (the United States) with the highest economic potential in the world."

"We want to transform the border into a great commercial, recreational and cultural avenue," Bermudez told the *Times*. "Through this great show window we must display what Mexico really is; it should be taken as an example to the world of friendship, of good neighbor relations and co-operation in every respect."

Teacher's View

Said a young, modern teacher, concerned with the "psychological effects of tourism" on border Mexicans: "The Mexican side of the border is a place where free-spending Americans go to do things they're not allowed to do at home. Loose money always attracts persons of questionable character, and the border cities have plenty of these."

"But the problem lies deeper than even the prostitution, dope traffic and extreme poverty indicate," he continued. "Paradoxically, though border town people know the economy is greatly boosted by the tourists, they somehow resent these free-spending pleasure-seekers."

"You see, you cannot have real self respect if you know you're making your living by selling services and merchandise which tourists themselves don't really respect."

Geared to Pride

The National Border Program's official goals, then, are geared to Mexican pride, and include the "improvement of the general environment of the border cities, their physical appearance and condition, that they may fulfill efficiently their urban functions both on behalf of their inhabitants and of national prestige, since they are entrance gates to the country."

"This means bluntly," the young teacher said, "that the federal government wants very bad to unsaddle the bad guys on the border and get the good guys in the saddle."

To do this, Bermudez emphasizes "creating the necessary conditions for the increase, in particular, of tourist family travel along the border."

Change Sought

"A change in the recreational aspect of the border cities must come about to include cultural festivals, high-quality Mexican movies and educational centers where foreigners may find evidence of our culture," a program report says.

The report admits that the program is ambitious, but says it is not unrealistic. Business is already booming in the area, it points out, but much of the profit goes back to the United States, which even sells U.S. gasoline to border cities — in a nation where the industry is nationalized.

"Products from Mexican industry in the interior must reach the border area in proper conditions of timeliness, quality and price," the report says.

"This must be done so that the dollars invested in our country by border visitors will not return instantly to the United States." With this added income the National Border Program (at least theoretically) can pay for itself.

Tijuana Gaudiest

What are the conditions on the border now? What are our neighbors like? Why must it be our business to seek answers to these questions?

I travelled the border from Tijuana to Matamoros on the Gulf of Mexico to find some of the answers. All of the big border cities were visited, plus many of the startlingly different smaller communities.

They include Tijuana, perhaps the gaudiest of all; Mexicali, a town whose people hold firm opinions concerning their American neighbors; Palomas, across from Columbus, N.M. (where a park has been dedicated to the once feared Pancho Villa); Juarez, the largest of the border cities, which in spite of all the Yankee dollars pouring into it is going broke; Ojinaga, where Mexico's newest and most exciting railroad begins; Santa Elena, a communal farm community across from the spectacular Big Bend National Park in Texas; and Matamoros, a city with a blighted beach on the Gulf of Mexico.

Murder of a Crusader Underlines Tijuana Choice: Reform or Go Red

January 8, 1962

TIJUANA, Mexico — The recent murder of a crusading local columnist has stirred the conscience of this gaudy town.

It was not only because the chief of police was jailed in connection with the killing that three state policemen were formally charged with the crime.

This, of course, was sensational enough, even in this naturally "wild" town.

But the thing that most disturbed Tijuana was the realization that journalist Carlos Estrada Sastre, columnist for *Noticias,* was apparently killed simply because he was writing about the city's most obvious problems — problems which were news to no one, but which were being glossed over by officials.

For weeks, now, the murder has been discussed by the people along Tijuana's Revolucion Ave., the city's main street, by people living in the exclusive residential area on the scenic hills just outside the city, by those living in the poor "colonias," by the peasants in the surrounding communal farms, by the many squatters in the city's foothills, and even by the tourists who can read the screaming headlines in Tijuana's newspapers.

One good thing has come out of the murder: it has given new impetus to the public's demand that the National Border Program be speeded.

This is the program which the federal government, under the revered President Lopez Mateos, says will change the 1,800-mile border into a "show window" of what's best in Mexico.

Improve or Go Red

"Either this program will be put into effect soon to bring about some dignity and respectability to Tijuana or we're headed for communism or anarchy," a worried businessman said recently.

Estrada Sastre, in his muckraking way, wanted everything the National Border Program stands for. He long ago associated himself with Tijuana's most controversial subject: the water problem.

The problem does not exist in the night clubs, bars or at the sports facilities frequented by tourists. These attractions have helped Tijuana — close to the California dollar — to achieve Mexico's highest "average" income.

But the people living in modest lodgings, the people living in poverty-stricken "colonias," and the squatters who came to Tijuana looking for the Yankee dollar and found nothing but a city already choked with too many people knew what Estrada Sastre was writing about.

Water Lack Desperate

Tijuana, with 166,000 population, has a water system adequate for a town of about 30,000 according to experts, and most people must buy water — if they can afford it — from "piperos" — water truck salesmen.

In what might be described as the "wettest" town in Baja California — alcoholically speaking — most of the residents ration their household water almost by the drop.

Columnist Estrada Sastre attacked this situation again and again in his pieces for the independent newspaper *Noticias*. He also wrote against a state law, Decreto 75, which was to finance the "permanent" solution — an aqueduct from Mexicali carrying Colorado River water, at a cost of $32 million.

Estrada Sastre wrote that Decreto 75 taxed most those who could least afford it. The Federal Supreme Court apparently agreed and declared Decreto 75 unconstitutional.

Police Corruption Hit

During the first two weeks of November, Estrada Sastre began attacking the state and local police for what he called "their active participation in the drug and prostitution rackets."

On Nov. 26, Estrada Sastre was killed in his hotel room with blows from, ironically, a length of water pipe. A few days later the chief of police found himself deposed and in jail and three state policemen were formally charged with the slaying and held without bail.

Border people often lose faith in local officials, but rarely in Mexico City. In travelling from Tijuana to Matamoros on the Gulf of Mexico, I often heard bitter criticism of local and state governments, but never once did I hear anyone say anything against President Lopez Mateos.

Water Please

The president has personally listened to Tijuana's desperate clamor for water.

When he toured Tijuana last May he saw the mayor's speech interrupted with yells of "We want water, not speeches!"

He also saw a weeping, elderly woman break through police lines during the presidential parade to approach Lopez Mateos' open car and plead: "Please give us water, Mr. President."

The president shook his head sadly and said: "We'll do everything we can."

Tijuana, according to Mexican government figures, has grown from a town of 30,000 in 1940 to a city of 166,000 in 1960. The "average" income of Tijuana's population is estimated at $980 per person, as compared to the national average of $280. The rub, of course, is that the "average" figure does not show that most of the money goes to a very few at the top of the economic ladder.

Job, Housing Shortage

Tijuana has an annual income of more than $160 million, yet the city cannot afford an adequate water system. It also cannot provide jobs, much less housing, for the thousands who pour in from the interior, thinking Tijuana is a city of gold.

"The gold is there," an economics professor from the University of Baja California said recently. "But social justice is not. There also is not a fair tax structure. American businessmen would drool at the thought of paying the low taxes Tijuana businessmen pay. But perhaps, most of all, we lack honest leaders on a local and state level."

In far-off Mazatlan, an editorial writer for *El Sol,* who—perhaps because of the distance—could be more objective than the economics professor, recently summed up the Tijuana situation this way.

Slap at Authorities

"In the northwest where life is easier, and where people should benefit from its advantages and so contribute to the national progress, it looks as if the opposite is true because of its people in authority who are going from bad to worse."

"(The development of Baja California) would have taken a better turn if it weren't for the absurd attitude of the successive authorities who, instead of helping, disrupt and frustrate the efforts of the federal government and private individuals."

"Two examples should suffice. One, the stubborn action of the state government to enforce at all costs the absurd and abusive Decreto No. 75 (the tax law designed to finance a water program), which has just been declared unconstitutional by the Federal Supreme Court."

"The other, the criminal attempts against four newspapermen who dared censure this and other actions by authorities, attempts which culminated in the murder of columnist Estrada Sastre."

Local Officials Fail

"It hurts and causes indignation that the efforts and sacrifices of President Lopez Mateos and the Mexican public to solve the problems of the nation are being frustrated by the people, the state and local officials, who are the ones who should be helping the most."

"These bad functionaries, with their selfishness and corruption, are merely opening the doors to Communist agents. . . ."

Juarez Falters Despite Yankee Tourist Dollar

January 10, 1962

JUAREZ, Mexico—As the largest Mexican city along the 1,800-mile U.S.–Mexican border, this community of 300,000 gets a big slice of the $520 million spent annually in border cities by American tourists.

Yet the town seems to be going broke.

Recently a 25% reduction in salaries of all city department heads, including Mayor Humberto Escobar, was approved at a special session of the Juarez City Council.

The mayor's expense account of 2,500 pesos a month ($200) was abolished altogether, and the police chief's salary was reduced from 3,000 to 2,000 pesos a month ($165).

Protest Late Pay

Policemen, teachers and city employees have complained that they are not paid for as long as 90 days at a time. Reformers claim that policemen make up for it by "mordidas" (bribes) from tourists, and point out that many teachers have been driven to part-time bartending and city employees to driving taxis.

Juarez is the national headquarters of the Partido Accion Nacional (PAN), a right-wing political party which charges that Juarez' government is spending all its money for projects which "smack of Russian ostentatiousness but which do not help the average citizen one bit."

"We have one of the fanciest and most expensive sports arenas in the world in Borunda Park," a PAN official said recently. "It's like the Russian subway — all show but with no direct benefit to the people."

Won't Answer Charges

The federal government will not answer PAN's charges, but points out that the National Border Program, which is supposed to "face-lift" and "clean up" the border, is providing a good look at the economies of the border towns.

"There are many reasons that border towns should be the most prosperous in the nation, and the border program will correct bad administration to bring this about," a program spokesman said.

Juarez, like Tijuana, suffers because its population ballooned faster than the city could successfully absorb it. Its dependence on the tourist dollar rankles many of the educated Mexicans and some insist that somehow the United States is to blame.

'Keep Your $2.50'

Jose Ramirez Sepulveda, a senior engineering student at the Juarez Agriculture College, explained it this way:

"What do you think of Kennedy's Alliance for Progress?* I think I would say, in all respect: Mr. Kennedy, keep your $2.50. You see, as I understand it, the plan will be initiated with $500 million. There are 200 million Latin Americans. If the 500 million is distributed equally, each Latin American would get 31 pesos and 25 centavos — or $2.50 American money.

"As I say, I think I would tell Mr. Kennedy to keep his $2.50. I would offer Mr. Kennedy a better solution. If he wants to sleep well, and not worry about communism in Latin America, I offer him free of charge this simple solution: Persuade his millionaires to stop buying our products so cheaply and selling theirs for so much. This theory of buying cheap and selling high is not conducive to good relations."

Juarez has had the border's biggest anti-American demonstrations in the wake of the abortive Cuban invasion, but Juarez and El Paso, Texas, across the Rio Grande, enjoy better relations than such sporadic demonstrations might suggest.

El Paso a Model

One of the reasons lies in the improved lot of El Paso's large Mexican-American population since the end of World War II. A town in which, for example, Mexican-American children were not allowed to swim in the same public swimming pools as "Anglo"-American children before the war, El Paso is now a model of democratic living.

Another example: ex–El Paso mayor Raymondo Telles, a Mexican-American, was the first member of his race to become mayor of an important Texas town — a thing undreamed of before the war — and is now President Kennedy's ambassador to Costa Rica.

The southwest is the area in which the American and Mexican cultures can blend most successfully because the Mexican side and the American side of the southwest are geographically really one. The only thing that divides the nations physically is an easily crossed bridge or a border line.

Seek Closer Ties

And ever since the war, both Mexicans and Americans seem to be looking for a closer association — perhaps as a result of mounting world tensions.

*The Alliance for Progress, initiated by President John F. Kennedy in 1961, encouraged political and economic reforms in Latin America as a way of countering potential revolutionary movements such as the 1959 Cuban Revolution.

Take the case of Columbus, N.M., a small border town about 60 miles west of El Paso.

The dedication of a state park to Pancho Villa in Columbus a few years ago was roughly akin to honoring the Mexican army at the Alamo. Yet it has happened — 45 years after Villa's army raided Columbus, killing 16 Americans and burning part of the town.

The day after the Columbus attack, President Wilson ordered a punitive expedition of 15,000 men under Gen. Pershing to go into Mexico and get Villa.

Hoped for Help

Wilson and Pershing had reason to believe that President Carranza would co-operate with the expedition for Villa was fighting Carranza's forces.

The Americans, though, didn't consider Mexicans' supersensitivity about having foreign troops on their land. (There was historic reason for the feeling: The French once attempted to put a dictator in Mexico. The Americans had taken about half of Mexico's territory after the Mexican-American War, and during the 30-year reign of dictator Porfirio Diaz, foreigners ran almost everything.)

Anyway, President Carranza voiced his objection to the entrance of U.S. troops — even if they were out to capture his deadly enemy — and on June 17, 1916, notified Gen. Pershing that further invasion would be resisted by arms.

The American troops withdrew without accomplishing their mission.

Forty-five years later, on March 18, 1961, the Pancho Villa Park was officially dedicated in Columbus.

Bill McGraw, outspoken editor of Columbus' *The Southwestern,* said of the dedication: "There's been rumbling that it shouldn't be named the Villa park at all. By some obscure reasoning, they say it honors Villa, a bandit, etc."

"Well, then, by the same spurious logic, I want the name of Virginia changed, because it honors a British queen and I am a democrat . . . and don't want New York to be called New York because it honors the Duke of York and I'm against him and his kind, too. . . ."

No Pollyanna Park

"If they want to build a Pollyanna State Park, let them put it in Santa Fe, or California, or Texas, or wherever else these 'fairweather' patriots are living."

"We in Columbus want it the Pancho Villa State Park for the simple reason that it is the only one that makes sense. Sabe?"

At the dedication ceremonies, however, Gov. Teofilo Borunda of Chihuahua tried to express more noble sentiments concerning the new park's significance. He said,

"You (people of Columbus) have risen above bitterness which came about as a result of times of violence experienced by all nations at one time or another. You have risen above any thought of revenge because you not only know democracy — you practice it."

Civic Leaders Troubled by School Dropouts

October 22, 1962

LOS ANGELES — Pablo Mendez, 17, who dropped out of high school this semester to keep his summer job, giggled nervously as he talked about his first brush with the law.

"Yeah, I was drunk. They told me at the lumber yard they would have to replace me with a union guy. They gave me my check and I got drunk with some buddies."

Pablo was in trouble only one week after he decided not to return to high school.

He says he quit school so he could work, but social workers, professors and law enforcement officials say the reason is much more complicated.

Many Reasons Cited

"The reasons for dropping out of school are many and complex, but it is certain that the 'official' reasons given are of little or no value in explaining the actual processes at work," Paul Bullock, researcher for UCLA's Institute for Industrial Relations, told an assembly subcommittee here last week.

"The simple fact is that the Board of Education either does not know or does not publicize the real factors underlying the high dropout rates in many of the schools, particularly in minority-group areas," Bullock said.

"Local school administrators unhesitatingly confirm that a significant proportion of the so-called dropouts are either encouraged or invited to leave school. These are not 'dropouts,' they're 'kick-outs.'"

In some schools, the number of pupils asked or required to drop out exceeds the number voluntarily quitting despite the fact that the school records themselves list only half of the total drop-outs as being "uneducable."

Productivity Wasted

Speaking before the Employment Opportunities Education Conference here earlier this year Dr. George R. Borrell said:

"At this very moment, the productivity of 350,000 Mexican-Americans is being wasted. This is the number who did not finish high school. They are caught in the age of mechanization, technological advances, and automation."

Pablo's father, Benito, knows his son is caught in a potentially tragic situation. What does he think of it?

"My son should never have gone to high school in the first place," Benito, a laborer, said. "Now he thinks he's too good for working with his hands like I do."

"School is all right if you're going to be a doctor or a lawyer or something. But look at this house, do you think I could ever afford to send him to college? He should have gone to grammar school and then started working."

Big Ideas, Then Job

"Instead, he gets big ideas at high school, then quits, then is thrown in jail as a drunk. Is this what his mother and I deserve?"

Pablo, with a little urging and only if you speak to him in Spanish, will probe a little deeper into why he quit school.

"I wanted to work . . . and I kept thinking about that damn algebra book. I kept saying, 'What has algebra got to do with me?' To me algebra always seemed to belong to the gringo world."

East Los Angeles is Pablo's world and he thinks it far removed from the rest of the United States.

Dr. Borrell touched on this problem when he said:

"What we need is the inclusion of that basic element that has been conspicuously absent in these discussions, the Mexican-American himself."

"For how can we presume to know what his needs, his fears, his problems, and his hopes are, unless he tells us? How can we even attempt to help, encourage and understand him, unless we are able to communicate with him?"

'Can't Get Through'

Ralph Poblano, president of the Council of Mexican-American Affairs, says the reasons for dropouts among Mexican-Americans revolve around "bilingualism and culture."

In terms of Pablo Mendez, Poblano makes sense.

Though he looks like a Mexican, Pablo is not. He's an American, but doesn't think of himself as one, and in many respects is not looked upon as one by non-Mexican-Americans.

Pablo's Spanish would sound ridiculous in a group of Tijuana high school students. And Pablo's English causes snickers among his "gringo" acquaintances.

For Pablo speaks a mixed Mexican-American lingo heavily peppered with "pachuco" slang.* He would be at home in any border town but a "foreigner" in either Guadalajara, Mex. City, or Des Moines, Ia.

According to Donald N. Michael, dropouts have the following choices: going back to school, "for which they are unsuited either by motivation or by intelligence; they can seek training that will raise them out of the untrained work force; they can compete in the growing manpower pool of those seeking relatively unskilled jobs; or they can "loaf" as Pablo is doing now.

"If they loaf," says Michael, "almost inevitably they are going to become delinquent. Thus, without adequate occupational outlets for these youths, cybernation (his word for both automation and computers) may contribute to further social disruption."

Lost to Further Schooling

Pablo has already caused some "social disruption." Because of his father's attitude, and because Pablo's mind is forever closed to the "gringo world of algebra," he is not likely to return to school.

Drop-outs and unemployment due to automation are a countrywide problem, but the Pablos of Los Angeles (and Mexican-American girls drop out as often as do boys) present a unique problem, according to Dr. Paul Sheldon of Occidental College.

---

*Beginning in the late 1930s in cities such as El Paso and Los Angeles, *pachuco* was the term for alienated young Mexican Americans who, besides facing poverty and lack of educational opportunities, also experienced the cultural tensions of being Mexicans and Americans. In response, the pachucos forged their own identity and street style. This included the invention of street slang called *caló* and the use by some of the zoot suit. Their defiant attitudes were often used by the police to justify police abuse in the barrios, most notably in the Los Angeles Zoot Suit riots of 1943.

In his report, "Mexican-Americans in Urban Public High Schools," Dr. Sheldon and colleague E. Farley Hunter pose the problem this way:

"Mexican-Americans in Southern California are represented in the higher levels of education and in the professions in much smaller numbers than their proportion in the population would warrant."

24% Dropped Out

Of the 2,061 students for whom the data was available, 403, or 24.4%, dropped out of school, Dr. Sheldon reports. Among the 947 Mexican-Americans, there were 294 dropouts, or 31%, as compared to 207, or 18.8% of the 1,114 non-Mexicans.

Of the Mexican sample, 42% graduated, as contrasted to the non-Mexicans, of whom 61% graduated.

". . . On the whole, Mexicans . . . are the ethnic group who do not accept the public school system as the ladder to climb within the social system. . . . The Mexican-American segment stands alone in having a school dropout rate in excess of its percent in the population, even below that of immigrants to the cities from Southern rural areas."

". . . The holding power of the school program is not as great for the Mexican-American as for other students."

Different Culture

Some educators, especially those who are Mexican-American, say teachers must bear in mind that Mexican-Americans are bilingual and of a different cultural background.

But, with a trace of impatience, one principal commented,

"First the minority groups want to be treated like everyone else and now they want to be treated differently. The experts should make up their minds."

The "experts," of course, realize the contradiction. Dr. Sheldon explains it this way:

"Interviews with Mexican-Americans also indicated a preference for the patterns of culture of the older generation, although many young people are now breaking away."

"While the Spanish background of the local culture and the proximity to Mexico are doubtless significant factors, this desire to cling to the old ways might be interpreted basically as a rejection of Anglo culture."

How to prevent more Mexican-Americans from becoming Pablos is called East Los Angeles' most important problem.

The experts know that the Pablos of Los Angeles hurt more than themselves. They hurt the whole community.

Commuting Mexican Farm Workers Stir U.S. Dispute 'Invasion' by 60,000 Every Day

November 25, 1962

SAN YSIDRO — Every workday from 4:30 to 7 a.m. an army "invades" the United States along the 1,800-mile Mexican-American border.

It is a friendly army of workers, many of whose 60,000 members wear the familiar straw sombrero of the Mexican farmhand. They are not to be confused with the 200,000 braceros who have worked across the vast farm areas of America this year.

The braceros (Mexican citizen farmhands contracted under Public Law 78) and this additional foreign labor force do, however, have something important in common.*

They are the objects of a far-reaching controversy which has sharp political overtones.

The controversy is, perhaps, more pronounced in California because the stakes are so high.

Essential to Farms

"Agriculture in California annually produces more than $3 billion in new wealth — an amount greater than the value of all gold mined in the state since the gold rush," according to O. W. Fillerup, executive vice president of the Council of California Growers.

The bracero and the "international commuter farmhand" are essential to keep our lush agriculture industry — the biggest in the state — going, most growers agree.

Yet on Oct. 4, 1961, President Kennedy reluctantly signed a bill extending the bracero program which he said does not include provisions "which I believe necessary to protect domestic farm workers."

The President said studies show that the Mexican labor program "is adversely affecting the wages, working conditions and employment opportunities of our own agricultural workers, large numbers of whom are unemployed or under-employed."

*The bracero program, which commenced in 1942, was a binational labor contract system whereby Mexico furnished field workers and common laborers to work principally in U.S. agriculture. The program, a World War II measure, was extended until 1964 at the request of U.S. agribusiness.

But he signed, he said, because he was aware that some Mexican workers still will be needed in some areas in 1962–63 and "am also aware of the serious impact in Mexico if many thousands of workers employed in this country were similarly deprived of this much-needed employment."

Because of the President's feeling, and pressures being applied by many diversified groups to end the bracero program, many, including State Senator Aaron Quick (D-Calexico), say the law probably will not be extended after it expires on Dec. 31, 1963.

The emergency Committee to Aid Farm Workers, formed in Los Angeles, however, says there is "an ominous" move by "certain self-interest groups" who not only want to retain the bracero program but increase it. The Rev. John G. Simmons, a Lutheran minister, is chairman of the committee.

But even should the bracero program—which Catholic Archbishop Robert Lucey of San Antonio calls "an international racket"—end, the more complex part of its controversy remains along the border states.

It is that of the "international farmhand commuter," the member of the labor army which crosses the border every daybreak.

Many are "green-card" carrying legal residents of the United States. However, they do not reside in the United States but use their highly privileged status to work for American wages and live cheaply in Mexico.

Labor Fights Them

The Texas state AFL-CIO has filed an injunction suit to end the international labor commuter, claiming the program is illegal and causes unemployment.

The litigation, Secretary of State [Dean] Rusk has told the U.S. District Court in Washington, is "jeopardizing the Alliance for Progress in Mexico and thus in all Latin America."

But first, who is this international farmhand commuter?

One is Rosario Contreras, 34-year-old native of Ojinaga, Mex., who became a legal U.S. resident because "I couldn't afford to be a bracero."

Also, though he holds the "green card" of an immigrant—with most privileges of an American citizen except voting—Contreras lives in Tijuana because, "I can't afford to live in the United States."

Contreras first worked in the United States as a "wetback" illegally sneaking across the Rio Grande, in the days when about one million desperate Mexicans bid against each other for jobs in this country.

On his return to Mexico he married, acquired a family of six and spent all his American earnings. By this time the U.S. Border Patrol had intensified its crackdown on wetbacks, and Contreras decided to become a bracero.

Had To Pay Bribes

"The mordidas (literally 'bites,' that is, bribes) I had to pay Mexican bureaucrats came to 600 pesos, but luckily I was able to borrow it from my brother who had just returned home from Texas as a mojado (wetback)," Contreras said.

"My bracero days 10 years ago were good. Americanos are muy extranos (very strange) to me, but they're generous. That's why I always wanted to return. I applied to be a bracero again, but I found out the mordidas were getting too expensive—1,000 pesos they wanted this time."

"So I again became a mojado, though this time I didn't wade the Rio Grande. I climbed the fence (on many parts of the border only a chain link fence separates the countries) and went to my old patron (boss)."

"When he heard I had jumped the fence he got paler than he usually is. He said he was glad to see a good worker back, but that he wanted no trouble with illegal workers. He told me to go back to Tijuana, and he would sponsor me with papers and everything."

"I finally got a tarjeta verde (green card) and was made emigrado (immigrant). I could live in San Diego, but who can at those prices? So I cross the line every morning at 4:30, am picked up on the American side by a truck from my patron's farm, and taken to work in the lettuce field. It's not too bad, except that by the time I get back home to Tijuana all I'm good for is bed. I have to get up at 3 a.m."

Contreras' right to be a legal U.S. resident, an actual resident of Tijuana and a worker in San Diego County irks domestic farmhands, especially the unemployed, and those who feel the letter of the immigration laws is being abused.

The San Diego Superior Court has ruled persons like Contreras are on good legal grounds. In 1961, some members of Laborers Local 89, AFL-CIO, picketed their hiring hall protesting the hiring of non-citizens. The union brought suit for an injunction to stop the picketing.

Judge Eli Levenson ruled that "the fact that a man is or is not a citizen of the United States . . . has no materiality. His membership in the local rises out of the type of work he does."

"The fact remains," says Kenneth Wilson, a San Diego merchant, "that these people, though legal U.S. residents, have no intention of ever living here and what's more never even buy anything here with their American wages."

On the other hand, many feel that international commuter workers are a natural phenomenon of border living. Rusk told the U.S. District Court in Washington that neighboring border cities "have grown into single economic communities."

Many who agree with Rusk say the issue is not one of whether these commuters have the right to work in the United States. The issue, they argue, is the effect these international commuters have on the economy of American border cities and what to do about it.

Pros and Cons

"If we cut out the resident aliens, we could not get enough Americans to replace them," says a farmer association official. "The more immigrants who come across the border and work, the less the number of braceros we import."

Dionicio Morales, former Labor Department compliance officer and Los Angeles Mexican-American leader, disagrees.

"The commuter worker and the bracero are killing employment opportunities for many, including Mexican-Americans in Los Angeles who are now in the position of having to compete for jobs against Mexican nationals with green cards who have wandered up from the border," he said.

"Just how long is the American public going to buy the idea that a foreign labor force is needed? We have vast unemployment in San Diego county and throughout the Southland. Automation is upon us and yet the foreign unskilled and farm workers are getting the jobs that American-born workers should get."

"Why? Because braceros and international commuter workers are willing to work for less."

Farm Workers' Lot Held Worsening in Southland

November 27, 1962

EL CENTRO—The farm worker has never been admitted to the "American Affluent Society."

In fact, the lot of the domestic farm worker "is worse now than

20 years ago," according to Catholic Archbishop Robert Lucey of San Antonio.

The reasons are so complicated that only dogmatic unionists, politicians and naive "do-gooders" claim to have pat answers to the problem.

2 Million Workers

Dr. Henry Anderson, labor expert, testified last year before the U.S. Senate Committee on Agriculture and Forestry that there are "at least 2 million American agricultural workers in the United States."

"With their dependents, they represent perhaps 6 or 7 million human beings," Dr. Anderson testified.

California's biggest industry is agriculture and it points out with pride that the state "annually produces more than $3 billion in new wealth — an amount greater than the value of all gold mined in the state since the gold rush."

Yet, Malaqueo Garcia, with a farm at San Ysidro, on the U.S. side of the border at Tijuana, says he can't make the grade and is about to give up his life's work.

He hires some domestic workers and Tijuana farmhands, but the latter usually find better work on bigger farms, where "green-card" holders (Tijuana's commuter workers) and braceros are hired.

Garcia could never hire braceros because he would never meet the standards set by Public Law 78 in order to get the much-wanted bracero.

Garcia's workers eat and sometimes sleep in a wooden building right out of "the Grapes of Wrath." Garcia admits that the structure is filthy, but says he's too poor to do anything about it. Besides, he has no fear of getting in trouble over unsanitary conditions.

Hires Americans

He doesn't hire braceros so he's not afraid of a visit from a federal compliance officer who would order him to clean up. He hires U.S. citizens — and no one seems to look out for them.

Scandalous sanitation in domestic agricultural workers housing is nothing new in California. Following World War II, the number of domestic agricultural workers increased and nationwide publicity was focused on the San Joaquin Valley, when 28 infants, mainly from families of agricultural workers, died. The deaths, the investigation showed, were due chiefly to diarrhea and pneumonia.

At that time Gov. Warren set up a committee for an intensive study of agricultural labor in the San Joaquin Valley. The committee noted that "the infant mortality rate is higher in the San Joaquin Valley than elsewhere in the state" and that "the problem, in addition to improving environmental conditions, is also related to inadequate health resources, and lack of maximum availability and utilization of medical facilities."

In July, 1960, Gov. [Edmund G.] Brown ordered the State Department of Public Health to study current health conditions and services for seasonal agricultural workers and to propose specific solutions. Dr. Malcolm H. Merrill, state director of public health, appointed Dr. R. Bruce Jessup of Stanford University School of Medicine to conduct the investigation.

How are things today?

Shocked at Conditions

Speaking at a California Farm Bureau Federation meeting in San Diego Nov. 13, Dr. Jessup said in part:

"After three years work, I, though filled with astonishment and profound respect for your accomplishment, remain at the same time shocked at the poverty, disease, and living standards which you still tolerate in many of your labor camps and rural fringe areas, housing an important segment of your seasonal farm workers' families. I am shocked at your apparent attitude of defeatism — with some notable exceptions — in not launching an attack with modern tools on basic farm labor problems in California."

"I refuse to believe that, notwithstanding your many problems and the difficulties involved, you cannot with your demonstrated heart and brains, develop over the next five years, with assistance from workers representatives and community representatives, a satisfactory, reliable domestic California farm labor force to meet the industry's needs."

Migration Unneeded

"This could be a work force with a truly adequate annual family income; whose families would not have to migrate and thus fall heir to the inevitable hazards and disruptions that will always attend family migration. With your programs for foreign workers and annual worker plans over the last decade you have proved that a work force of this type can be kept working, can be recruited, transported and that it can fulfill the industry's demands."

"It can be done with domestic California workers; further, it can provide a force in the future; with increasing mechanization — but inevitably continuing need for unskilled hands."

Argument Given

California farmers say they can't get along without braceros and "international commuter farmhands" because there is no domestic work force to do the work. Domestic workers are called lazy and undependable. Besides they won't do "stoop" work such as picking lettuce, they add.

There is a garrulous and angry physician in Brawley who disagrees with the fury of a crusader. He is Dr. Ben Yellen, who claims the "domestic farmhand was forced out of his home and job."

"In the old days, there were labor contractors who would bring crews of domestic farm workers to different farms," he told the *Times*. "These domestic farm workers had their permanent homes in the Valley. In the summer they left to work in Northern California."

"But the big farmers did not want to pay decent wages, so they started a campaign of propaganda saying that there were not enough domestic farm workers and they needed to import Mexican farm workers."

"This amounts to a government handout to the big farmers, the handout being Mexican labor. You do not see the government importing Mexicans to factories so that the manufacturers can have low labor costs. If the lettuce growers need farm workers, let them pay decent wages and they will get farm workers. But they do not want to pay American wages. They want the cheap labor from Mexico."

Two Worlds Seen

Mike Miranda, 89-year-old Brawley patriarch, puts it another way:

"I have seen two worlds in my lifetime of farming. In the old world, the good world, the little guy like me had a chance. In the new world, now, you're discriminated against because you're an American citizen."

Miranda says that "50, 30, 20 years ago the little guy could make a good living. My wife Benita and I used to pick figs for $30, $35 each week," Miranda said. "Twenty years ago that was good money. Then I started contracting workers, Brawley people mostly, and at one time furnished from 300 to 500 workers to the farmers here. Just last year I lost the housing in which my workers used to live in the old world — because I couldn't pay the taxes."

Can't Compete

"Who can compete with the braceros and the people that come from Mexicali to work for cheap wages? Mexicali is swallowing us." (The Mexicali area has a population of about 250,000 compared to Imperial Valley's 75,000.)

"They say they must hire Mexican nationals because there are no domestics to do it. They're right. There are no domestics because they forced us out of business. They say domestics won't do stoop labor like the braceros. I ask you, who did all the stoop labor when the Imperial Valley was just starting. We, we Mexican-Americans, Japanese and the Chinese before that. But they all lived here. They were part of the valley. They weren't brought in like machines and sent back to where they came when the harvest was done. . . ."

Good Old Days

Luis Cureil, a friend of Miranda, also talked about the "old, good days in the valley."

"You see East Brawley, now," he said sadly. "Well, it was not this run down in the old days. When we did the picking in the valley, we weren't rich but our town looked better, because we had the jobs and they paid pretty good."

"It could be like the old days if they wanted. The war is over, the boys are back. But the braceros and Mexicali people have forced us out."

How about those 2 million migrant workers who are still supposed to be roaming about the country looking for jobs in the fields? Where are they? Why don't they come to California any more?

In October, the Bread of Life Rescue Mission in Brawley served 2,316 meals to 758 men, women and children. Many of them were migrant families from Texas, Oklahoma and the deep South.

One was Robert Louis Kramer of East Texas, father of two. "We came to the Imperial Valley 'cause they told us it was the land of plenty," he said.

"We got jobs, OK. The law says we domestics must get the jobs before foreign people. But I didn't last. You can't keep up with these Mexican nationals. They work harder and for less than anyone else. Maybe they can live on $1 an hour and can work without stopping for a little rest."

"I have nothing against the Mexican nationals. All I'm saying is how can domestics compete with guys who will work harder and for less?"

Negro May Win Roybal Seat in City Council

December 16, 1962

LOS ANGELES—Los Angeles councilman Edward R. Roybal, for 13 years the "Papacito" of local Mexican-American politics, may be replaced by a Negro because of a lack of Latin etiquette.*

When Roybal moves to Washington in January as the new Democratic congressman from the 30th District, he will leave the 9th Council District in a radically different situation than when he first took over.

Once inhabited predominantly by Mexican-Americans, the 9th District—bounded roughly by Main St. on the west, Valley Blvd. on the north, Indiana St. on the east and Slauson Ave. on the south—is fast becoming another Los Angeles Harlem.

According to recent estimates, of the more than 260,000 persons residing in the 9th District, 50% are Negro, 35% Mexican-American and the remainder are Oriental, Jewish and other ethnic groups.

Roybal Aware

No one is more aware of this than Roybal, who recently warned a large Mexican-American political meeting that Latins should stop thinking of the district as their very own.

However, the meeting, called by Juan Acevedo, vice president of the statewide Mexican-American Political Assn., unilaterally chose its candidate—Richard Tafoya, Mayor [Sam] Yorty's field secretary for Latin American affairs and Roybal's cousin.

"This was the biggest mistake a Mexican-American could have made," Roybal told *The Times*. "It probably hurt Tafoya's chances to succeed me."

The meeting of about 250 Mexican-Americans at the Alexandria Hotel not only incensed some Negro leaders, but split the Mexican-American vote as well.

---

*Roybal was elected to the Los Angeles City Council in 1949, the first Mexican American to serve in that council since the nineteenth century. In 1962 he was elected to the U.S. Congress, where he served until 1992.

Tafoya, 38, personable, and reportedly favored by Mayor Yorty, already is making speeches as the Mexican-American community's favorite son.

Claims Enough Votes

But Gilbert W. Lindsay, 62, a Negro deputy to Supervisor Kenneth Hahn, says he may not "be making as much noise now as Mr. Tafoya but I have the votes, the support and the council's ear."

"If a showdown came now in the City Council, I would win the appointment," Lindsay says. "The council knows that it's about time the 400,000 Negroes living in the city of Los Angeles should get some representation."

Lindsay says Tafoya's selection by a strictly Mexican-American group "was the best thing that ever happened to me."

"It only unified the Negro vote that much more," Lindsay said.

Other Negro leaders point out that though Mexican-Americans have about 50 Mexican-American organizations throughout Los Angeles County, the Negroes have a "large and powerful organization in the NAACP."

Negro leaders say they got a "fast shuffle" when Joe E. Hollingsworth, a Caucasian, was appointed 10th District city councilman Aug. 25, 1961, to replace Charles Navarro, now city controller.

Solid for Lindsay

Hollingsworth won appointment by an 8–6 vote after a bitter debate in the City Council. At that time, Councilmen Roybal, James Harvey Brown, Everett G. Burkhalter, John S. Gibson, Jr., Gordon R. Hahn and Mrs. Rosalind Wyman voted for the appointment of George Thomas, a Negro.

Norman O. Houston, president of the Golden State and Mutual Insurance Co., largest Negro insurance company west of Chicago with a home office here, says Negro leaders "are watching very closely to see we're not neglected again."

"We've got more votes than the Mexicans in this area and I think the Negro community is solidly behind Mr. Lindsay," Houston said. "The *Sentinel* and the *California Eagle* (Negro newspapers) are for Mr. Lindsay and also such leaders as Dr. H. Claude Hudson, president of the Broadway Federal Savings & Loan Assn. I don't think we can or should be ignored this time."

Wants All Represented

Mexican-Americans and Negroes might have backed a single candidate, acceptable to both groups, if that meeting of Mexican-Americans at the Alexandria had listened to reason, Roybal now says sadly.

"I told them that they should think of ways to select a liberal candidate to succeed me," Roybal told *The Times*. "I warned them against selecting a candidate unilaterally."

"I told them they should select someone who would represent all groups — not just Mexican-Americans. I even went so far as to say I would prefer a liberal Republican candidate for the post than a reactionary democrat."

Tafoya, caught in the middle, says he doesn't feel his selection by a Mexican-American group should isolate him from other ethnic groups. "I agree with Congressman-elect Roybal that who-ever gets the post should represent all ethnic groups, and that's exactly what I intend to do should I be appointed or elected to the 9th District's seat."*

Parley Airs Problems of Mexican-Americans

January 18, 1963

PHOENIX — About 500 community leaders are gathering here to spell out why they think the American Dream has eluded most of the 3.5 million Mexican-Americans in the five southwestern states.

The conference, mostly of educators from California, Arizona, New Mexico and Colorado, will air theories on why Mexican-Americans generally are doing poorly educationally, economically and socially.

With emphasis on education, the seminar will probe causes of school drop-outs among Mexican-Americans, who, according to statistics, quit school earlier and in greater numbers than any other ethnic group.

Remains a "Foreigner"

In a paper submitted to the conference, Marcos de Leon, teacher of Spanish at Van Nuys High School, said educators "can no longer accept the school's usual educational program . . . developed for the English-speaking student as a valid educational approach with the Mexican-American."

---

*Gilbert W. Lindsay was elected to replace Roybal on the city council.

He charged that even though the Mexican-American tries to "identify himself with the representative culture, he still remains a foreigner, a stranger and, for all intents and purposes, a 'Mexican' with the common stereotyped connotations brought on by some 100 years of cultural conflict."

"Moreover," de Leon said, "the partial disintegration of the parent culture and the fact he has been taught through social pressure to be ashamed of and even to disown his ethnic ancestry, has made the Mexican-American a victim of confusion, frustration and insecurity."

Census Analyzed

In an analysis of the 1960 U.S. census for the conference, University of Notre Dame sociologist Dr. Julian Samora said that Spanish-speaking people in the United States number "at least 6 million."

He reported that in the past 10 years the number of Spanish-speaking people has increased 88% in California, 41% in Texas, 8% in New Mexico, 6% in Arizona and 5% in Colorado.

According to Dr. Samora, the census shows 1,426,534 persons with Spanish surnames in California, most of whom live in the Southland. And, he adds, only 24.4% of these have a high school education or more, as compared with 54.8% for the "Anglos" and 39.8% for the non-whites, including Negroes.

Much of the blame for the large [number of] school drop-outs among Mexican-Americans must fall on the schools, Dr. Samora charged.

"The lower-class and the minority students who do not fit the mold are less likely to be educated and more likely to become dropout statistics."

Few school systems can, or do, gear their curricula to the needs of the Mexican-American, Dr. Samora said.

"It is easier and safer to prohibit the speaking of Spanish on the school grounds and in the school (the need being to learn English) than to take the imaginative step of teaching both English and Spanish to both Anglos and Spanish-speakers beginning in the elementary school," he said.

Spanish-speaking Angelenos: A Culture in Search of a Name

February 24, 1963

Los Angeles has one of the largest Spanish-speaking urban populations in the Western Hemisphere. Most are "Mexicans," but historians tell us this does not accurately describe these people because in many respects they are "indigenous" to Southern California and the Southwest. Though they also help make up what generally is known as California's "Spanish heritage," Spain is not their "mother country." They are so highly heterogeneous they can not be adequately understood by studying the cultures of Spain or Mexico. This is an attempt to trace where they came from, what they are and where they are going — first of six parts.

Three guys were arguing in an East Los Angeles bar and one said angrily: "The trouble with you is you're just a Mexican with a gray-flannel serape."

"That's better than being a cholo who professes love for 'la raza' and Mexico and yet came here to live, work and have your children," was the heated retort.

The third man argued against all such "self-defeating" terms as Mexican-American, cholo (slang for a Mexican immigrant), pocho (slang for an American-born Mexican), Spanish-American and Latin American.

Being from Texas he especially resented the last term because in parts of Texas a saying goes that a "a Latin American is a Mexican who has paid his poll tax."

"No, you're both wrong," he said. "We're American. . . . We're Spanish-speaking Americans."

Demonstrate Problem

However ludicrous such arguments may seem, they demonstrate how difficult it is to pinpoint just what more than 700,000 Los Angeles area residents really are. The complexity of definition is further aggravated by those who speak of Los Angeles' "Spanish heritage."

Romanticists like to think that El Pueblo de Nuestra Senora La Reina de Los Angeles de Porciuncula was settled by Spanish grandees and caballeros, sophisticated descendants of the "conquistadores."

Some story-tellers assure us that Spanish Gov. Felipe de Neve, leading a detachment of soldiers proudly bearing the banner of Spain, and followed by the original settlers, entered our city on Sept. 4, 1781, in a flurry of glory.

Not so, says Father Zephyrin Engelhardt, OFM. In his authoritative "San Gabriel Mission and the Beginnings of Los Angeles," a Mission

San Gabriel historical work published by the Franciscan Herald Press, he writes:

"It is a pity, and rather cruel, to spoil this [romantic] description of the founding of Los Angeles; but our duty is to supply accurate information and to correct misstatements or errors."

Lacked Enthusiasm

According to Father Engelhardt, Gov. de Neve had hoped to settle Los Angeles with Spaniards, but being unable to muster any enthusiasm from them he ordered the settlement made by whoever was available.

As a matter of fact, continues the Franciscan priest, the "sorry crowd of settlers" were led practically at gunpoint by a "corporal and three soldiers."

Father Engelhardt says Los Angeles' first settlers were "Jose de Lara, 50, a Spaniard, with an Indian wife and three children; Basilio Rosas, 68, an Indian, with a mulattress wife and six children.

"Antonio Mesa, 38, a Negro, with a mulattress wife and five children; . . . Antonio F. Felix Villavicencio, 30, a Spaniard with an Indian wife and one child; Jose Vanegas, 28, an Indian [Los Angeles' first 'alcalde' or mayor], with an Indian wife and one child."

"Alejandro Rosas, 25, an Indian, with an Indian wife; Pablo Rodriguez, 25, an Indian, with an Indian wife and a child; Manuel Camero, 30, a mulatto, with a mulattress wife; Luis Quintero, 55, a Negro, with a mulattress wife and five children; and Jose Moreno, 22, a mulatto with a mulattress wife."

Of the original settlers, then, including their wives, there were two Spaniards, one mestizo, two Negroes, eight mulattoes and nine Indians. Their children were four Spanish-Indian; five Spanish-Negro; eight Negro-Indian; three Spanish-Negro-Indian and two Indian.

Overshadowing Aspect

All of this, of course, is nothing to raise the eyebrows of anyone living in a democratic society. But it is curious how the "Spanish heritage" of Los Angeles has overshadowed all other historical aspects concerning the founding [of] our city.

Dr. Paul M. Sheldon, director of the Laboratory in Urban Culture, Occidental College, calls this "Spanish heritage" the "patina of romantic misinformation which attributes to the Spaniards a venture which was essentially Mexican-Indian and remained substantially so until the village (Los Angeles) and surrounding 'ranchos' were taken over lock, stock and barrel by Anglos during the years from 1818 to the 1880s."

California itself was discovered by a Portuguese, Juan Cabrillo, who was in the employ of Spain. He came here in 1542, but it was not until 1769 that Father Junipero Serra came to establish the famous missions.

All told, however, only a few hundred Spaniards settled. Since then immigration from Spain has been negligible. (For 120 years — from 1820 to 1940 — the total Spanish immigration to the United States was about 175,000, most of which came after 1900.)

Historians say that though the Spaniards transplanted their language, their religion and many of their institutions in the Americas, they did so through other groups. Spanish culture, they say, was superimposed and inflicted on native peoples in the Americas, some of whom already were in the Southwest.

Even so, "Spanish heritage" is always stressed when the history of Mexican-Americans is honored in Los Angeles. Last year at an Olvera St. fiesta, for example, a much respected hotel owner and descendant of Hernando Cortes was named "padrino" or protector of the Mexican-American colony.

This was a well-intentioned gesture meant to please the many Mexican-Americans (for lack of a better term) in Los Angeles. But a Mexican-American community leader called *The Times* to complain that this was "historically grotesque."

"Naming a descendant of Cortes as a 'protector' of the Mexican-American population is like naming a descendant of King George as a 'protector' of the descendants of American revolutionists," he said with a chuckle.

Question Rises

If Mexican-Americans in Southern California are not "Spanish" or even their first cousins, then what are they — besides being Spanish-speaking Americans?

The Times asked this question recently of Dr. George I. Sanchez, University of Texas expert on ethnic groups in the Southwest.

"They defy categorical classification as a group and no term or phrase adequately describes them," he said.

"Biologically, they range over all the possible combinations of first their heterogeneous Spanish antecedents and, then, of the 'mestizaje' (interbreeding) resulting from the crossing of Spaniards and various indigenous peoples of Mexico and the Southwest."

Were Already Here

(That in many respects the Mexican-Americans are "indigenous" to the Southwest is often mentioned by historians. They like to point out that the Spanish-language minority did not come from Spain and Mexico. They were already very much a part of the Southwest when the Anglo-Americans arrived here, experts tell us.)

"Historically," continued Dr. Sanchez, "they are both old and new to this region—some came with Onate in 1598, others with missionaries of the 18th century; some were part of the gold rush of '49, others came to build railroads a few decades later; many came as contract-labor during World War I."

"Culturally, reflecting their varied biological and historical backgrounds, they are many peoples—the 'californios,' the 'hispanos,' the 'mexico-tejanos,' and numerous other cultural personalities produced by the range of their antecedents and their environments, by their occupations, by their culture-contacts."

Language Not Single

Even their language, Dr. Sanchez points out, is heterogeneous.

"Their mother tongue, their vernacular, is usually Spanish—of every conceivable variation, that is. In fact, for some the home-language is English; for others a part-English, part-Spanish vernacular is the rule."

The reason the "Spanish heritage" is propagandized out of proportion at the expense of the Mexican-Indian heritage is the Anglo-American's attitude toward the so-called non-white races, several educators charged at a recent Mexican-American seminar in Phoenix.

"The Mexican-American is a victim of confusion, frustration and insecurity because he has been taught through social pressure to be ashamed of and even disown his ethnic ancestry," says Marcos de Leon, teacher of Spanish at Van Nuys High School.

Road to Disaster

"A very practical teaching of mental hygiene is that one cannot run away from himself, or what he is. To do so is to invite disaster."

"Somewhere along the way the Mexican-American must make a stand and recognize the fact that if there is to be progress against those barriers which prevent and obstruct a more functional citizenship, he must above all retrieve his dignity and work as a person with a specific ethnic antecedent, having a positive contribution to make to civilization."

"No man can find a true expression for living who is ashamed of himself or his people."

Leader Calls Effort to Aid Mexican-Americans Failure

Second of a Series

February 25, 1963

Salvador (Macho) Chavez, 19, is Mexican-American, anti-social and a bum.

Los Angeles taxpayers have provided him with schools, four of which have kicked him out; rehabilitation centers, where he scoffed at sincere attempts to help him, and jails, where his criminal habits were fired up.

Gov. (Edmund G. "Pat") Brown wishes he could do something for Macho. Mayor Samuel W. Yorty is on record for uplifting him. All city councilmen have supported legislation tailored to help Macho out of the gutter. All members of the County Board of Supervisors work hard to answer his dilemma.

There's only one thing these officials have not done, charges Dr. George R. Borrell, East Los Angeles physician active in Mexican-American affairs. They have not really communicated with Macho.

"It's not only that these officials don't speak Spanish," Dr. Borrell said, "though that presents a problem in understanding this complex bum."

Sense of Fair Play

"It's that, ironically, because of their sense of fair play and democratic feelings they refuse to think of Macho as anything other than 'an American boy of a minority group in trouble.'"

"If Macho had been born Irish, Negro, Hungarian, Anglo or Italian he still might have grown up to be a bum."

"But because he's a Los Angeles-born Mexican-American bum, his problem is unique."

"There's no panacea for all diseases. Each has to be looked at separately."

Militant Hate

His admirers tagged him Macho, a nickname derived from "machismo" (which has been defined as a feeling of overwhelming masculinity), because of his militant hate of the established order.

Is it so important that Macho is a bum?

Aren't things better generally for the Mexican-American?

Haven't more Mexican-Americans assimilated successfully since the end of World War II?

Haven't the freeways done away with many East Los Angeles slums?

And isn't it significant that you no longer see pachucos walking the streets in their zoot suits?

Standing in Hoyo Mara ("Marvelous Hole"), a "barrio" (neighborhood) in unincorporated East Los Angeles, Dr. Borrell made a wide arc with his arm as if to introduce someone to the slums around him.

"Look at this," he said. "Also listen to this. In the 1950 census it was determined that three-quarters of the Mexican-American population had not finished high school. In the 1960 census it was determined that three-quarters of the Mexican-American population had not finished high school."

"You call that progress?"

"Surely there must be something radically wrong with our leadership—including, of course, our Mexican-American leadership—when in 10 years there has been no improvement in our school drop-out problems."

Tuberculosis Threat

"And do you know that tuberculosis is a serious threat in Mexican-American ghettos? Yes, in our space age, tuberculosis is a serious problem among Mexican-Americans."

"Crime? Ask the police if it's not too high in Mexican-American ghettos."

"Narcotics? Recently released statistics show 54% of all Californians in institutions for dope addicts are Mexican-Americans. Who do the dope peddlers prey on if it's not the frustrated, uneducated and unhappy?"

"No, things aren't as peachy as some of our so-called leaders would like to make us think. Look around you."

(Dr. Borrell's contentions were checked with city, county and state statistics. They mirror the doctor's facts if not his feelings.)

To look at the problems of the Mexican-Americans "separately," Dr. Borrell, chief of staff at Bellavista Hospital, has helped form the Equal Opportunities Foundation.

Officers Installed

Working in conjunction with UCLA's Institution of Industrial Relations, the foundation's officers recently were installed by George Siros, representing President Kennedy's Committee on Equal Opportunity.

Dionicio Morales, the foundation's consultant, is a longtime Mexican-American leader in Los Angeles. He has been executive director of the Council for Mexican-American Affairs and has been honored by the Board of Supervisors for his "outstanding service to the Mexican-American community."

"When I look at the beautiful scroll the supervisors gave me I feel a tinge of frustration," Morales says. "Somehow I feel we so-called Mexican-American leaders have failed seriously. I worked hard to form this new foundation because it seems to me Mexican-American community problems will never be solved by certain professionals, would-be politicians and the perennial self-appointed leaders who do nothing but sit on their hands and give this huge minority sugar-coated lip service when called upon to help."

Problem Urgency Felt

Others feel the urgency, if not the passion, about bringing swift action in tackling Mexican-American problems.

Supervisor Ernest Debs has gone on record for scrutinizing the problems of Mexican-Americans apart from those of other minorities. He has pledged that he will work to see that funds available to the Youth Opportunities Board of Greater Los Angeles will go to that end.

Occidental College, whose Dr. Paul M. Sheldon and E. Farley Hunter have published a study on Mexican-American school dropouts, has announced a spring conference on "Educational and Social Problems of Urban and Rural Mexican-American Youth."

Many of the experts who will take part at Occidental attended the recent conference on "Mexican-Americans in the Southwest" in Phoenix. At that conference a new approach was much discussed under the pedagogic title of "Acculturation."

Dr. George I. Sanchez of the University of Texas explained, smiling, that acculturation means Mexican-Americans have the obligation to become Americanized and "Anglos have the obligation to become Mexicanized gringos."

The Southwest, educators pointed out in Phoenix, means not only the Southwestern states of the United States but also northern Mexico because both "are one geographically, climatically and in many respects culturally."

After *The Times* printed reports of the Phoenix conference a reader wrote the newspaper in part:

"This country has been settled by foreigners from all over the world. Excluding those from England (even they had some adjustments to make) their children had to adjust themselves. The parents, for the most part, went to night school, read our English newspapers, spoke English at all times. . . . Furthermore, supposing for instance, the Chinese and Japanese among us wanted their language spoken on the school grounds . . . ?"

"Do the Mexican parents go to night school: Do they read the English newspapers?"

Wrong Perspective

"Why do Mexican parents speak Spanish in public. . . . I hear them around the shopping centers. Why do they give the children tortillas, etc., for their school lunches? Why do they not give them the kind of sandwiches, etc., that the other children have so that they do not feel embarrassed when they take out their lunches? The parents could do a great deal to help the children feel 'American' by themselves adopting the American way. You know, when in Rome . . ."

"This reader," claims Dr. Borrell, "looks at the problems of the Mexican-Americans from the wrong perspective. Many well-meaning people like him are saying in effect, 'All you have to do is be American, speak American.'"

"Hell, Mexican-Americans aren't interlopers. They were in the Southwest and borderlands hundreds of years before the descendants of the people who now tell Mexican-Americans to 'Americanize.'"

"Mexican-Americans are not immigrants to the Southwest in the sense that Japanese, Chinese, Irish, Anglos, Italians, Jews, southern Negroes, etc., are immigrants. Mexico, after all, is part of the Southwest. How can you blame Mexican-Americans for in many ways rejecting the Anglo culture when theirs was here first?"

"How can we ever understand Latin America and woo her away from communism when many of us don't understand that Mexican-

Americans are bicultural, not through accident but through nature? The two cultures have fused in them and nothing is going to tear them apart."

"Why is it all right to continue to call many of our cities and streets by Spanish names, encourage Mexican-Spanish architecture, praise and eat Mexican food and still expect Mexican-Americans to become wholly Anglicized?"

"And how is a person who in his youth was not allowed to enter certain restaurants and movie houses going to feel 'American' now just because he is being told things are different now?"

Serape Belt Occupies City's Heart

Third of a Series
February 26, 1963

The heart of Los Angeles could be called the Serape Belt.

Here in a six-mile-square area live most of metropolitan Los Angeles' 700,000 Mexican-Americans.

You can stand at Brooklyn and Rowena Aves. for an hour and not hear a word of English. In a neighborhood church the mass is celebrated in Spanish.

Handmade tortillas are bought here by people who don't think of them as exotic food. And at night you can go to a cantina to drink tequila con limon and listen to a mariachi band, relatively certain that no tourists will gape at you.

The Serape Belt is bounded by the Los Angeles River, Broadway, Huntington Dr., Alhambra Rd., Garfield Ave. and the Santa Ana Freeway.

Included are parts of the city of Los Angeles, all of the unincorporated county section known as East Los Angeles and parts of such adjoining communities as Montebello, Monterey Park and Alhambra.

In the heart of the Serape Belt, encircled by the Golden State, San Bernardino, Long Beach and Santa Ana Freeways — are a dozen census tracts with a population from 75 to 99% Mexican-American. Surrounding tracts vary from 30 to 74%.

Sarita, age 2, lives there. She has tuberculosis.

In her area, 440 cases of tuberculosis were recorded by the City Health Department in 1962. It is the same in other parts of the Serape Belt.

In Sarita's neighborhood last year 32 cases of TB were discovered in the age groups of 1 to 4. Twenty-seven cases of active tuberculosis were reported in the 5 to 9 age group. Nineteen teenagers were found to be tuberculous.

Live Close Together

Other TB statistics for the same neighborhood: 68 active cases in the 20–29 age group; 88 in the 30–39 age group; 64 in the 40–49 age group; 62 in the 50–59 age group; 50 in the 60–69 age group; and 27 in the 70 and over group.

"This is only the number we know about," emphasizes Al Torribio, assistant to City Health Officer Dr. George M. Uhl. "Who knows how many others go undetected? Mexican-American families are large. TB is infectious, and East Los Angeles families live close together from infancy to old age."

Because of ancient prejudices, uneducated Mexicans consider tuberculosis something to be ashamed of, Torribio says. It's a word to be whispered, something somewhat sinful. And so, in many cases, it goes undetected.

"We're trying to educate these people to take advantage of free chest X-rays yearly," Torribio said, "But old ways, old prejudices are hard to overcome."

These are crowded neighborhoods with many children. Sarita once lived in a house with 12 other persons whose ages ranged from one to 68. A Regional Planning Commission study shows that of the total East Los Angeles population 14.6% were under 5 years of age, as compared to 10.1% for the rest of Los Angeles.

East Los Angeles Trails

The study also shows that in the 20–64 age group East Los Angeles is behind the rest of Los Angeles by 7%. One explanation: The age group able to acquire better jobs moves away.

Sarita's father, a laborer, made $4,689 in 1962. The average for East Los Angeles is higher, $5,434 — but even this is far below the city average of $7,066.

Sarita's grandfather is a university man, but he never made it above pumping gas and writing letters for a fee. To escape the Mexican Revolution he came here from Guadalajara in 1911. But he never was assimilated in the Anglo world. Why?

"When I came to Los Angeles I discovered I was thought of as more or less a peon," he says. "I learned that the word Mexican was kind of a dirty word. . . . You know. I was treated like my class in Mexico treated and treats the peon. So I guess I kind of gave up. It's hard to progress, when no one around you is. . . ."

Elsewhere in the county are other—and interesting—Mexican-American areas.

Another Large Area

One is a section north of Pico Rivera bounded by Whittier Blvd. on the south, Whittier narrows on the north, Rio Hondo on the west and the San Gabriel River on the east. Four census tracts there vary from 35% to 90% Mexican-American.

Other heavily concentrated areas: Los Nietos (south of Whittier), up to 59% in some tracts; in the San Gabriel Mission area (south of Las Tunas Dr.), up to 44% in one tract; in Wilmington (between Pacific Coast Highway and Cerritos Channel), up to 74% in one tract; in San Pedro (between Miraflores Dr. and 10th St.), three tracts with up to 59%; and in South Azusa (between Foothill Blvd. and Arrow Highway), one tract with up to 59% Mexican-Americans.

In most of western Los Angeles County the Mexican-American population is under 3%. The same holds true in Burbank, Glendale and Pasadena. In the extreme eastern part of the county (La Puente, Covina, Glendora) the percentages run from under 3% to 20%, the latter in one or two census tracts.

The second largest concentration of Mexican-Americans is in the San Fernando-Pacoima area of the San Fernando Valley. A large tract there has 60% to 74% concentration with street boundaries sharply dividing Anglo and Mexican neighborhoods. Other tracts, including the San Fernando Mission area, are from 45% to 59% Mexican-American.

Similar to Sonora

The intersection of Hewitt and Kalisher Sts. in San Fernando reminds one of San Luis in the Mexican state of Sonora. There is no hectic movement so characteristic of big cities. There is a tortilla factory, a Mexican record and magazine shop, a dreary cantina. Children play quietly in the sidewalks.

You have to remind yourself that you're in the San Fernando Valley, the fastest growing area of Los Angeles.

But things are not all placid in this Mexican-American pocket in the valley, according to the Rev. Luis Sada, pastor of the Iglesia Metodista (Mexican Methodist Church) at 467 Kalisher St.

"There must be 10,000 Mexican-Americans in my area and they all seem to be living in the past — or in a modern hell," says Mr. Sada. "Most of the people here are good, but they seem to have given up. There seems to be no opportunities for them because they're Mexicans. And the young! Drunkenness, narcotics, crime."

"Sometimes I can't believe I'm in a modern city. We seem to be forgotten."

Speaks in Spanish

Mr. Sada spoke in Spanish, his only language.

Mexican-Americans, then, live all over the county, but the vast majority can be found almost exactly in the center of Los Angeles County — the Serape Belt.

They most certainly are the least mobile of Californians.

Buy why?

Dr. Paul M. Sheldon, director of the Urban Culture Laboratory, Occidental College, thinks he knows:

"Between 1910 and 1930 the population of East Los Angeles was increased by an influx of Mexicans fleeing the revolution," he says. "Many of these were middle or upper class businessmen and ranch owners who left behind business and property in communities where they have been citizens of high status."

"In Los Angeles, as in other cities along the Mexican border to which they came, they were faced with prejudice, loss of status, and inevitable poverty since only menial labor was available for Mexicans."

Within the Mexican-American community was established a way of life which involved little participation or interest in the larger Anglo-dominated community, Dr. Sheldon says.

"A stereotype grew up, a concept of the Mexican as an unskilled laborer, uninterested in education, political activity or union membership."

"The long history of disenfranchisement of the Mexican-American reached its depth during the depression. Faced with a heavy relief load, Los Angeles officials sought to solve the problem, by rounding up hundreds of thousands of Mexican-Americans, men, women, and children — with dogs, cats and goats, half-opened suitcases and rolls of bedding and shipping them back to Mexico."

"All this tended to bring about attitudes of resignation and hopeless-ness," Dr. Sheldon claims and long-standing bitterness broke out with the "zoot-suit" riots on June 3, 1943.

(The racial riots were between Mexican-American youths, wearing outlandish "pachuco" clothing, and Anglo servicemen.)

"On June 11, a formal inquiry by the Department of State, requested by the Mexican Ambassador in Washington and followed by the action of the Navy in declaring downtown Los Angeles 'out of bounds' finally brought the local press and city officials to the realization of the disas-trous international effects of the riots and the consequences of their own actions," Dr. Sheldon said.

"We're still trying to correct complicated consequences of past actions which have tended to isolate the Mexican-Americans."

Mexican-Americans Lack Political Power

Fourth of a Series
February 27, 1963

Politically, our Mexican-Americans are like a fighting bull—but a fight-ing bull made of paper. On paper their political potential appears fierce—they are the largest minority group in California.

But, unlike the Negroes, the second largest minority in California, Mexican-Americans have no real political cohesion.

"Unity, my friends, what you need most is unity," former Supervisor John Anson Ford recently told a Mexican-American banquet.

On issues concerning all of the more than 1.5 million Spanish-speaking population in the state, their political force invariably crumbles like a "piñata" struck with the stick of feuding factions.

This is not true in Texas and New Mexico where Mexican-Americans have been elected to municipal, state and federal offices for many years.

Ezequiel de Baca was elected governor of New Mexico in 1916. The late Dennis Chavez was elected a U.S. Senator from that state in 1936 (he was U.S. Representative before that) and remained in the Senate for more than two decades.

1962 Victories

Raymundo Telles was elected El Paso (Tex.) county clerk after World War II, later became mayor and now is our ambassador to Costa Rica. Henry Gonzalez was elected to Congress from San Antonio during the

Eisenhower administration even though the President campaigned for Gonzales' [*sic*] Republican opponent.

It was not until last year that California, supposedly more "liberal" politically than Texas and New Mexico, started catching up.

In 1962 Councilman Edward Roybal, a Democrat, was sent to Congress and John Moreno (D-51st District) and Phil Soto (D-50th District) were elected to the state legislature.

Even so, the Mexican-American political "piñata" often crumbles because they can often agree on the worth of Anglo politicians, but rarely on the worth of their own.

When Roybal was elected to Congress he left a local political vacuum for the Mexican-Americans. For 13 years their political "papacito," Roybal warned a large political gathering of Mexican-Americans that "unity" in the endorsement of a candidate to run for his place was very important.

He also reminded them that his 9th Council District was not to be considered exclusively Mexican-American, as in the old days. Negroes are there in great numbers, now, and they must be considered when selecting a candidate, Roybal told the meeting.

List Approved

Nevertheless, the informal gathering went on record supporting a list of Mexican-American candidates because, as Mayor Samuel W. Yorty put it in a television interview, "Mexican-Americans have always thought of that district as their own."

The "piñata" really crumbled a month later when a Negro, Gilbert W. Lindsay, was appointed by the City Council to take Roybal's place.

Angry, hurt and anxious to take some kind of action, leaders of the statewide Mexican-American Political Assn. (MAPA) called a meeting which they hoped would endorse a strong Mexican-American candidate to run against incumbent Lindsay.

The MAPA endorsement meeting was held Feb. 8 in the Alexandria. After a spirited all-night caucus at which charges of everything from "packing the house" to "Communist techniques" were made by various factions, the meeting ended with no endorsement.

None Strong Enough

None of the several Mexican-American candidates could muster the necessary three fourths of the total votes.

MAPA, however, which is pledged to raise the Mexican-American political star, did endorse — by acclamation — an Anglo candidate for the City Council in the 12th District.

The lack of unity was perhaps best dramatized in 1961 when the proposed incorporation of East Los Angeles failed in an election.

MAPA claims that Mexican-Americans have a better than average record in registration and voting. In the April 25, 1961, election to incorporate East Los Angeles — populated mostly by Mexican-Americans — only 46% turned out to vote.

At a time in Southern California when new cities are popping up like toadstools after a rain, East Los Angeles — which perhaps had better reasons to incorporate than other areas because of its supposed homogeneity — turned down incorporation by 340 votes.

Too Many Factions

Some of the reasons, pundits said later, were that too many fighting factions were running candidates for the city's council, the Citizens Committee to Incorporate was overly confident, that Mexican-Americans would realize it was "natural for them to vote yes," and the opposition of the Committee on Political Education (COPE) — political arm of the AFL-CIO.

(COPE said at that time that it opposed all new incorporations because "rapid growth of cities has resulted in great confusion and overlapping of services at an increased cost to the taxpayer.")

The vast majority of Mexican-Americans are Democratic and helped substantially in the "Viva Kennedy" and the "Re-elect Gov. [Edmund G. "Pat"] Brown" campaigns. Recently, however, some rumbles of dissatisfaction with the Democrats have been coming from Mexican-American leadership.

The Mexican-American Committee to Re-elect Gov. Brown reorganized as the Mexican-American Citizens Committee of California. At an open meeting, members of the committee charged that Gov. Brown had not appointed enough qualified Mexican-Americans to positions in his administration. This, they charged, was not in keeping with Gov. Brown's campaign promises.

Dr. Francisco Bravo, adviser to the committee and a Los Angeles police commissioner, later said members of the committee "met with two top officials of Gov. Brown's office in a very amicable and understanding meeting. This committee agreed to assist Gov. Brown in filling present and future state vacancies with qualified persons of Mexican-American descent on the basis of merit and qualifications only."

'Image at Stake'

Another member of the committee, however, Municipal Judge Leopoldo Sanchez, said the problem of the Mexican-American "image" was at stake and should not be discussed with "a governor's aide; but rather with the governor personally."

Sanchez, first Mexican-American to be elected municipal judge in East Los Angeles, says a meeting between Mexican-American leaders and the governor "is important now if the amicable relationship with the governor is to continue."

MAPA, from Sacramento to Los Angeles, has gone a step further and charged that the governor's office is throwing a "smoke-screen" to hide the growing dissatisfaction of the Mexican-American population with the Brown administration.

Arthur Sutton, who served as Richard M. Nixon's campaign consultant on Mexican-American affairs in 1962 and was active in the movement to incorporate East Los Angeles, says it is his studied opinion that "neither the Democrats nor Republicans take Mexican-Americans seriously."

"In their more honest moments, leaders in both parties will admit — off the record, of course — that the Mexican-American is far below the Negro as a figure of political importance, as a group whose wishes must be respected and whose views must be heard," Sutton said.

Born in Port Limon, Costa Rica, and a writer on Latin American affairs, Sutton is a member of the board of directors, Community Council for Greater East Los Angeles, Inc., MAPA, and the Council of Mexican-American Affairs.

"Riddled with bitter feuds, sour jealousies and deep rivalries, Mexican-American leadership has failed to unite in a solid front dedicated to the advancement of the Mexican-American community at large," he says.

Sutton, who is working on a new attempt to incorporate East Los Angeles, said the "fragmentation of the Mexican-American community has been a gold mine for the Democratic Party."

"It has allowed Democratic leaders to count on Mexican-American votes without the bother of having to take their views into consideration when making party policy, or, it might be added, when passing out patronage."

Few ethnic groups in the United States supported Kennedy in 1960 as did the Mexican-American communities in California, Texas, Arizona, New Mexico and Colorado, according to Sutton.

"But is there any substantial evidence of appreciation from the Kennedy Administration? There is not. Sure, a few Peace Corps positions, a judgeship or two. But nothing really important. And many of the Kennedy appointees that the administration points to as 'honoring the Mexican-American people' are, upon closer examination, men and women of Puerto Rican or Spanish extraction, not Mexican-Americans."

The Republican Party, Sutton claims, long has written off the Mexican-American vote as "lost." And he adds, "Thanks to the Birch issue,* the California GOP is itself in a hopeless mass of internal feuds, too."

Sutton, a lifelong Republican, says that Nixon made "a real bid for Mexican-American support last November but even that was a case of too little and too late." †

"The budget for the Mexican-American approach was $5,000 — a mere pittance — and the East Los Angeles Republican Center closed down right after the election," Sutton said.

"The political aspirations of the Mexican-Americans are grossly misunderstood, perhaps understandably so, considering the many feuding factions involved."

"But not even people who should make it their business to know what these aspirations are take the trouble to find out. Test my theory."

The Times did by asking a high elected official what he thought of the Mexican-American Political Assn. He answered:

"The stressing of the words Mexican-Americans strikes me as an organization much like the Muslims" (the white-hating Negro group).

And in the next breath he said:

"The Mexican-Americans need a strong organization which will help them present a solid front."

Mexican-Americans Succeeding

Fifth in a Series

February 28, 1963

"They're building Mexican-Americans better than ever."

The East Los Angeles car dealer got up from his desk, chewed on his cigar and walked to the large show window.

---

*The John Birch Society is a right-wing political group that was especially active in the early 1960s. The "Birch issue" to which Sutton refers was the rise of the ultraconservative group, which had a greatly disruptive effect on the California GOP.

† In 1962, Richard Nixon unsuccessfully ran for governor of California.

"There are too many sobbing do-gooders, piddling politicos and lazy opportunists saying we've got to do this and that for the Mexican-Americans," he said puffing clouds of smoke.

"Nobody ever helped me. I'm a Mexican-American. I made the grade. But I didn't do it by sitting on my behind thinking up ways of chiseling the public. I worked for what I got. Many others are doing the same and they'll get there. Anybody can make it in this country."

"Just don't use my name — it's not good for business."

Statistics show Mexican-Americans ARE "being built better than ever."

Spread Over County

Though most live in the eastern part of the city and county and in the Pacoima area of the San Fernando Valley, some Mexican-Americans live in every part of the county.

There are rich Mexican-Americans. There are Mexican-American movie stars. Mexican-Americans are also doctors, dentists, musicians, scientists, police and sheriff lieutenants and captains, businessmen, insurance men, educators, building contractors, government officials, etc.

Mexican-Americans can be found in almost every walk of life which spells the American Dream.

Successful Named

To name a few, an impressive list of successful Mexican-Americans here would include:

Superior Judge Carlos Teran; movie star Anthony Quinn; Arthur Rendon, civic leader and architect; Municipal Judge Leopoldo Sanchez; Juan Acevedo, director of the California Youth Authority Board; Ray E. Gonzalez, chief of replacement and recruitment for the civilian personnel division of Space Systems Division, U.S. Air Force; and Dr. Francisco Bravo, surgeon, rancher and Los Angeles police commissioner.

The rub is, according to Occidental College's Laboratory in Urban Culture:

"The low ratings of the majority of Americans of Mexican extraction in Southern California on the usual socioeconomic scales despite their long residence and the high achievements of some members, has been a major concern in the Los Angeles community."

"Mexican-Americans in Southern California are represented in the higher level of education and in the professions in much smaller numbers than their proportion in the population would warrant."

Many Are Agreed

Many who have succeeded, however, agree with the East Los Angeles car dealer that a great number of Mexican-Americans are coming up in the world and that if you'll just let nature take its course they'll continue to do so.

Since the end of World War II, they argue, the Mexican-American has made great strides. Why all this soul-searching over the lack of Mexican-American ethnic power?

"The price of assimilation, after all, is the loss of ethnic identification," said a journalist. "And it's a cheap price to pay."

Carlos Borja, who has made the grade, doesn't agree.

"We should assimilate socially but not politically," he says.

Borja was born in central Los Angeles and attended grammar school there.

"My father and mother came from Mexico and were very proud of the named Borja," he said. "The name dates back to Rodrigo de Borja, a Spanish noble, who in 1492 became Pope Alexander VI. Before he became Pope he fathered Cesare Borgia, the famous Italian politician and art patron, and his sister, Lucrezia."

"Don't let the name throw you, though. My father was a waiter."

Unique Problems

"But he was a Borja and was determined to see that I succeed. When I was a boy I belonged to a Mexican-American gang — my school used to be where the freeway cloverleaf is now — and we used to fight Anglo gangs. But we didn't live as ethnically isolated as some Mexican-American boys now live in parts of East Los Angeles."

"I went to Hollywood High and then to USC — thanks to the sacrifices of my parents."

Carlos Borja, now a deputy attorney general of California, who has been investigating alleged harassment of Mexican-American voters in Imperial County, says Mexican-Americans have "unique" political problems.

"Many of us, after all, are of peon stock and have remnants of a folk culture in which the family and one's little clique are more important than the populations as a whole," Borja said.

Ethnic Pull Used

"Mexican-Americans need political education. Many of them, for instance, do not complain about abuses against them because they don't really feel themselves part of our whole political structure."

"That's why I'm for Mexican-Americans banding politically. They best know their problems and if they gain political strength they can best solve these problems themselves. That's the American way."

"American electioneering has always given special attention to the ethnic and religious interest of the voters," according to "Our Own Kind," a pamphlet published by the Center for the Study of Democratic Institutions.

"History demonstrates that Americans bring to the polls their special backgrounds and pull down the levers congenial to their national origins and religious ties."

Some who have made the grade — especially the younger successful Mexican-Americans — feel an urgency to identify themselves with the less fortunate by attempting to help them.

"Too many times Mexican-Americans who become successful suddenly become 'Spanish' and forget about their brothers in Mexican-American ghettos," one said.

Not Realizing Dream

Frank Macias, a biochemist and micro-biologist at Northrop Space Laboratory, says Mexican-Americans are not fulfilling the American Dream in as many numbers as they should.

"Those of us who have a good education and economic stability have an obligation to help others of our kind who are less fortunate," he says. "We, who are on our way up, so to speak, must continue to associate ourselves with the problems of those who for many reasons are stagnant — in order that they realize that they too can make it."

A sociologist told *The Times* that successful Mexican-Americans who talk about "working for the good of all" — as compared to tackling Mexican-American problems separately — are "naive do-gooders."

Groups Differ

"Answers to problems of one group are not necessarily transferable to another group," he said. "The importance of solving Mexican-American problems unilaterally can not be overemphasized."

According to Municipal Judge Leopoldo Sanchez, what bothers many young Mexican-American leaders is that "the image of the Mexican-American is not good and must be improved."

Dr. Ruth Landes, former professor of anthropology at Claremont Graduate School, puts it another way:

"The Russian threat and the election of an Irish Catholic President have made racial prejudice unfashionable, but the supposed beneficiaries don't know about it."

"Today in our California, docility is no longer wanted by Anglos or younger Mexican-Americans. This is the newest evidence of American 'equality.' Public opinion in advanced responsible groups — education, government, social work — is for this equality and the law says that it must come about."

Understanding Needed

The educated and the economically stable must be trained to understand the "personal and group dynamics of relationships with the under-privileged" and the responsibility — of the educated and economically stable — to the underprivileged, she continued.

Dionicio Morales, consultant to the Equal Opportunities Foundation, likes to quote William Saroyan on this subject:

"'Be the inferior of no man, nor of any man be the superior,' Saroyan wrote. 'Remember that every man is a variation of yourself. No man's guilt is not yours, nor is any man's innocence a thing apart. . . .'"

"The isolation of the Mexican-American must be broken, for his own good and that of the community," sums up Morales.

Mexican-Americans Have Culture Protected by 1848 U.S. Treaty

Last of Series
March 1, 1963

In the peculiar pedagogical language of some educators, impoverished Mexican-Americans are "culturally deprived."

Presumably they want to save these poor people from this terrible void by giving them culture.

What they don't seem to realize is that Mexican-Americans have a culture, one that is protected by the Treaty of Guadalupe Hidalgo.

Signed on Feb. 2, 1848, after the Mexican-American War, the treaty guarantees Mexicans, who become Mexican-Americans, the right to retain their language, religion and culture.

A close study of the treaty and of the Southwest could clear up a lot of misunderstanding in Anglo-Mexican relations, some scholars say.

It also could give the Mexican-American the status he so desperately seeks.

"When I was very young and discovered at school that I was a Mexican-American and consequently 'different,' I vowed to become an American without the Mexican part," says Jesus Hernandez, a Los Angeles social worker.

"I systematically forgot any Spanish I knew, I even changed my name. I soon discovered, however, that even though I knew no Spanish and though I had a ridiculous new name — Joe Hernan — I was still thought of as a Mexican. After all I look like a Mexican."

Unique Position

"So one day I said to myself: So I'm a Mexican — so what? What's wrong with that? Nothing, I discovered. I relearned Spanish, I went back to my old name and found out that I could still be a good American and have my Mexican cake, too. . . . Being bicultural can be an advantage in this complicated new world, you know?"

The Treaty of Guadalupe Hidalgo clearly shows why the Mexican-American minority is "unique" and why Mexican-Americans can not be thought of as "foreign."

Mexicans, with the exception of the American Indians, are the only minority in the United States who were annexed by conquest. The rights of Mexicans, again with the exception of the Indians, are specifically safeguarded.

The fact that Mexicans lost the Mexican-American War — a war, incidentally, called "unjust" by generals from U.S. Grant to Atty. Gen. Robert F. Kennedy — does not change the fact that Mexicans are very much of the Southwest. They are no more foreigners to the Southwest than the cactus that grows there.

Rankled by Loss

It still rankles Mexicans that this "unjust" war cost them California, Arizona, New Mexico and Texas — half of the territory of Mexico in 1821 or an area larger than Germany and France combined.

Educators who abhor the term "culturally deprived" prefer another pedagogical term: "Acculturation."

That, says Dr. George I. Sanchez of the University of Texas, means that Mexican-Americans should become Americanized and that Anglos should become "Mexicanized gringos."

People who have given Anglo-Mexican relations a lot of thought feel strongly that "acculturation" is the answer. The best way for Mexican-Americans to become Americanized, of course, is to leave the Serape Belt of eastern Los Angeles and really integrate in the community.

Eventual Change

This eventually can be done, according to Paul Bullock of UCLA's Institution of Industrial Relations, by ending the de facto segregation in the schools.

"Observation would indicate that most of the elementary and secondary schools in the Los Angeles system — at least three-quarters — contain few, if any, Negro or Mexican-American students," Bullock says.

"Examination . . . shows that four of the Los Angeles high schools are overwhelmingly Negro, and two are overwhelmingly Mexican-American."

"There is no doubt that housing segregation is responsible for much of the segregation evident in the schools. The San Fernando Valley (outside of Pacoima), west and northeast Los Angeles, and other parts of the city contain so few minority-group residents that there is little possibility of integrating the schools. . . ."

"Acculturation," if it is to come, is in the future.

What is important now, according to the Council of Mexican-American Affairs (CMAA), whose president is Edward Vega, is doing something about problems facing Mexican-Americans today.

The CMAA lists the most pressing problems as:

Children of "countless Mexican-American families present challenging problems in education" and need "special attention which elementary school teachers are not always trained effectively to meet."

Highest Dropouts

Junior and senior high school dropouts among the Mexican-Americans "in most Los Angeles metropolitan areas are the highest of any other ethnic or racial group."

The County Probation Department, in a 1961 survey, determined that the Mexican-American youth is the most gang-minded, and commits more killings than any other group.

The California Adult Authority revealed that 54% of the adult narcotic addicts in California institutions are of Mexican background.

Some of the reasons for these problems, the CMAA says, is that "too frequently the community agencies and institutions do not reach the citizen of Mexican background and so he becomes 'isolated.' This isolation deprives him of having proper social values."

Salazar Praised and Panned for Articles on Mexican-Americans

March 4, 1963

It certainly is a commendable thing for *The Times* to publish the factual series on the Mexican-American problems. Ruben Salazar has done a tremendous job on his research and unbiased factual presentation. My friends and I have found this series to be very interesting and educational.

I believe that those of us that follow this series will broaden our minds in the overall problems and will motivate us to try to help solve those of our community.

Some of us may not like the opinions on some of the issues that have been brought to light. When the nerve of a tooth is tapped, we feel the pain. Therefore, it will tend to motivate us to take better care of our teeth. Perhaps this series will have the same effect to those who are really interested.

Rafael C. Flores, Pico Rivera

The series that *The Times* ran on the dimension of contemporary Mexican-American life has been called to my attention by many of my supporters in the last supervisorial election. In describing the manner in which the East Los Angeles community is presented, I would consider myself conservative in using the word outrageous.

Your reporter managed to "poison the well" before he even developed this presentation by using a barroom dialogue as a point of departure. The second article was also of poor journalistic vintage — describing an alleged "Mexican-American bum" of 19 years of age who is anti-social. The reference to the "Hoyo-Mara neighborhood" was very vulnerable to a hasty generalization by the reader who is not acquainted with East Los Angeles. It is a very insignificant and inarticulate section of East Los

Angeles. The third article was a Cape Canaveral flop in that it was entitled "The Serape Belt."

Manuel Lopez, Los Angeles

I have read the Ruben Salazar series on the Mexican-American of the
Los Angeles area with interest, and I must say that a great service is being
done on our behalf by the writer.

The Salazar series shows what we have always known. The opportunities that this country has given us have been a sorry waste of time and
energy. It is easy to crucify the political parties for our plight, the blame
lies wholly on us individually and as a community.

Carlos B. Gil, San Fernando

In reference to your article pertaining to so-called "Mexican-
Americans," I am very much in favor of any means that might advance
the social and economic standing of Americans of Mexican ancestry. I
do not believe that your articles are accomplishing these ends.

I am aware that these articles are not intended to be derogatory in any
way, but they are giving an incorrect picture of the American of Mexican
ancestry in this area.

We, of Mexican ancestry, born in the United States, are Americans.
"Mexican-Americans" implies dual-citizenship, and nothing could be
farther from the truth.

We, in East Los Angeles, resent our area being referred to as "Little
Mexico." This is an American community, lived in by Americans.

Richard L. Valdez, Los Angeles

The articles written by Mr. Salazar have motivated me to anxiously
await the next article daily.

We in Pico Rivera are tremendously thrilled at the articles' content,
for we feel that in Pico Rivera we are to set the tone for the rest of
the Mexican-American community in terms of unity, cohesiveness, co-
operation, and desire.

Mrs. Margaret Perez, Pico Rivera

I have been reading your articles and want to let you know that they
have been very informative, and I certainly hope that Mr. Salazar keeps
on writing such articles. I know there are a lot of people that do not like
the truth to be printed or that it be revealed openly, but it's about time

most of the other people really find out the truth about the Mexican-American and his many problems.

Mrs. Dolores Cendejas, Los Angeles

This is the first letter I've written to a newspaper but I feel I have to thank Ruben Salazar for the articles he has written. I am glad he works for a newspaper such as *The Times* that allows him to write blunt truth.

Mrs. Julia Cereceda, Montebello

'Uneducable' Get Assist in Fighting Frustrations, Gaining Some Success

April 8, 1963

It was "War Ball" time at Jackson High School. Thirty boys, evenly divided on each side of the basketball court, were throwing volley balls at each other with a vengeance.

Wham! One got clobbered and retreated. The impact of the speeding ball shook him a bit but didn't hurt him.

The thrower smiled. Wham! The ball struck him right on the mouth, wiping off his smile.

"You know, we've never had a fight resulting from our weekly War Ball?" school coach Pete Martinez said proudly. "It helps them work off their frustrations."

The boys at Jackson High have many frustrations to work off.

They are youthful failures in the eyes of a society hell-bent on its idea of success.

Work Against Dropouts

They are the prime candidates for the newest badge of dishonor, the school dropout.

Andrea Jackson High School, 2821 E. 7th St., is dedicated to the idea that a high school diploma, in many cases, is not as important as saving a boy's self-respect.

Not that Jackson High doesn't pass out diplomas. Twelve boys, kicked out of other schools as uneducable, were graduated in February.

The present enrollment at Jackson High is 379, but principal Wendell Lorbeer doesn't like to think in terms of numbers.

"I think of them individually," he says. "You name any problems —
from family trouble to narcotics — and these kids have had it."

Lorbeer says problem children are often spotted as early as in the second grade, but that our schools are not geared to help the "unaverage"
child.

Give Them Credit

"The reason they are at Jackson is that they didn't understand what was
going on in their regular schools," Lorbeer said.

"But at least they had the spunk to raise a ruckus so someone would
know they didn't understand. You've got to give them credit for that —
they raised hell instead of just sitting there daydreaming."

"They have to succeed at something, even at raising hell, and they
need the recognition of their classmates as much as anyone else. When
they come here and discover there's no 'stage' or 'audience' for them they
settle down and start to learn."

Manuel went to Jackson High in 1960 because, according to a teacher's report, "he is not benefiting from his high school attendance."

"Manuel has been in my class for one year and has not progressed at
all, either socially or educationally," the report says. "He has made no
friends in class. . . . In my opinion he is uneducable and should be excluded (from school)."

Shows Progress

Jackson High vice principal William L. Van Sistine didn't agree in 1960
that Manuel was a hopeless case and this year wrote a report pointing
out his progress.

Manuel's grades, according to Van Sistine, were: leather shop, B;
crafts, B; English I, B; physical education, A; and math, B.

"He never could have made those grades in his old school, of course,"
Van Sistine says. "But we grade him in relation to his own intelligence,
not on what a manual says he should be doing."

The rub, according to those who oppose schools such as Jackson, is
that the school is a six-year high school and that teaching Manuel simple
things which his intelligence can grasp cost $1,186 last year as compared
to $604 for the "average" student.

The Difference

"But it must also be kept in mind that if Manuel had not been helped and if he had gotten in trouble with the law, it would have cost the tax-payers $3,000 a year to keep him in custody," Lorbeer says.

The reason it cost so much is that Jackson High must, of necessity, have very small classes and special teachers.

"But it keeps them off the streets and gives these boys self-confidence and ability in at least one trade," Van Sistine emphasizes.

Though Jackson High is in East Los Angeles, students come from as far as West Los Angeles, Hollywood, South Gate, El Sereno, Highland Park and other parts of Los Angeles.

All ethnic groups are represented at Jackson, where the curriculum is mostly vocational geared to non-academically inclined boys.

When a boy is just about to drop out or be expelled from high school, he may be sent to Jackson.

Favorable Environment

"Boys referred to Jackson are sent here because of a need for a change of school and instruction," principal Lorbeer says. "The primary purpose of Jackson is to provide a favorable environment for the pupil with prob-lems in which he may be helped and to experience success instead of failure. We have small classes and provide a wide choice of industrial arts and other activities."

Lorbeer says the disadvantages and dangers in such schools as Jack-son could be that "adjustment schools" might be used as threats or punishment.

"Improper screening of placement cases has brought us students with high IQs, health problems and habitual truants," Lorbeer says. "We feel these children should be dealt with in their own schools."

Other "adjustment center high schools" are Ramona, Betsy Ross and Garden Gate Schools for girls and Jacob Riis and William T. Aggelar High Schools for boys.

Won't Fix Blame

Jackson's Lorbeer doesn't like to argue about who's to blame for the dropout problem: schools, parents, students, society, etc.

"Jackson can't do anything about society, bad educational philosophies or parents," Lorbeer said. "But we can attempt to help an individual child who needs sympathetic understanding."

Mrs. Rachel Hayes, principal at Ramona High School, Jackson's counterpart for girls, also worries more about the individuals than about the controversy over dropouts and American education.

"We try to help the girls because we know that in many cases these girls are not only not wanted by their parents but even hated by them."

Youths Study Problems of Mexican-Americans

April 10, 1963

A group of Mexican-American student leaders have put a new twist on Easter vacation by mixing fun with serious social problems.

Meeting at Camp Hess Kramer, 40401 Pacific Coast Highway, 110 Mexican-American high school and college students Tuesday ended a three-day conference on "Spanish-speaking Youth at the Crossroads."

Sponsored by the County Commission on Human Relations and Industrialist Tobias Kotzin, the youthful leaders tackled such questions as "Are Mexican-Americans timid and hesitant in aspiring to advance?" and "Should agencies other than those existing be set up to help these people?"

Summing up what one thought students learned in workshops, Lucila Carrasco, a student at East Los Angeles Junior College, told the conference:

"The isolation of the Mexican-American home must be broken. Too many times Mexican-American families feel that as long as they — as a family unit — are happy that's all that counts."

"We are apathetic too often and must become much more aware of our civic responsibilities. But we need more legislation to help us (in problems such as school dropouts) and the Mexican-Americans need an organization much like the NAACP."

First Attempt

Tony M. Sanchez and William O. Gutierrez of the County Human Relations Commission said the conference was the first local attempt to help "young Mexican-Americans focus their role on the brink of entering and becoming a member of community life."

Sally Alonso, 16, of Roosevelt High School, said that her study group found that "many times we're embarrassed at being Mexican-Americans when we should be proud."

"Actually, we're very fortunate in being bilingual and bicultural," she said. "Let's take advantage of these instead of worrying about it."

Negro Drive Worries Mexican-Americans

July 14, 1963

A growing concern over the relation of the Southland's Mexican-Americans to the accelerated drive by Negroes for civil rights was aired Saturday at a closed meeting in the Hall of Administration.

Some Los Angeles area Mexican-American leaders, *The Times* learned, are worried that Negroes' victories in their fight against racial prejudice, ironically is adversely affecting the Spanish-speaking people.

About 60 leaders of the Mexican-American community Saturday night presented their grievances to the Los Angeles County Commission on Human Relations.

Ray Mora of the California Democratic Central Committee told *The Times* after the meeting that a "dangerous situation" is brewing because employers are now "afraid" to discriminate against Negroes and are firing Mexican-Americans.

"This should not be interpreted to mean that Mexican-Americans are against the fight Negroes are waging for better opportunities," Mora emphasized. "I bring it out so that this ironic side-effect should not be used to pit one group against the other."

"The pressure Negroes are applying on employers has had this effect: When Negroes apply for jobs, employers are afraid not to hire them for fear of retaliation and so, in some cases, fire Mexican-Americans to make space for the Negro."

"It's a problem that will get worse and we must talk about it if it is to be solved."

It was learned that several of the more conservative Mexican-American leaders strongly oppose any "mixing" of Mexican-American and Negro grievances.

One Mexican-American leader was quoted as telling the commission: "The Mexican-Americans have no problems. Just leave us alone. Any problems that might arise we'll take care of them ourselves."

Carlos Borja, a California deputy attorney general and Mexican-American leader, told *The Times* he disagrees.

"We should not disassociate our problems from those of the Negro," Borja said. "How long are we Mexican-Americans going to sit here and say we have no problems? We have them and the greatest one is the lack of education of many of our people."

Mexican-Americans' Problems Evaluated

July 21, 1963

Too many Mexican-Americans are "functionally illiterate" and their problems are aggravated by "cheap labor flowing in from Mexico" which depresses their wages, according to a report released by Occidental College.

The report on the April 6 conference held at Occidental College to probe social and educational problems of rural and urban Mexican-American youth, also listed the following critical areas:

"Housing — The Spanish-speaking people (in the five southwestern states) rent more than the Anglos, they get less for their money, and the houses they live in are, more often than not, deteriorating, dilapidating and overcrowded, without basic sanitary facilities."

Employment Limited

"Employment — Opportunities are limited, income status is lower, and there are few opportunities for apprenticeship training."

"Administration of Justice — Frequently unequal."

"Voting — Practices vary widely, but there are still barriers to voting (by Mexican-Americans) in some parts of the Southwest."

"Public Accommodations — Less discriminatory than in the past but the problem still exists."

"Leadership — Effective leadership among the Spanish-speaking has yet to develop."

The report of the conference, at which 150 Southwestern leaders in Mexican-American affairs participated, was prepared under the direction of Dr. Paul M. Sheldon, conference director and head of Occidental College's Laboratory in Urban Culture.

"The (education) level of the Spanish-speaking has increased only about one grade in the past 10 years," the report says. "While other populations have increased in relatively the same proportions, the level of the Spanish-speaking is so much lower that they remain terribly disadvantaged and the gap between them and even the non-whites is fairly large. A large proportion of the population, then, is really functionally illiterate."

Dr. Julian Samora of Notre Dame University reported to the conference that 52% of the Mexicans in Texas have less than fourth-grade education, 35% in Arizona, 24% in California and Colorado and 30% in New Mexico.

"If we take Los Angeles–Long Beach as a standard metropolitan statistical area, 19% of the Mexicans have less than fourth-grade education, (as compared to only) 3% of the Anglos and 9% of the non-white (primarily Negro)," Dr. Samora said.

As for job opportunities among the Mexican-Americans, the report says that "cheap labor flowing in from Mexico in the bracero and 'green card' programs depress wages and create innumerable social problems."

The status of the Spanish-speaking people in the Southwest is shattered, according to Dr. Samora, by "the effects of domestic and foreign agricultural labor systems; the effects of the open border; the effects of the commuter worker system in the border cities, and the effects of illegal entrance for employment purposes."

Unfair Competition

"These effects," continued Dr. Samora, "consist of: Unfair competition for domestic laborers, the depression of wages, exploitation of labor, the deprivation of civil rights, categorical retardation in education, and the perpetuation of a vicious social system which is detrimental to our society."

The solution to these problems, according to Dr. Samora, "is relatively simple."

"Namely, stop the commuter system (Mexican citizens crossing the border everyday to work in the United States), which is illegal anyhow; place restrictions on the issuance of green cards (issued by the Immigration Service) to Mexicans wanting to come to this country; and do away with Public Law 78 (bracero)," the Notre Dame sociologist said.

The recommendations made by the conference, which was the 12th annual at Occidental College, included:

"School curriculum should include recognition of the cultural heritage of the Mexican-American. This is especially important in the primary grades, where children often face a new world and the necessity of learning a new language, and where permanent attitudes and work habits are formed."

"The present leadership of the numerous Mexican-American organizations should be brought together, perhaps under the auspices of Occidental College, for the purpose of developing coordinated, nonpolitical action toward securing primarily community organization staff services that will make it possible for the people to express their views about needed services. . . ."

Johnson to Hear Plaint of Minority

July 29, 1963

When Vice President Lyndon Johnson comes here Aug. 9, he can expect the traditional "abrazo" (embrace) from the Mexican-American community, but it will be tempered with Latin skepticism.

As chairman of the President's Committee on Equal Employment Opportunity, Johnson has agreed to meet with Mexican-Americans to discuss a gnawing concern that the Spanish-speaking population is lagging.

About 50 top Mexican-American leaders are planning strategy for the conferences with the Vice President at the Statler-Hilton.

The consensus seems to be:

"We're grateful that the Vice President is coming, but we're not going to let him get away without letting him know that we've got grave problems which the Democratic administration seems to be ignoring."

Cite Negro Example

It is no secret that Los Angeles area Mexican-American leaders are impressed with the results militancy has brought the Negro community.

Some Mexican-American leaders express the opinion that perhaps they have been too "polite" and that "maybe the Democratic party has taken us for granted for too long."

Dr. George R. Borrell, controversial Mexican-American chairman of the Equal Opportunity Foundation, puts it this way:

"Who is not aware of the plight of the Negro? Conversely, who is aware of the plight of the Mexican-American?"

Will Attend Luncheon

"Do you know that 18% of the Mexican-American males in California are employed as laborers in comparison to 8% of all California males?

What is worse, 24%, or nearly one-fourth, of all Mexican-American laborers are farm workers. Compare that to only 5% of all California male laborers.

"And one must remember that 'all' California male laborers includes, of course, the Mexican-American, making the comparison that much worse."

Mexican-American leaders promise that at least 1,000 Spanish-speaking citizens will attend a Statler-Hilton luncheon honoring Vice President Johnson.

'Forgotten Minority'

But the promise came only after they were assured that a select group of Mexican-American leaders will get a private meeting with the Vice President to discuss, among other things:

1 — Charges that Mexican-Americans are being ignored by the Kennedy administration in political appointments.

2 — Contentions that the reason 50% of Mexican-Americans in California have less than an eighth-grade education is that they are the "forgotten minority."

3 — That Mexican-Americans are not getting equal opportunities in employment.

George J. Seros, a representative of the Vice President here, has assured the Mexican-American leaders that Johnson is aware of the problems facing the Spanish-speaking citizens in the Southland.

He also emphasized that for the first time an official of Johnson's stature will come to Los Angeles exclusively to discuss the problems of Mexican-Americans.

Scheduled to attend the Aug. 9 conferences are Sen. Clair Engle (D-California), Rep. Edward Roybal (D-Los Angeles), Rep. George E. Brown Jr. (D-Monterey Park), and Rep. Henry Gonzalez (D-San Antonio, Tex.). The list may later include Gov. Brown and city and county officials.

More education and better employment opportunities will be stressed publicly at the luncheon and conferences, but other — more touchy problems undoubtedly will be discussed in private.

Latin America Hurt

They include contentions by a few Mexican-American leaders that Negro stepped-up demands for civil rights have ironically hurt the

Mexican-Americans because employers are now "afraid" to discriminate against Negroes and are, in some instances, displacing Mexican-Americans to hire more Negroes.

Such a charge was made at a recent meeting of the County Human Relations Commission with 50 Mexican-American leaders, but most disclaimed the charge as a "dangerous contention which would pit one group against the other."

The other touchy problem that might be discussed with the Vice President is the effect of Public Law 78 on Mexican-Americans.

Occidental College recently released a report which claims that the bracero program and other "cheap labor flowing in from Mexico depress wages and create innumerable social problems" for Mexican-Americans.

Los Angeles Rep. Roybal and Texas Rep. Gonzalez were instrumental in killing an extension of the bracero law in the House. The law is scheduled to expire Dec. 31.

Dr. Borrell of the Equal Opportunity Foundation, Dr. Francisco Bravo, Los Angeles police commissioner and rancher, and most California big growers are for an extension of the bracero law.

Dr. Borrell, for one, says he doesn't want "Mexican-Americans to be doing the stoop labor braceros are willing and anxious to do."

Latins Here to Protest Bracero Law

August 5, 1963

A committee of Mexican-American community leaders announced Sunday it will take the occasion of Vice President Lyndon Johnson's visit here to go on record against Public Law 78, which allows the importation of braceros.

Johnson, as chairman of the President's Committee on Equal Employment Opportunity, will speak at a luncheon and conference Friday at the Statler Hilton.

The Mexican-American Education Conference Committee, composed of leaders of most of the Los Angeles area Spanish-speaking organizations will host the affair.

Oppose Extension

In a strongly worded resolution passed by 49 of the 50 members of the committee, the Mexican-American leaders urge the Vice President to use his influence in defeating a proposed extension of the bracero law, which is due to expire Dec. 31.

"Public Law 78 takes advantage of hunger and hardship in Mexico to provide for recruitment of a captive, docile and exploitable foreign farm labor force," the resolution reads.

Twenty top Mexican-American leaders, who hope to meet with the Vice President in private to discuss Public Law 78 and other controversial issues, pushed for the resolution.

A spokesman told *The Times* the resolution was passed "in the hope that planned picketing of the hotel where Johnson will be speaking will be called off."

Urge Dignified Action

"The committee is in sympathy with the persons who want to picket (mostly labor-backed organizations) but we hope to discuss it with the Vice President in a dignified manner," the spokesman said.

The resolution claims the bracero program "creates a large surplus labor pool which misplaces and adversely affects American farm workers."

Braceros, the committee claims, "depress laborers' wages, aggravate severe unemployment and underemployment, and help create wretched living conditions."

Labor Shortage Denied

Denying the contention that there are no American farmhands available to replace the braceros, the resolution says: "Most of the California farm workers are Mexican-American. These workers can furnish all the labor needs of the California growers."

Mexican-American leaders also hope to discuss with the Vice President in private what one called "our disappointment in the New Frontier because we are literally forgotten once we helped the administration get into office."

Members of the committee claim that the Viva Kennedy Clubs across the Southwest substantially helped the President get elected, but that the administration has not kept its promises of appointing more Mexican-Americans to federal offices.

Carlos Borja Jr., president of the Council for Mexican-American Affairs and state deputy attorney general, will be master of ceremonies at the luncheon. Mrs. Georgian Hardy, president of the Los Angeles Board of Education, and Dr. Francisco Bravo, police commissioner, will speak at the conference.

Among the organizations forming the committee at the luncheon and conference are the Equal Opportunity Foundation, League of United Latin American Citizens, Council for Mexican American Affairs, Community Service Organizations, GI Forum, Mexican-American Political Assn., the Los Angeles Mexican Chamber of Commerce, the Welfare Planning Council, the County Commission on Human Relations and the Mexican-American Lawyers Assn.

Johnson Urges Latin Citizens to Report Bias

August 10, 1963

Vice President Lyndon B. Johnson instructed Mexican-American community leaders here Friday to help the federal government uncover any instances of racial discrimination in employment for presentation at a conference in November.

Johnson met with 20 Los Angeles area Mexican-American leaders in his suite at the Statler-Hilton following a speech before more than 1,000 persons at the luncheon sponsored by the Mexican-American Education Conference Committee.

Johnson said Mexican-American problems may stem from the fact that they don't complain enough.

Minority Voice

He said he has received 4,334 complaints of discrimination in the two and a half years as chairman of the President's Committee on Equal Employment Opportunity, but "only 90 have been from Spanish-speaking persons."

"I'm not asking for more complaints," Johnson said smiling, "I have plenty of those. But it seems to me that perhaps you have not been successful in making your needs known . . . and by that I mean facts, not mere grumblings. . . ."

The only thing that marred the otherwise genial and informal meeting with the Vice President was the walking out of Dr. Francisco Bravo, Los Angeles police commissioner, who was told his presentation was not in order.

Dr. Bravo wanted to tell the Vice President that Mexican-American voters in California "have not received appointments to federal jobs even though we helped substantially in the 1960 Presidential campaign."

The Vice President said he did not want to get involved in politics at this meeting and "besides I don't make any appointments myself."

Dr. Bravo, a large contributor to the Democratic Party, has been vocal in his dissatisfaction with both the state and federal officials in "their neglect of the Mexican-Americans even though we worked hard to get them elected."

Poor Housing Area

Martin Ortiz, of the Planning Welfare Council, told the Vice President that "25% of all Mexican-American families have annual incomes below $4,000 and about 10% have incomes below $2,000."

"Fewer than half (47%) of all families own their own homes," Ortiz said. "In East Los Angeles only 29% of the Mexican-Americans own their own homes." Ortiz said the "greatest concentration of poor housing in Los Angeles County is found in and around East Los Angeles, the hub of the Mexican American population." Johnson was reluctant about discussing the controversial proposed extension of the bracero program. Anthony P. Rios, vice president of the Los Angeles Community Service Organization, told Johnson that all the 143,562 different braceros in California in 1962 were employed by only 7,694 growers, 8% of the 99,000 farmers in California.

"Most of this 8% used only a few of the total number of braceros, while the largest growers used the great majority of braceros."

Americans Available

"There is not a shred of evidence," Rios said, "that these large operators cannot afford to pay the cost of hiring American workers. And there is incontrovertible evidence that California's under-employed and unemployed seasonal farm workers are available to fill the jobs of braceros."

The Vice President said extension of the bracero law is up to Congress and noted that Sen. Clair Engle (D-Cal.), Reps. Edward Roybal (D-Los Angeles), George Brown (D-Monterey Park) and Chet Holifield (D-Montebello) were in the room.

Johnson said he and his committee would "come in force" to hear the problems of the Mexican-American community in November.

Latin Leaders in Five States Map Strategy

August 11, 1963

Los Angeles Mexican-American leaders Saturday began contacting Spanish-speaking leaders in the five Southwestern states — where more than 4 million Mexican-Americans live — to plan strategy for a second meeting with Vice President Lyndon B. Johnson in November.

The plight of agricultural workers and Mexican-Americans' lag in education will be high on the agenda when the President's Committee on Equal Employment Opportunity, with Johnson as chairman, meets here in the fall.

Johnson instructed leaders here to "get the facts on the problems facing Americans of Mexican descent."

Oppose Braceros

The 20 leaders, members of the Mexican-American Educational Conference Committee, were hosts at a luncheon and met with the Vice President. They called for ending the bracero program as the first step in "bettering Mexican-American chances."

A resolution from the committee, presented to the Vice President, said Mexican-Americans "throughout the Southwest of the United States, consider the (bracero program) to be the most harmful and repressive government sponsored program that has ever been imposed on the Mexican-American community."

The committee claimed braceros are displacing American agriculture workers (mostly Mexican-Americans) and that "regimented importation of farm workers, from a moral standpoint, [is] inhumane and cruel" and that "economic benefits to both countries would be a legitimate consideration only if it were right to treat labor as a mere commodity."

Accused by Growers

Some California growers immediately took the Mexican-American committee to task for using the "visit of Vice President Lyndon B. Johnson as a sounding board for attacks" on the bracero program.

The growers Saturday challenged Mexican-American leaders to "make good on their claim that they could supply needed agricultural workers in California."

"We have received telegraphed confirmation of bona fide job offers for 48,000 workers," said R. H. Daniels of Corona, chairman of the California Farm Labor Committee Domestic Recruiting Program.

"These offers are on file with the State Department of Employment now and many of them have been on file for months," Daniels said.

Lack of Education

As for education, Dr. Francisco Bravo, committee member and Los Angeles police commissioner, reminded the Spanish-speaking population in Los Angeles that:

"The level of education of Mexican-Americans here is the 8th grade (a little better than that in other Southwestern states) as compared to the 12th-grade level for the general population."

"Three out of four Mexican-American children disappear from the school rolls by the time they reach the high school level."

Senators to Hear Woes of Latins

September 10, 1963

A Los Angeles Mexican-American community leader will tell a Senate sub-committee in Washington, D.C., Wednesday that California's Spanish-speaking population is the worst-off minority in the state.

In a prepared statement to the Senate Subcommittee on Employment and Manpower, Dionicio Morales, consultant to the Equal Opportunity Foundation, will charge that:

The problems of the more than 1.5 million Mexican-Americans in California have "received little attention from public officials, businessmen and educators."

Mexican-Americans constitute about 10% of the California population (the largest minority in the state), outnumbering Negroes by about 500,000, but little has been done to "promote more effective communication between Anglos and Mexican-Americans," Morales will testify.

Problems Listed

Morales, who recently coordinated a meeting between Vice President Lyndon Johnson and Mexican-American leaders in Los Angeles, will tell

the Senate group the most pressing problems of the Mexican-Americans
include:

1 — "Figures on the occupational distribution of Southern California
demonstrate conclusively that they, like Negroes, are now concentrated
in the blue-collar job categories and are underrepresented in the white-
collar fields. . . . About 79% of the Mexican-Americans are in the crafts-
man, operative, laborer and service categories, compared with 51% for all
workers surveyed. More importantly, 60.7% are in the lowest three of
these categories in contrast with only 24% for all workers."

2 — "The Mexican-American averages less than a ninth grade education while Negroes average 10th grade and the population as a whole
averages a little more than 12th grade. In metropolitan Los Angeles, 10%
of the Mexican-Americans have less than four years education. In other
words, while the average Anglo-American has had at least some college
experience, the average Mexican-American has had no more than an elementary education."

3 — "The median family income for Mexican-Americans in the Los
Angeles area is substantially below that of the population as a whole. In
1960, the federal census showed that the Mexican-American median income for 1959 as $4,990, compared with $8,670 for the whole population
of the metropolitan area. It should be noted that the latter includes both
the Mexican-American and Negro populations, and that a comparison
of the Mexican-American and Anglo incomes would necessarily show an
even more striking gap."

Relive Sweat Shop

4 — "Recent immigrants from Mexico are re-living the cruel sweatshop
conditions in various areas of Los Angeles County which immigrants
suffered in our country a half-century ago. Strangers in the land, ineli-
gible for relief or unemployment insurance, with hungry families to feed
in their native land, they are desperate for any income."

5 — "Serious, adverse effects created by Public Law 78 (Braceros) have
affected the lives of thousands of Mexican-Americans in California. . . .
The Mexican-American leadership in California is concerned about the
sociological effects of the bracero law and are opposed to the type of
population movement represented by it. . . . Such an infusion of the unassimilable has been an overwhelming burden on Mexican-Americans
and has retarded the process of integration so essential for the blending
into the total American community pattern."

Immigration Increase

6 — "A dramatic increase of immigration to the United States from Mexico has presented immense employment problems and need for special assistance. The problems created by a near 500% increase in Mexican immigration has posed an acute concern for placement of these newcomers. The increase of immigration from 6,841 in 1950 to 32,684 in 1960 plus the fact that some 48,000 are waiting to be processed in Tijuana are creating a heavy and confusing responsibility on the various communities in California."

Morales, who has 20 years experience in the field of California Mexican-American community relations, concludes in his statement to the Senate subcommittee that the Mexican-American "finds himself in a peculiar and uncertain position as the product of two cultures."

Cultural Handicaps

"Because our society and our educational system often fail to give proper recognition to the values of the culture, the bilingualism and dual cultural background which ought to be advantageous are turned into handicaps," Morales will testify.

"In most schools, the educational program is now directed toward the Anglo students, mainly middle-class, who have no special problems of language or culture. The Mexican-American youngster and parents feel uncomfortable, perhaps even unwelcome, in a school setting designed entirely for a different group of Americans."

"Language difficulties often prevent this youngster from demonstrating his native abilities on tests which require verbal facility in the English language. Teachers, counselors and administrators often tend to categorize the Mexican-American as, at best, a 'vocational pupil,' unfitted for academic training."

"A bold program, therefore, is essential to eliminate discrimination, improve vocational counseling and training, promote more effective communication between Anglo and Mexican-American citizens and expand the educational horizons of Mexican-American youngsters."

The Senate group to which Morales will make his presentation is part of the Senate's Committee on Labor and Public Welfare. Leading members include Sens. Jacob Javits (D-N.Y.), Barry Goldwater (R-Ariz.), Wayne Morse (D-Ore.), Ralph Yarborough (D-Tex.), and Edward Kennedy (D-Mass.).

Vice President Johnson told a meeting of Mexican-American leaders in Los Angeles in August that the President's Committee on Equal Opportunity, which Johnson heads, will open hearings here in November to discuss problems of minorities in Southern California.

Problems of Latins Seen Thing Apart
New Policy for U.S. Spanish-speaking Students Urged

September 16, 1963

A Mexican-American ad hoc education committee said Sunday "assimilation" is not the answer to problems of Spanish-speaking students and urged the Board of Education to consider Mexican-American problems apart from those of Negroes.

The Mexican-American committee statement was issued in response to the school board's ad hoc committee report on equal education opportunity which was made last Thursday.

The Mexican-American group declared that in some ways the school board's findings were constructive but charged that Mexican-American educational problems "were mentioned only in an incidental or secondary matter."

"We recognize that an educational philosophy based primarily on the principal of assimilation has proven historically inadequate," the Mexican-American committee said.

Want Policy Stated

"Accordingly, in order that schools may meet the needs of the Mexican-American community, we hold that school boards should establish a strong positive statement of policy and philosophy towards the acculturation of the Mexican-American child."

Unlike assimilation, acculturation is "basically the acceptance of the plurality of culture as a functional principle," the Mexican-American committee said. "This entails the implementation of both cultures (Mexican and Anglo) to the greatest advantage possible in creating a personality who will find dignity in both."

The Spanish-speaking committee said it "regrets very much" that no Mexican-American testimony was heard during the year-long public hearings by the school board's ad hoc committee on equal educational opportunity.

Requests Listed

The school board's committee report pointed out that "late in August, spokesmen for the Mexican-American community (largest minority in the Southland) presented to the board a list of 15 requests."

"These requests," the report continued, "were received too late for thorough study by the committee or for recommendation. . . ."

The Mexican-American committee Sunday agreed on this point and said the lack of Mexican-American presentations to the school board's committee is a just "indictment of the Mexican-American community."

"It is not as well organized or as vocal as other minority groups in Los Angeles," the Mexican-American committee said. "However, we propose to have speakers at the three hearing dates before the school board makes its final decision Sept. 26 on the recommendations made by the board's ad hoc committee on education."

Stresses Curriculum

Ralph Poblano, an educator and member of the Mexican-American ad hoc committee, said Sunday that school boards must be made to realize that the problems of Mexican-American students do not necessarily stem from de facto segregation or inadequate school boundaries but from curriculum.

"A curriculum should take into consideration the needs of the Mexican-American in accordance with his cultural heritage," Poblano said. "English and Spanish should complement one another as foreign languages throughout the elementary level utilizing the child's vernacular as an asset and not labeling it as a handicap."

Marcos de Leon, head of Van Nuys High School's foreign language department and chairman of the Mexican-American committee, said Sunday "assimilation" and "end of de facto segregation," as commonly defined, are not the crying needs of the Mexican-American community.

"What is needed is a new educational philosophy for the Mexican-American," he said. "Whatever progress in education and community consciousness has been achieved by Mexican-Americans can be attributed to:

"1. — Becoming realistically aware of their non-acceptance by American society."

"2. — Finding personal dignity and worth in their ethnical and cultural background."

"3. — Sacrificing immediate ethnic integration and assimilation by excelling in education and the professions, thereby making a greater contribution to American democracy."

De Leon charged that the process of acculturation has been left "unguided and without direction."

Attacks Melting Pot

"The idea that the United States is the 'melting pot' of the world does not necessarily hold true," he said. "The frustration and insecurity brought on by a 'melting process,' carried on at random and conditioned by cultural conflicts, are too great to permit this 'catch as catch can' philosophy to reign over and control the life of the Mexican-American any longer."

"The school cannot continue to function as an isolated unit, or continue to carry on practices based on tradition for the bicultural community, under the present 'all or none' concept as an educational philosophy."

In order that the process of acculturation be carried out, the Mexican-American committee asks the school board to, among other things:

1. — Provide the teaching of Spanish at all levels, including elementary grades.

2. — Introduce in lower levels of instruction Mexican, Spanish and Latin American Literature.

3. — Provide an intensive English oral language enrichment program preferably in the pre-kindergarten years and continued in the elementary grades.

4. — Develop continuing and flexible programs of testing and guidance which will permit the discovery as early as possible of the potential of each child and the identification and development of academically able students, motivating and guiding them toward definite educational goals, and thus preventing them from becoming misplaced within the schools as to ability and interest and thereby becoming dropouts.

5. — Expand and modernize the vocational programs of the comprehensive high schools so as to give a student adequate adaptability to a technologically changing community.

6. — Recruit, hire and place bilingual teachers, counselors and administrators who have an understanding of the Mexican-American child and his community.

Besides de Leon and Poblano, committee members include Hilario S.

Pena, supervisor of foreign language department, Los Angeles City Schools; Antonio Sanchez of the County Human Relations Commission; Arnold Martinez, field representative for Supervisor Ernest E. Debs; William C. Lopez, union representative; and Mrs. Geraldine Ledesma, housewife.

Farm Labor Setup Faces Vast Change

October 20, 1963

FRESNO — California growers are "in a state of shock," according to Don Larin, executive secretary of the state's Agricultural Labor Commission.

They're shaken because though farming last year brought the Golden State $3,340,747,000 in cash receipts, it came with bundles of labor problems.

Whether Congress will extend the bracero program or not, a new era of agricultural labor seems to be approaching and with it the "shock" that comes with change.

"When the bracero program ends, as it must, there will be a sizeable decrease in farm acreage and a radical change in the labor picture," says Larin.

System at Stake

But more than the bracero program is at stake.

A farm labor system which has served California growers for more than 90 years is being aggressively challenged daily by organized labor, politicians, clergymen and idealists who say the American dream must reach the agricultural worker.

Experts generally agree that California's dependence on foreign and migrant farm labor should be replaced with a modern system.

But with what? ask exasperated growers who say that among their many problems is the "cost-price squeeze" in agriculture.

Mechanization won't soon affect the growing labor needs in California's crop-specialization farming, growers contend, and American domestic workers will not do "stoop" labor as braceros will.

Basic Problems

Not so, say anti-bracero forces, adding that there are many domestic agricultural workers who would gladly do it "if conditions were right."

The structure of California agriculture, which is basic to farm labor problems, dates back to 1870, and is made up of crop specialization, large-scale land ownerships, foreign laborers and seasonal migration — a structure radically different from the "family farm" system in most other states.

If one substitutes the word "Mexican" for the word "Chinese" in the following, it will illustrate how the California farm labor structure has not changed.

In May, 1918, Charles E. Warren, a fruit grower, told the San Francisco Commonwealth Club:

"We all know we (growers) need labor. . . . There is only one thing that will furnish the labor for the state of California. . . . What we need is 40,000 to 50,000 good young Chinamen. . . ."

Noted a state Senate Fact-Finding Committee in a massive report published in 1961 and 1963:

"Although the nationality of the 'solution' varied, the 'solution' itself remained constant. The 'solution' was to obtain new labor supplies which fitted the agricultural structures, rather than fitting the structure to the supplies."

After the Chinese Immigration Exclusion Act of 1882, California farmers did not have to face up to the end of the "solution" because the Japanese played a similar role.*

The "Gentlemen's Agreement" of 1908, according to the State Senate committee, "shut off the supply of Japanese." † Laborers of European origin, Italians, Spaniards, Portuguese, Russians, German Russians and Armenians, served as farm laborers in California after that. These soon found better jobs or acquired farms of their own.

In World War I, thousands of Mexicans were imported for the war emergency. After the war unrestricted Mexican immigration furnished the needed agricultural workers.

---

* Promoted by nativists in California who called attention to a "yellow peril," the Chinese Exclusion Act of 1882 singled out Chinese on a racial basis and excluded further Chinese immigration to the United States. The law was finally repealed during World War II when China became an ally of the United States against Japan.

† After the Chinese were excluded in 1882, their place as immigrant workers, particularly in California agriculture, was taken by Japanese immigrants. However, in time the increase in Japanese immigrants led to the renewed allegation of a "yellow peril." Nativists once again promoted exclusion laws. The 1908 Gentlemen's Agreement between the United States and Japan accomplished this goal by restricting, although not fully excluding, the entry of Japanese laborers into the United States.

Braceros Declining

The "solution" of encouraging foreign immigrants to do farm work, this time Mexicans, continued.

The Mexican population of California, for instance, increased from 121,000 in 1920 to 368,000 in 1930, according to U.S. Immigration Commission reports.

A great depression starting in 1929 furnished California with a new farm supply, the "Okies" and "Arkies." But as World War II approached, agricultural workers entered the service or got better jobs.

In 1943, Congress passed the bracero bill, Public Law 45. This was superseded by PL 229 in 1944, PL 893 in 1948 and PL 78 in 1951 which will expire Dec. 31 unless extended.

Under the present law, the number of braceros in the United States grew from 52,000 in 1943 to 433,000 in 1958 and reached a peak in 1957 with 467,000. Since then the number of braceros imported has been declining. In California, for instance, 143,562 braceros entered the state in 1962.

"Wetbacks," Mexicans who entered the country illegally to do farm work, also accounted, according to some sources, for as many as 1,000,000 farmhands in the Southwest from 1942 to 1954.

The U.S. Immigration and Naturalization Service deported 84,000 wetbacks from California in 1954.

Whether the bracero program ends Dec. 31, most California farmers are bracing themselves for the apparently inevitable end of the 90-plus year "solution" to farm labor problems — that is, dependence on foreign labor or migrant labor or both.

In coming years it may be noted that a revolution involving Mexican-American agricultural workers started in Vice President Lyndon B. Johnson's suite at the Statler Hilton here on Aug. 9, 1963.

An intense group of Mexican-American leaders had this message for the Vice President:

"The bracero program must end because it's taking jobs away from our people."

Johnson looked around the room at Sen. Clair Engle and Reps. Edward Roybal, George Brown and Chet Holifield and answered:

"Tell your congressmen of your wish. It's up to them."

Whether the request in that message was justified and whether it will be carried out remain to be seen.

For one thing, also at the Statler Hilton that day were representatives of California growers who held a press conference to debunk the anti-bracero message.

Old Arguments

R. H. Daniels, chairman of the California Growers Farm Labor Committee, told newsmen that the bracero program was needed because there were not enough domestic farmhands to do the work.

Then he hung out a verbal help-wanted sign for 48,000 domestic workers and challenged the anti-bracero Mexican-American leaders to make good their claim that they could supply the needed work force.

J. J. Rodriguez, one of the Mexican-American leaders present when the anti-bracero message was delivered to the Vice President, immediately answered the challenge with:

"We could easily supply the 48,000 agricultural workers — but only if growers are willing to pay American wages and offer American conditions, not bracero's."

The arguments on both sides were not new.

What was new was that the anti-bracero message came from 49 out of 50 Mexican-American leaders — a highly individualistic and faction-ridden breed.

For the first time a large number of Mexican-American leaders had agreed on an issue important to Mexican-Americans in general but not necessarily to the city-bred leaders themselves.

Why did they pick on the bracero issue?

One reason is that they were influenced by unionists who want to organize the domestic agricultural workers (mostly Mexican-American) and use the foreign bracero program as a natural whipping boy.

Another reason is that southwestern Mexican-Americans have new aggressive leadership in Reps. Edward Roybal of Los Angeles and Henry Gonzalez of Texas who are committed to help better the "plight" of the Spanish-speaking people.

But probably the biggest reason for the interest in the agricultural workers by the cities' Mexican-American leaders is that the Negro revolt of 1963 has given impetus to a Mexican-American revolution which is far less spectacular but perhaps as important.

Like the Negroes in the South, Mexican-Americans in the Southwest (especially California and Texas) comprise most of the domestic agricultural workers. It is their one common issue throughout the Southwestern states.

For Domestic Farm Hands 'Shape-Up' Is at 4 a.m.

October 21, 1963

STOCKTON — It's 4 a.m. and 5,000 men as cheerless as the pre-dawn are milling about the farm labor office in Skid Row.

At least 100 drab busses parked and double-parked choke the narrow streets.

Late comers are still spilling out of the nearby flop houses in the incongruously named S. El Dorado St.

It's "shape up" time for domestic agricultural workers. None are braceros.

Some are family men. Some are Mexican immigrants. Some southern white and Negro migrants. Some Filipinos. Some white Texans and Oklahomans. A few are winos.

Most want to work. Their jobs require stooping, digging, cutting, pulling, walking, climbing, reaching, lifting and carrying. They do all this at one time or another in an environment of dust, heat, cold, rain and mud.

Their work is often made more arduous because of scratches, blisters, cuts and insect bites.

It's 4:30 a.m. now and labor contractors are motioning the men they have picked to start boarding the busses which will take them to work.

All is confusion. Men try to board busses as other busses try to drive out. Pickets carry signs saying the "shape-up" system is lousy.

"It's like a mechanized slave market," says a bitter labor organizer.

The busses finally roll. Several hundred men still mill about the Farm Labor Office or hang around the dilapidated coffee shops or in front of the as yet unopened saloons. Some say they couldn't get work that day. Some sit in a vacant lot sipping wine.

"Do you know that there's a hard core of about 200 bums who come every morning, not to look for work but to mooch from the field hands for a bottle of wine?" asks the organizer.

'Unpleasant' System

Farm Labor Office people will tell you that the "shape-up" system can be unpleasant, but that things used to be worse.

Willis Osterlie, manager of the Stockton Day-Haul Farm Labor office, says that a Department of Labor policy of screening and registering day-haul workers started in 1961 appears to be resulting in more stable practices in the day-haul market. For example, there is less milling about in the streets.

The busses that leave the "shape-up" area may pass federally regulated bracero camps where the Mexican nationals are in their barracks getting up to go to the fields, too.

Domestics (permanent residents in the Stockton area, migrants and immigrants) and braceros (Mexican nationals contracted for agricultural work) have much in common. For one thing, they help harvest the specialized crops in the lush San Joaquin Valley.

Many domestics, though, will tell you that braceros are displacing domestics and dragging down wages in general.

Some persons, like Rep. Henry Gonzalez of Texas, claim that braceros, through no fault of their own, have been "used to bring the misery of a people in one country to further depress the misery of a people in another country."

Contrast Startling

Norman Smith, official of the Agricultural Workers Organizing Committee AFL-CIO, tries to prove this by pointing out the immaculate stables for transient horses at the Fresno County Fair and then takes you a few blocks away to show where the transient field workers live.

The contrast is startling. But the problem of housing for domestic farm workers is complicated.

For instance, in Weedpatch, south of Bakersfield, a domestic farm worker's family of nine lives in two 12 × 16-ft. wooden cabins with cement floors and two beds.

Mr. and Mrs. Manuel Humada and their seven children have lived in these two shacks for three years. They pay the Housing Authority of Kern County $33 a month for the cabins. All toilet and washing facilities are outside.

"But our biggest problem is that the two big boys have to sleep in the bed in the kitchen cabin and the rest of us [five] have to sleep in the other bed," says Mrs. Humada.

Humada makes about $64 every six days when there's work in the fields, does odd jobs when there are no crops to pick and goes on county relief the rest of the time.

"Some day we hope to live in a house in the city of Weedpatch," says Mrs. Humada. "But rents are too high and our work too uncertain."

Represents Best Housing

The Rev. Russell Paulson of the Lamont Lutheran Church, who visits the Humadas occasionally, says the camp where the family lives "probably represents some of the best housing for permanent domestic farm workers in the state."

"At least there's plenty of space for the children to play in and as you can see the camp is relatively clean," says Mr. Paulson.

In Firebaugh, *The Times* team found far worse conditions. The housing furnished by the grower consisted of one-room shacks for large families. They rent for $35 a month. The rent is deducted from the agricultural worker's paycheck.

The children, unlike those in Weedpatch, must play near a highway and debris is found throughout the housing area.

Condemned Shack

In Tracy, a permanent domestic farm worker's family of six live in a condemned shack.

"We didn't have enough work in the fields this year," says the mother, "so I don't think the growers, or unions or anyone else will ever change things for us."

In a report to Gov. Brown by the California Department of Public Health, it was noted that in Fresno County agricultural areas "the prominence of chronic diseases was striking" among farm families.

"One half of the families had no family physician," the report said. "Eighty-seven per cent had no health insurance of any kind."

The report also noted that:

Fewer than half of the agricultural families interviewed had a water tap in their homes. Seven families had to haul water and the rest used community taps located outside the dwellings.

About two-thirds of the families had no private flush toilets; less than one-third had community flush toilets. About one-fourth of the families interviewed had private privies and six families used community ones.

One-fourth of the families interviewed had no means of refrigerating their food.

More than half of the families had two or three persons to a room and 22 families had four or more persons per room.

Since the report was made, Gov. Brown has signed Senate Bill 282, which provides limited funds for expanding health services to domestic seasonal farm workers and their families.

A report released this year by a State Senate fact-finding committee, says, however:

"For the last 50 years, roughly, the health and medical care needs of California's seasonal farm workers has been studied and restudied. Recommendations on top of recommendations have been issued. Yet with only four recent exceptions, little has been done to effect long-range and permanent solutions."

Braceros Guaranteed More Than Domestics

October 22, 1963

FIREBAUGH — Stooping braceros picked pear tomatoes nearby as a $125-a-week "pusher" talked about a system which makes him a comfortable living but leaves a bad taste in his mouth.

"Of course there aren't enough domestic workers to pick tomatoes," he said. "There's not enough idiots around, even in the sticks."

Farm work has become so disreputable in our affluent society, he complained, that "I'm known as a 'pusher' now instead of a foreman as in the past."

Why is farm work looked down upon?

"You see those braceros? The rate for picking those pear tomatoes is 25 cents a box. This crop isn't too good, so they're not picking more than 2-1/2 or 3 boxes an hour."

Hate-filled Battle

"Say they work the usual 10 hours a day at this rate. They'd be making $32.50 to $37.50 a five-day week. But because these men are braceros they're assured at least $1 an hour under international agreement."

"So they'll make at least $50 a five-day week."

"Not the domestic, though. He's not protected by a minimum-wage law and must pick this crop at 60 to 75 cents an hour. A domestic would make $32.50 to $37.50 a five-day week on this crop — not $50 like the bracero."

"You see why the domestic will not pick these tomatoes?"

Around such arguments — and figures, of course, vary from field to field — revolves a bitter, hate-filled battle between big growers and labor unions.

But the fact remains that, unlike the bracero, domestic agricultural workers are not protected by a contract minimum. The wage-and-hour provisions of the Fair Labor Standards Act do not cover agriculture.

The Council of California Growers points out, however, that wages of California agricultural workers are the highest in the nation and insists that braceros are not driving down domestic farm wages.

J. J. Miller, manager of the Agricultural Producers Labor Committee, a grower organization, says that if the agricultural workers' wages are low—and he'll debate that—it is because "the agricultural economy is not in a healthy or prosperous condition."

Farm Income Down

Testifying before the California Agricultural Labor Commission, Miller said:

"During the 10-year period between 1947 and 1957, farm wages rose 32%, which is approximately one-half the increase in industrial wages. But during this same period of time manufacturing income and profits rose more than 32% while farm income was decreasing, and the prices the farmer had to pay for all the goods and services he had to buy were increasing."

The farmer and his laborers, Miller continued, "are in the same economic boat. They are both victims of the depressed state of agriculture, but of the two, the laborer has fared better the past 10 years than the farmer. In that time farm wages have increased substantially while farm income has declined."

"The problem of employer-employee relations in agriculture is the problem of the farmer and of agriculture generally."

Problem Still Unsolved

"To try to raise the level of farm wages by organization, unionization, collective bargaining, political or economic pressure, does not solve the basic problem involved, but only aggravates it, and adds to the miseries and inequities already oppressing the American farmer."

Besides, says Miller, a "large segment of (agricultural) workers" believe "they are better off in farm work than in being herded like cattle and sheep into union corrals."

Speaking to domestic agricultural workers from Weedpatch to Stockton, a *Times* reporter-photographer team didn't find any noticeable enthusiasm for unionization.

Cesar Chavez, general director of the National Farm Workers Union, says labor organizers are "aware of this apathy."

"But let's face it: Most agricultural workers are in the lowest educational level and don't even understand what unionization means," he said. "Many are Mexican immigrants who think joining a union could get them in trouble."

"We're now in the process of educating agricultural workers in the importance of organizing."

A member of the Emergency Committee to Aid Farm Workers added, "It cannot be denied that domestic agricultural workers have no protection at all."

"The bracero at least has a contract backed by international law," the member said, "but the domestic worker has nothing."

Deserves Protection

"Surely the domestic worker deserves some kind of protection so he can have guaranteed work for a specified period at a guaranteed minimum wage, plus transportation and housing — things which the bracero has now."

Al Green, director of the AFL-CIO Agricultural Workers Organization Committee, says that if there is a shortage of domestic farm workers it's because braceros are treated better than domestics.

But he denies that the "labor shortage" is anywhere near as acute as "the farm lobby and the Department of Employment contend it is."

"There's no job that Americans won't do if they get paid for it," Green said. "The argument that braceros must be brought into the country because domestics won't do the work is ridiculous."

"How many braceros do you find working as floor layers, cement masons, roofers? What is worse than working as a roofer, with that hot tar stinking in your face all day, or cleaning out the sewers? But you find Americans doing this work because they get paid well."

Growers Hit 'Meddling' With Bracero Program

October 23, 1963

TRACY — "All the do-gooders love the bracero, but they want to take away his livelihood."

Speaking was a grower who feels that "meddlers," especially clergymen and "ignorant city slickers," are trying to kill the bracero program out of hypocritical sentimentality.

The end of the bracero program, many growers contend, will bring more social problems than it will solve.

This is debatable but growers, domestic farmhands and union organizers seem to agree that the bracero "is a good guy" caught in a bad situation.

All along the San Joaquin you hear domestic agricultural workers complain about the bracero system, but immediately temper this with "of course, I have nothing against the bracero himself."

Therein lies a touchy human problem which agricultural workers, mostly Mexican-Americans, hate to face.

"I suppose it's wrong in a way to want the bracero program to end," said Juan Contreras, an unemployed farmhand. "It means the end of jobs they probably need very much."

"But they sure have loused up the valley so a guy can't make a living. Or did they do it? I really don't know."

Racial Brothers

Because Mexican-Americans and braceros are racial brothers, the former are sensitive about opposing the bracero program.

"After all," Contreras said. "many of us and our parents came from Mexico not too long ago."

But that's not the point, according to the Committee to Aid the Farm Worker, which sees it more from the economic and social point than from the emotional.

Suppose, said the committee whose membership includes John Steinbeck and Carl Sandburg, that Congress had enacted a law drafted by consumers for the purpose of "stabilizing food prices." Suppose it provided that whenever U.S. farmers failed to furnish American consumers with fruit and vegetables, at the "prevailing price," the Secretary of Agriculture was authorized to import fruit and vegetables from foreign countries and sell them directly to housewives' associations.

The "prevailing price," continues the committee, would mean whatever the housewives' associations were accustomed to and willing to pay.

Under those circumstances the price of food would be "stabilized," the committee said. It might even decline. Housewives could always find reasons why they could not afford to pay more. The Secretary of Agriculture could always find cheap produce overseas, the committee contends.

"The price of everything else might go up steadily, but the price of food would not," the committee said. "American farmers might complain that this was bitterly unfair, large numbers of them might have to leave their farms and go on welfare in the cities, but the Secretary of Agriculture would point to the law and say 'that's the law.'"

"A bad dream?" asks the committee. "A nightmare?" Of course. It could never happen. . . . In 1951, however, strange to relate, the U.S. Congress did enact such a law—except that workers rather than vegetables were the commodity involved, growers rather than housewives were the consumers, and the Secretary of Labor rather than the Secretary of Agriculture, the purveyor.

"Public Law 78 (bracero law) says in effect, 'we shall artificially add to the supply of farm labor without influencing the price of farm labor.'"

If Congress wants to extend the bracero law it should then try "to demonstrate how the law of supply and demand can be successfully repealed. The burden should be upon the Department of Labor to prove how the hundreds of thousands of braceros it certifies can possibly have anything but an adverse effect on the hundreds of thousands of Americans denied those jobs."

Also, other opponents of the bracero law say, the bracero is not only "dragging down" Mexican-Americans but in many cases the bracero himself is "being dragged down too."

"I was a federal compliance officer for the bracero law last year," says Mariano Arevalo.

"I got sick of it. Though I was supposed to see that braceros were protected under the law, pressure was always applied by growers and I was often instructed to take it easy."

"After all, the bracero could not hurt me and the grower might." At a recent Community Service Organization debate here, a program proponent challenged an opponent to show "how the bracero is dragging down the Mexican-American."

The answer was a quote from Congressman Henry Gonzalez of Texas who says that the "language problem is always blamed for Mexican-Americans' lag educationally, economically, and socially."

Yet, Gonzalez argues, these same people don't see any "inconsistency in importing thousands of unassimilable braceros most of whom are illiterate."

According to Samuel H. Cavanaugh, a retired Tracy farmer, the bracero has helped stop the "undesirable" from coming to California.

"From the human side, too, let's remember that you don't see as many labor shanties, barefoot and hungry children as you did when I was farming."

Tent Cities Gone

"You also don't see those dusty tent cities that were so common in the San Joaquin Valley in the 30's. If the bracero program ends you'll see a lot of 'undesirables' coming from Texas, Oklahoma and the Deep South."

"And you know what? They'll be on relief—at the taxpayers' expense—in no time."

Not so, says the Committee to Aid Farm Workers, which claims that "an increase of many thousands of local domestic field workers boosted the California farm labor force during the past year."

"Statistics based on a count of Social Security accounts as reported by employers show that an average of 35,000 more American farm workers had worked in agriculture between October 1, 1962, and March 31, 1963, than during the period October 1, 1961, and March 31, 1962."

This proves, says the committee, that a domestic labor force is available if recruited. But it never will be if the bracero is there to compete with.

Johnson Speaks Here for Fair Employment

November 15, 1963

Vice President Lyndon B. Johnson told an Equal Employment Opportunities conference here Thursday that the answer to job discrimination is not to "promote" minority groups, but to make everyone a member of a huge majority group.

"What we really seek," Johnson told 1,000 delegates at the Ambassador, ". . . and I believe what really lies in all our hearts—is a system where all of us from the standpoint of opportunity are in the majority, and there is no doubt in my mind that when artificial barriers are removed, we will find that all of us are in the majority after all."

Sincerity Challenged

The sincerity of the Vice President's words was challenged by one delegate, Dr. George Sanchez, a University of Texas professor, who charged that Johnson had "managed the conference."

"He (Johnson) gave the minorities a pat on the back," Sanchez said, adding that he questions the Vice President's sincerity in dealing with minority problems.

Johnson, who heads the President's committee on equal employ-ment, said he was here to study the problems of Mexican-Americans, Negroes and Orientals in the southwestern states.

He was joined at the conference by Gov. [Edmund G. "Pat"] Brown and Secretary of Health, Education and Welfare Anthony L. Celebrezze.

Mending Fences

Johnson didn't say, but it was clear, that he also was here to mend fences with Mexican-American leaders who have expressed discontent with the administration's handling of their problems.

The discontent was made apparent when Ramon Castro, spokesman for a group of Mexican-American leaders meeting at the Ambassador's Oval Room Thursday evening, said that Mexican-Americans had been "taken" at the conference.

Castro said he felt the problems of the Mexican-Americans in the five southwestern states had been articulated by "experts" — who happened to be Negroes and members of the Jewish community.

Castro made it clear he did not question the "experts'" ability to dis-cuss Mexican-American problems but did "resent the fact that Mexican-Americans were not invited to articulate their own problems."

Celebrezze came under fire from spokesmen of the Mexican-American group when Martin Ortiz, of the City Welfare Planning Council, and Philip Montez, of the El Rancho School District, charged that the secretary was "ill-prepared to listen to Mexican-American problems."

Montez said Celebrezze assumed the problems of the Mexican-Americans revolved around integration, when in fact, they do not.

"Mexican-Americans," Montez said, "must retain their cultural back-ground because they are indigenous to the country."

60 Leaders Attend

The leaders' meeting at the Ambassador was attended by more than 60 Mexican-American leaders from California, Arizona, New Mexico, Colorado and Nevada, including as local representatives Arthur Rendon, City Health Commission president, and Richard Tafoya, recent City Council candidate.

The group agreed to meet in Phoenix next Feb. 1 to discuss plans for the formation of a permanent Southwestern Mexican-American organi-zation to express their views.

At the opportunities conference, charges of discrimination in the local

Small Business Administration office were leveled by Henri O'Bryant, Negro president of the City Board of Fire Commissioners.

Loan Trouble Told

"It is easier for a Negro student to matriculate at a white college in Alabama than it is for a Negro businessman to negotiate a loan from the Small Business Administration in the City of Los Angeles," O'Bryant said.

Charging that both the SBA and local banks had made it difficult for him to negotiate a loan for the operation of his choir robe manufacturing business, O'Bryant said to him "it is quite clear that the Negro businessman cannot look to white lending institutions for the development of his business."

The regional conference on equal opportunities was keynoted by Celebrezze who said:

"Our goal is a society in which all men are free — free from poverty and deprivation, free from disease and ignorance, free from injustice and discrimination."

At a luncheon meeting following a series of panel discussions, Gov. Brown called on Congress to "lay aside its sectional prejudices" and approve President Kennedy's civil rights bill.

Papacitos Era Seen on Way Out

June 13, 1964

FRESNO — The 745,000 Mexican-American registered voters in California are ridding themselves of their political "papacitos" (bosses) and giving the Democratic Party notice that it can no longer consider Spanish-speaking people in its pocket.

So claimed Dr. Manuel H. Guerra, keynote speaker Friday at the Mexican-American Political Assn. state convention here.

Dr. Guerra, a USC assistant professor of Spanish, said Mexican-Americans are no longer "seduced by benevolent 'papacitos' demagogues and pseudo liberal apostles of the welfare state bossism and emotional appeals at the expense of reason, logic and facts."

'Promises Not Kept'

He said that Mexican-Americans are disillusioned in the state with federal Democratic administrations "which have not kept their promises to Spanish-speaking voters."

Dr. Guerra said MAPA, with 24 chapters from San Diego to San Francisco, is becoming "militantly bipartisan."

"We have discovered that conservative candidates tend to keep their promises more than so-called liberals," Dr. Guerra said. Our people are beginning to look toward the Republican Party as a possible ally."

Dr. Guerra said 18 Spanish language radio stations throughout the state and Los Angeles Spanish language television station KMEX have pledged themselves to informing the listeners of the benefits of bipartisanship in the November elections.

Latin-Negro Unity Move Launched

July 5, 1964

Negro and Mexican-American politicos have launched a shaky trial marriage.

After numerous meetings in Los Angeles, San Francisco, San Diego, Fresno and Pico Rivera, the "activists" in both groups are ready to test each other.

"You help us defeat the initiative to repeal the Rumford Housing Act," the Negroes ask of the Mexican-Americans.*

"Yes," they answer, "if you help us elect a Mexican-American to the State Assembly from Imperial County."

What comes from these challenges to cooperate may determine whether Mexican-Americans and Negroes can develop what optimists on both sides call the "balance of power" in many elections.

Vow Cooperation

The Mexican-American Political Assn. at its state convention in Fresno on June 14 sent out the first trial balloons by passing resolutions condemning the anti-Rumford Housing Act initiative and pledging "cooperation with Negroes in areas of common concern."

Negro Assemblyman Mervyn M. Dymally (D-Los Angeles) followed this up with a pledge at a Los Angeles "coalition" meeting June 25 that he and other Negro legislators would "personally campaign" for Mexican-American Cruz Reynoso in his bid for Imperial County's 75th Assembly District seat, now held by Republican Victor Veysey.

---

*The Rumford Housing Act was a fair housing law prohibiting racial discrimination adopted by the California State Legislature in early 1961. Efforts to repeal the law were unsuccessful.

Mexican-American politicians are particularly interested in Imperial County because of its high proportion of Spanish-surnamed residents — 33.1%.

24% Farm Laborers

Also, points out Carlos Borja, president of the Council for Mexican-American Affairs, "24% of all Mexican-American males are employed as farm laborers, in contrast to 5% of all California males."

Presiding at the coalition meeting with Dymally were Assemblyman Phil Soto (D-La Puente) and Eduardo Quevedo, state chairman of the Mexican-American Political Assn.

Soto reminded the "coalition" gathering that after the recent defeat of Assemblyman John Moreno (D-Santa Fe Springs), he was the only Mexican-American left in the State Assembly.

Dymally and Los Angeles Councilman Billy Mills offered Reynoso help on the spot.

Dymally, Mills and two other Negro politicians, Assemblyman F. Douglas Ferrell (D-Los Angeles) and Los Angeles Councilman Albert Lindsay head what they call the Democratic Community Organization.

This organization, Dymally said, turned the primary tide for Democratic U.S. Senatorial nominee Pierre Salinger against State Controller Alan Cranston in the Negro community.

Councilman Mills, who called the Negro and Mexican-American "coalition" gathering June 25 "probably the most important meeting I've ever attended," almost saw the "coalition" disintegrate before it began.

For followers of Dymally and Mills were in a bragging mood and reminded the "coalition" meeting that they helped beat Cranston in the June 2 primary.

This infuriated the Mexican-American politicos who had supported Cranston. They later charged that the "coalition" meeting was a move by Dymally and Mills to "brainwash" Mexican-Americans into the camp of Assembly Speaker Jesse Unruh, who supported Salinger, at the expense of Gov. Brown, who supported Cranston.

Coalition Opposed

The Salinger supporters also piqued the followers of Negro Congressman Augustus Hawkins (D-Los Angeles), a Cranston supporter, who plans to form a Negro political organization of his own and is also wooing Mexican-American support.

After the "coalition" meeting, Mexican-American supporters of Cranston and Brown got to work and were instrumental in passing a resolution at the state convention of the GI Forum in Pico Rivera on June 27 which put that Mexican-American veterans' organization on record against a formal Mexican-American and Negro coalition at this time.

This was a blow to Dymally, who together with Unruh was a guest at the GI Forum convention banquet.

Thanks to Quevedo's and Dymally's groups, however, the political trial marriage between Mexican-Americans and Negroes is still on.

But it is shaky on still another point.

Many Negroes say Mexican-Americans have been "conspicuous by their absence" in the fight for civil rights.

On the other hand, many Mexican-Americans say that they have had a long, painful and lonely battle for acceptance and that a coalition with Negroes now would set them back.

It's when they think of themselves as Americans, instead of as Negroes or Mexican-Americans, that both sides visualize the political marriage as a step toward joining the mainstream of the American political family.

And it's when they function as practical politicians, instead of as faction ridden cliques, that both sides see the coalition as a potentially great political muscle.

Reynoso, who beat Brawley Mayor Nick Pricola for the Democratic nomination for assemblyman, reminded the "coalition" meeting that the Negro and Mexican-American vote in Imperial County could be the difference between victory and defeat in November.

The trial marriage, then, could become lasting if Mexican-Americans fight hard to help Negroes defeat the anti-Rumford Housing Act initiative.

And the marriage could produce a political offspring if Dymally, Ferrell, Mills, Lindsay and their Democratic Community Organization really help Reynoso financially and in a registration drive.

Mexican-American Lag in Schooling Income

July 20, 1964

Mexican-Americans — more numerous in California than Negroes but less analyzed — lag seriously behind the majority of Californians in schooling, jobs and income, a state report revealed Sunday.

The study, published by the state Fair Employment Practice Commission, points out that "although attention has been centered on the severe social and economic problem of Negroes," Californians of Spanish surnames are "not participating really in the mainstream of California's economy."

The report is the first of its kind to be made by a state agency on Mexican-American population.

Hard-Core Unemployed

"Displaced more and more from the farming and laboring occupations that were their mainstay in the past, they (Mexican-Americans) are among the hard-core unemployed in some areas," the report says.

"Their young people are often discouraged or alienated from preparation for skills — thus the circle of poverty is closed."

The report, based on the 1960 census, reveals that Californians of Spanish surnames — mostly Mexican-Americans, but also including some Cubans, Puerto Ricans, Central and South Americans — represented 9.1% of the state's population in 1960, compared to 7.2% in 1950. Negroes formed 5.6% of California's population in 1960.

According to the FEPC, California's Spanish-speaking population grew much more rapidly between 1950 and 1960 — by 88.1% — than did the state's total population, which grew by 48.5%.

Lack of Opportunity

Commenting on the economic status of the Mexican-Americans as reflected in the report, Mrs. Carmen H. Warschaw, FEPC chairman, said a higher-than-average unemployment rate and lower-than-average median income indicates Mexican-Americans are confronted by lack of opportunity.

"Sometimes the reason is discrimination," Mrs. Warschaw said. "Sometimes it is the absence of a marketable skill. In either case there is a problem, and the Mexican-American needs help to reach the point where he can share equally in the opportunities and rewards of our society."

The 54-page study, "Californians of Spanish Surname," shows that the median income in 1959 for Mexican-American men was $3,649 compared to $5,100 for the total white population.

Almost one-fifth of Mexican-American families had incomes under $3,000 in 1959, the report said.

In Los Angeles County, where 44% of the total California Mexican-American population lives, the median family income in 1959 for

Spanish-speaking people was $5,759 as compared to $7,046 for the total population, the FEPC said.

"Social and economic discrimination against newcomers from Mexico and other Spanish-speaking countries, and against their children and grandchildren — especially if their skin is dark — continues to affect the status of this large minority in California," the report said.

"Despite that fact that Spanish and Mexican people pioneered this area and made important contributions to its history, hundreds of thousands of Mexican-Americans are relegated, like non-whites, to inferior jobs and poverty-stricken neighborhoods."

Housing Issue Ignored by Mexican-Americans

August 30, 1964

A large percentage of Mexican-Americans here have no knowledge of the issues in the controversy over discrimination in housing, a survey made by a UCLA group has revealed.

A total of 101 Mexican-Americans were polled in the "working-class" East Los Angeles area, which has 75–90% Mexican-American population, and in the "middle and upper-middle class" area of Monterey Park, which has 15–20%.

The largest racial minority in Los Angeles and in the state, the Mexican-Americans were questioned on their attitude toward Proposition 14.

Made by UCLA

The proposition on the November ballot would nullify the Rumford Housing Act and would prohibit city, county and state governments from enacting further laws on discrimination in housing.

The survey, made by a UCLA student team headed by Jesus Chavarria, a UCLA Fellow in the history department, and Richard Maullin, a research assistant in the UCLA political science department, showed, among other things that:

1 — 76% of those polled in the "working-class" area and 53% of those polled in the "middle and upper-middle class" area had no knowledge of Proposition 14.

2 — The Spanish-speaking community, in general, does not express an interest in politics or this particular election as a means to realize ends advantageous to the Mexican-American communities.

3 — The Spanish language is still of great importance even to Mexican-

Americans who have a good command of the English language, and Mexican-Americans formulate political thoughts mainly in Spanish.

In the Monterey Park area flanking East Los Angeles Junior College (15–20% Mexican-Americans), it was found that 52% of those polled do not know whether the Rumford Housing Act (which Proposition 14 seeks to repeal) protects Mexican-Americans from housing discrimination.

Some 24% said the Rumford Housing Act does protect Mexican-Americans, and 24% said it does not.

In the lower-income area lying between Soto and Indiana Sts. and Brooklyn Ave. and 3rd St. (75–90% Mexican-American), the survey showed that 45% of the registered voters do not think Mexican-Americans are discriminated against when looking for housing.

Chavarria and Maullin, both working toward a Ph.D. in history and political science, conclude that the survey suggests discrimination in housing is not a "gut issue" in the Mexican-American community.

Feel No Need for Law

In the Monterey Park area, for instance, the survey suggests that a large number of Mexican-Americans have not felt the need to resort to the fair-housing law, or even know that they could.

"However," say Chavarria and Maullin, "there is still a residual feeling that somewhere, someone of Mexican-American descent is going to run into discrimination."

In the East Los Angeles area, the survey shows that there is a "great lack of information on Proposition 14" among Mexican-Americans but that when the issue is explained in terms relevant to the Mexican-American situation, the potential vote runs highly in favor of the No vote on Proposition 14.

Interest in Mexican-Americans' attitude toward Proposition 14 was intensified recently when the Mexican Chamber of Commerce of Los Angeles voted to support Proposition 14 and then rescinded its stand under pressure.

Mexican-Americans Protest Santa Fe Springs Projects

September 7, 1964

Santa Fe Springs, winner of the All American City award, is having urban renewal problems with explosive Latin overtones.

On Thursday, the city, located in the Pico-Rivera-Downey area, will hold its third public hearing on a proposed urban renewal project.

It promises to be like the other two—a fiery protest by Santa Fe Springs Mexican-Americans who claim the project is aimed at kicking them out of the All American City.

The National Municipal League in 1960 honored this industrial city for citizen participation in civic improvements. But it now has become apparent that some of its citizens are highly subjective about "improvements."

Gov. Brown Booed

Gov. Brown, for instance, was roundly booed by demonstrators in February when he visited a training class for voter registrars in Santa Fe Springs and volunteered that urban renewal is a "good thing."

He quickly added that he didn't know anything about the Santa Fe Springs situation and invited a delegation of the protesters to Sacramento to explain their problem.

Most Santa Fe Springs officials are as puzzled as Gov. Brown over the violent objection by many in the low income bracket to the use of federal money to "improve" their area.

Richard Weaver, city planning director, has pointed out that the city's 65-acre Flood Ranch area, overwhelmingly Mexican-American, has 131 "deteriorating" dwellings, 86 "substandard to a degree warranting clearance," 103 houses in need of "major rehabilitation," 70 "indicated for demolition" and 96 which "require minor repairs up to $2,000."

59 Passable Dwellings

Only 59 dwellings may be considered standard and only eight need no repair, Weaver says.

Of the 65 acres in the project area, officials say, about 16 would be devoted to public streets, and 44 of the remaining 49 to residential development.

The other five acres would be used for a public plaza area, including recreational facilities, church facilities and commercial development.

And, officials point out, the federal government would carry three-fourths of the financial load. Acquisition of the land would cost $1,942,934 with the city paying only $700,000.

At the first public hearing Aug. 27, Massey Herrera, director of the Santa Fe Springs Redevelopment Agency, told a crowd of 300—almost all against the project—that residents displaced by the urban renewal plan would:

1—Receive certain benefits they would not otherwise get if relocating, including cash for their equity and payment of closing and escrow costs.

2—Get assistance in finding new homes.

3—Get loans at lower rates than otherwise obtainable through conventional financing.

4—Receive prices for their property based upon "fair market value" derived from two individual appraisals by private firms.

Militant Opposition

At the two public meetings held so far, however, militant opposition to the plan appears to be representative of the 1,200 Mexican-Americans living in the Flood Ranch area.

Sarcastic picket signs reading "Move Out Mexican—We Need Your Land" and "Chavez Ravine All Over Again" appear at the public meetings.*

And, warns the Rev. Manuel Magana, chairman of the protesting citizens group, "violence could very well erupt if the city insists on pressing for a program which the area people clearly do not want."

Will Defend Property

A vow to defend property with arms was voiced Aug. 27 at the public hearing and pickets outside carried signs reading, "I Will Fight for My Land," "Arms Are Used in Defense of Freedom, We Will Defend Our Homes," and "When You Bring Your Bulldozers, Don't Forget Your Guns."

One of the reasons for this militancy, it has been said, is that the area is one of the original settling grounds of the people who once worked in the orange groves and were able to buy property at greatly reduced prices.

Many of these, who have low incomes, feel the project will result in grave economic hardship.

Mr. Magana, a Pentecostal minister, charges the project is the city's method of getting rid of "unwanted Mexicans."

---

*Chávez Ravine in Los Angeles was a Mexican American barrio before the residents were displaced to make way for the construction of Dodger Stadium in the early 1960s.

"I think the date the Flood Ranch area was annexed to Santa Fe Springs and the date this urban renewal project was first brought up, are suspiciously close," said Mr. Magana.

"I'd like to know whether Flood Ranch was brought into the city just to wipe us (Mexican-Americans) out."

Mr. Magana charges that the housing proposed for the project would be too expensive for the people now living there and they would have to get out.

At one of the public meetings, officials showed colored photographs of Newport Beach town houses which, officials said, resemble, the type of "moderately priced" housing the Flood Ranch area would get. The audience laughed derisively.

Albert Cisneros, 9019 Miller Grove, told the hearing: "You (city council) have a wonderful plan, you spent $160,000 to develop it. But why didn't you even ask the opinion of the people?"

"We were born poor and will stay poor. There will always be poor people. You can only displace them. You will not improve them by moving them around."

Mr. Magana also charges that additional housing created by rehabilitation of the area would put too heavy a burden on the schools, both financially and in facilities.

John Alvarado, 9212 Danby St., told a public hearing that he "is more interested in my civil rights than in a new home."

"As a Mexican I have been studied all my life. And it always comes out the same. Somebody has a plan to help me. But I have no voice in it. I'm the person they're trying to help. Why don't they ask me how?"

Interested observers at the public hearings have been members of the Congress of Racial Equality, who have advised the people to exert more militancy, and members of the John Birch Society, who have described what they call the evils of urban renewal. No members of either group, however, have spoken at the public hearings.

Harassed redevelopment director Herrera has one theme: "We merely aim to provide better housing and commercial facilities for approximately 300 families living in the Flood Ranch area."

He vehemently denies all of the charges made by Mr. Magana and his group.

The city council has repeatedly contended that it has not made up its mind about approving the urban renewal project and won't until it hears all sides.

Mr. Magana's group, however, resents the city council's apparent view that the Flood Ranch area needs drastic "rehabilitation."

Scoffed Mr. Magana at a public hearing:

"I don't believe we are so retarded in our progress that we need the Great White Father to come build us a teepee."

Crux of the controversy, however, may have been expressed best by Robert Mitchell, attorney for the Flood Ranch Improvement Assn., who told the public hearing:

"Urban renewal is new and is evolving daily. Some rules and concepts are being developed right now that have been mentioned here, such as gaining the consent of the people living and owning property in the area."

"You (city council) have crossed all your t's and dotted all your i's, but failed to get the consent of the people."

Roybal, Feder Clash on Issue of Braceros

October 15, 1964

Rep. Edward R. Roybal (D-L.A.) and his Republican opponent Jack Feder clashed Wednesday over what the farm labor controversy means to their highly urbanized district.

Roybal charged that Feder is misleading the voters of the 30th District by backing the distribution of a campaign leaflet which says Roybal's opposition to the bracero program is detrimental to the Mexican-American community.

Meanwhile, Roybal and Dionicio Morales, member of President Johnson's Citizens' Committee Relations, objected to a statement attributed to Republican senatorial candidate George Murphy on the bracero controversy.

Murphy Statement

This week's *Time* magazine quotes Murphy as saying that foreign farm labor programs are necessary to California because, among other reasons:

"You have to remember that Americans can't do that kind of work. It's too hard. Mexicans are really good at that. They are built low to the ground, you see, so it is easier for them to stoop."

Sandy Weiner, Murphy's campaign manager, said the candidate emphatically denies the statement.

"I never said such a thing, privately or publicly," Weiner quoted Murphy as saying. "I haven't even thought of it."

Weiner said Murphy will protest vigorously to *Time* magazine.

Morales said Murphy's reported statement is the "same old stereotype farce which tries to make people think that Mexicans are physically and biologically different and so can do stoop labor easily."

"Actually Mexicans do stoop labor because they have to," Morales said. "The issue is really that growers prefer Mexicans because they'll do stoop labor for low wages. Domestic farm workers, who include many Mexican-Americans, would gladly do the stoop work if wages and conditions were good."

As for the campaign leaflet, distributed by the Mexican-American Agricultural Protection Assn., Feder said he agrees with it that Roybal has hurt his Mexican-American constituents by opposing the bracero law.

"Your representative (Roybal) voted against the bracero program and the Mexican-American community," says the leaflet.

"He has denied your families and friends the right to work in the United States. He has denied them the right to earn money and feed their families."

Feder said the bracero controversy is important to the 30th Congressional District because many produce workers live there who would lose their jobs if California had to cut back on its agricultural production if the bracero program ends.

Roybal said that, on the contrary, the bracero program has been especially harmful to California Mexican-Americans because it has meant pitting Mexican nationals against Mexican-Americans for low paying jobs.

"Historically, the bracero program fits into California's 90-year pattern of dependence on cheap imported foreign labor to work in the fields."

"First it was the Chinese, then the Japanese, the Europeans — Italians, Spaniards, Portuguese, Russians, German-Russians, and Armenians — then the so-called 'Okies' and 'Arkies' of the depression years. Now it is the Mexican national."

"In my opinion, California agriculture, and agriculture in other parts of the country as well, has lived long past the day when it should be leaning on the crutch of a foreign labor subsidy at the expense of hundreds of thousands of fellow Americans."

Feder said domestic farm worker recruitment campaigns have failed and the end of the bracero program would mean a "serious unemployment problem among Mexican-Americans in agricultural allied fields."

The 30th Congressional District has about a 30% Mexican-American population.

Last Braceros Leaving as Job Program Ends

January 1, 1965

EL CENTRO — Hundreds of Mexican braceros started streaming across the border to their native land on New Year's Eve — the last of more than 100,000 who helped harvest California crops in 1964.

Whether they will return to the United States still is up in the air as the controversy over braceros versus domestic farm workers continues.

All of the remaining 9,000 Mexican braceros now leaving California must be back in Mexico by Tuesday, according to Walter Francis, manager of the large, government-operated reception center here.

1,000 Loss Daily

About 1,000 have been repatriated daily for the last four days and the deadline may be met if no major transportation problems arise, he said.

Braceros worked in the fields Thursday until late afternoon, picking Imperial Valley lettuce, but quit at the end of the day because the 13-year-old Mexican farm labor import program died at midnight.

At the reception center, braceros loaded their belongings on buses for the 14-mile trip to the border and many voiced sadness at leaving the country, possibly for good.

Happy With Job

Typical was Guadalupe Becera Tapete, 33, who said that working as a bracero was "the best job I ever had. It was good for me, my wife and my children."

Wearing a new black leather jacket, Becera said that about two weeks ago the braceros were given hope "unofficially" that they might remain in California when the labor import program expired.

"But apparently the governments of Mexico and the U.S. could not get together on an agreement, and we must go home."

"But we may be back. I don't think the locals want to do this kind of work."

Statement Disputed

Meanwhile, however, the hundreds of jobless American workers who flocked to the state employment offices to replace braceros on the farm jobs disputed Becera's statement.

And harassed officials of the Department of Employment continued to complain that some growers don't want to give domestic American workers a chance to prove they can replace braceros.

Edwin H. Peters, state farm placement supervisor for San Diego and Imperial counties, said he was "puzzled and angered" by the Imperial Valley lettuce growers' decision not to co-operate in a state-federal recruitment drive for American farm workers.

Growers' Reaction

Herbert Lee, president of the Imperial Valley Farmers Assn., Wednesday told the State Department of Employment that lettuce growers would not continue in the crash recruitment program because "the caliber of worker being referred to us these last few days would make our harvest problems even greater than the impending labor shortage."

"I don't know what H. Lee is up to, but it is very confusing. We tried to help them replace the braceros because of their claim that a labor shortage crisis is coming. Now they don't want to co-operate," Peters protested.

Peters said Imperial Valley growers are complaining because the local farm office is sending them too many domestic workers.

"This is not true," he said.

"In December, 1963, the local office referred 195 workers to farm jobs in El Centro area."

"This year, in the same period, we have referred 238 workers, and this certainly does not appear to be a large number considering growers' claims that they need 1,800 farm workers."

As of Wednesday night, the Department of Employment had signed up 2,586 U.S. citizens for the jobs, and had placed 1,002.

THREE

FOREIGN CORRESPONDENT, 1965-1968

Los Angeles Times

Dominican Republic

Dominican Leader Denies Red Charge

May 17, 1965

SANTO DOMINGO — Hector Florentino Olivarez, one of 53 men considered dangerous Communists by the U.S. Embassy here, lives just around the corner from rebel headquarters.

I was inspecting a captured U.S. paratrooper jeep in front of the headquarters of "provisional Presidente" Francisco Caamano Deno when I was introduced to Florentino.

Speaking very quickly, he invited me to his apartment on Calle Santone just around the corner.

Florentino, 22, doesn't look dangerous. He's slight of build, dark complexioned and sports a thin mustache. He looks like thousands of Latin American university students.

Student, Party Member

And that is what he is — an economics student at the University of Santo Domingo. But he is also a militant member of the 14 de Junio political party, which he describes as a Socialist organization, but which the American Embassy considers an international Communist front.

Florentino smiled wryly when he recalled that American government sources call him a "fervent admirer of Mao Tse-tung."

"One can admire without being taken in," he said.

The obvious questions: "Are you a Communist and are you influential in Caamano's rebel movement," were quickly disposed of.

"No, I'm not a Communist. Yes, there are probably a few Communists involved in the rebel movement — but these are domestic Communists and not imported."

"No, I can't be considered too influential with Caamano. We even belong to different political parties." (Caamano belongs to ex-President Juan Bosch's Dominican Revolutionary Party.)

"How come you live so close to Caamano's headquarters?"

"It's just a coincidence. It used to be the Canadian Embassy just before the rebels took it over, you know."

Florentino's modest ground floor apartment has the romantic look of a Bohemian's pad. Two tastefully done etchings adorn his bedroom. Books are all over the place, from heavy economic tomes to the collected works of Oscar Wilde.

In one corner was a briefcase with protruding papers and a pistol with loose ammunition around it.

Picture of Christ

His sitting room in front, however, is quite different. It is very conservatively furnished and a large picture of Christ is on the wall.

"The list," he said calmly, "was made up during the reign of President Cabral Reid. I was put on it because I was a militant member of the Federation of University Students.

"I'm still an officer in the organization. Students have to agitate in this country to try to improve things. Remember, the Trujillo terror reign lasted a long time."*

Just then sniper rifle bullets cracked in the outside air.

"We'll all die before we let it happen again," he said quietly.

"But I understand you have been to the Communist bloc countries and to Red China," I reminded him, "and that you may be a trained Communist who may help lead a Communist take-over if Caamano's forces win."

"I have never been to those countries," Florentino said. "I was in Bahia, Brazil, in 1963 to attend a seminar of the University Students of Underdeveloped Countries organization. And I attended a similar conference in Paris."

"You admit that there are Communists in the rebel cause," I said. "What about the contention then that the Dominican Republic could become a Cuba?"

"Ridiculous," he said in his quiet intense manner. "Cuba had a Communist party for 30 years before Castro, who of course is a Communist. And Cubans were well organized in labor unions. It was easy for the Communists to take over.

"But the Dominican Republic has not had Communists for that long. The situation is very different."

---

*Rafael Trujillo was military dictator of the Dominican Republic from 1930 until his assassination in 1961.

Simple, Honest

"What about Caamano and Hector Aristy, said to be the rebel leader's right hand man?"

"Caamano is a simple, honest man who wants nothing but a return to constitutional government, not necessarily under him," Florentino said leaning closer. "Aristy is just an intelligent opportunist, not unlike many politicians. The good thing about him is that he's for the people's rebel movement."

"But do you admit that there are Communists in Caamano's organization?"

Florentino smiled, a tolerant, almost supercilious smile.

"Of course. As Castro himself has said, where did you expect the Communists to go — to (Gen. Elias Wessin y) Wessin's side?"*

"If you're not a Communist, then you must admit that your affinity for communism makes you less than a friend if not an enemy of the United States?"

Florentino leaned back on his bed and began to formulate one of his careful, quiet, intense answers which overflow with impressive but artificial logic.

"I want the Yankees out. I want the illegal junta to be dissolved so that the many Dominicans who want to but are afraid to, can join us."

"I want a return to the constitution of 1963 and a president to be legally elected under it."

"Wanting these things I can't ignore the way the Soviet Union voted in the U.N. on intervention of Yankee troops. And, I can't ignore the way the United States voted and acted."

"If that makes me an enemy of the United States, well?"

"Even if you were right that the Communists here are of a domestic type, are you, as a Dominican who says you're interested in Dominican Sovereignty, not worried about international communism?" I tried again.

"Look," he replied, "the Rockefeller, duPont, General Motors and General Electric organizations are international in nature. They dominate much of the economy of countries."

"It's only natural that there has to be a counterpart for the working class."

"Communism, you mean?"

* General Elias Wessin y Wessin's faction of the Dominican military overthrew the constitutionally elected administration of Juan Bosch in 1963, which led to the civil war and U.S. intervention in 1965.

"Oh, that word again," he said, rising.

We went out into the street. We could still hear sniper fire. Florentino went back to the spot in front of Caamano's headquarters where I had met him.

I went away wishing we had done something to win him to our side.

Who Would Get U.S. Fire, Junta, Rebels?

May 20, 1965

SANTO DOMINGO — What will American troops do if caught in cross-fire between rebel forces and those of the five-man junta now fighting in northern Santo Domingo?

The question became a pressing one Wednesday as rebels in the northern residential and industrial sections of the city were being pushed toward the American safety zone by junta forces advancing slowly but effectively from the northwest in house-to-house fighting.

If hit, will American marines and paratroopers return the fire at the rebels? The junta troops? Both, because it will be hard to tell which is which?

Or will Americans retain their officially neutral position?

Protect U.S. Lives

Thousands of leaflets have been dropped over rebel and junta areas which read (in Spanish) in part:

"The American forces have arrived in the Dominican Republic. Our action was necessary to protect the lives and properties of American residents here and to assure the salvation of all citizens of the Dominican Republic, until peace and stability prevail in the country."

The protection of "all citizens of the Dominican Republic" is getting very difficult for American troops as fleeing citizens from the northern working-man areas are caught in the cross-fire between junta soldiers and armed rebels.

For about five days now, hundreds of unarmed Dominicans, older men, women and children, have been fleeing the Villa Consuelo, Ensanche La Fe and El Ensanchito as the fighting gets closer to their homes.

Many of them carry with them as many possessions as they can in cars, carts, bicycles, motorcycles, motor scooters and on foot.

American troops permit these fleeing people to enter the safety zone and help them as much as they can. Marine and U.S. Army hospitals have treated the wounded and sick coming from the north.

Americans also have distributed food among the Dominican people who live in rebel-controlled areas but who are caught in the middle, politically and militarily.

Refuse to Disarm

But the armed rebels are not dropping their arms, as urged by the American government, to enter the safety zone where they have been assured full protection.

Col. Francisco Caamano Deno, the *Nacional* (a rebel but moderate-sounding tabloid), and the extreme leftist organization, the 14th June Revolutionary Movement, urge the rebels—who prefer to be called "constitutionalists"—to resist.

Neither are unarmed civilians fleeing to the safety zone. Many are now taking arms, when they are available, and joining the rebels in the fight.

People in the Villa Consuelo area, for instance, are caught in the dilemma of whether to flee or take their chances with the rebels.

This reporter had Sunday dinner at the home of a Dominican reporter-photographer, Ramon Laro, in the Villa Consuelo.

Laro, who worked on the *Listin Diario* (founded in 1889) until it was closed during the first days of fighting, says he will never go to the "Yankee side."

On Sunday, as we ate fried chicken, a very rare delicacy in that area now, Laro and his pretty wife talked happily of "when all this is over."

"We'll invite you to a fiesta like you've never seen before," Laro said.

After dinner we sat outside under a large shade tree, sipped rum and conversed all afternoon with the neighbors and teen-age soldiers from the near-by neighborhood rebel command.

There was much joking and laughter.

Laro and I had been north of his house before dinner where Laro had risked his life to take a picture of a man covering a dead rebel on the street with a Dominican flag.

We had seen a large helicopter hovering about, which had no markings on it at all. Laro was convinced it was an American helicopter "pinpointing rebel positions for the junta forces."

American newspapermen had confronted U.S. embassy sources with similar charges, for many American newsmen had also seen helicopters over areas where rebel and junta forces were fighting.

The American newsmen had been assured that the helicopters were American all right but that they were there only to see how close the fighting was getting to the American safety zone.

American newsmen agree that this is a good answer to the charges because the United States has to make an important decision when and if the fighting gets closer to the American lines.

Laro Sunday conceded that "This is possible."

But on Wednesday he said bitterly: "I was right all the time. You Yankees have been helping the enemy."

(He calls me "Yankee" when he's mad at me and "Mexican" when we're on good terms.)

I knew something was wrong when I met Ramon in front of the Hotel Commercial, a few blocks from Caamano's headquarters, on Wednesday.

"I had to take my family (wife, father-in-law and mother-in-law) out of the house last night," he said.

"It's awful up north, men, women and children are running."

"But we men are not. We're going to stay and fight the junta and Yankees."

I remembered that on Sunday Laro's father-in-law had sat in his rocking chair and said with confidence, even as we heard rifle fire in the distance:

"The war won't come down here. We're safe here."

On Tuesday night, Laro said, his father-in-law "was barely able to get our women out of the area."

"They took what belongings they could carry (they have no car) but I guess by now the junta troops have gotten to our house and destroyed everything," Laro said.

But not all are running says Laro.

"The young men are going to fight to the end," he said with a newly acquired militancy in his voice.

"And we're not running toward the American line. We're going to reform in the districts north of Villa Consuelo."

Some of these districts to the extreme north of the city are called the Ensanche Luperon, the Presidente Espaillat and the La Caridad and El Algibe.

"There, the rebels will fight off the junta troops," Laro said. "We're not beat yet."

People here tell me that those extreme northern districts are "even poorer than Villa Consuelo" and that the houses, "mostly wooden shacks," will be impossible to defend.

The rebels in the working man's districts have only two choices: fight or put down their arms and go to the American safety zone.

They can get little help from the rebels downtown who are on the other side of the American lines — in a pocket of about 25 blocks square with the Ozama River to the east and the Caribbean Sea to the south.

And what about the rebels downtown, who so far have a solid stronghold on a good part of the business district?

They're getting restless.

Many will tell you that the Yankees will allow the junta troops to cross the safety zone to attack the rebel stronghold.

But not many responsible people — American or Dominican — feel this way.

The 14th of June Revolutionary Movement, considered a front for international communism by embassy sources, however, is getting more active every day in the downtown rebel area.

And they are taking advantage of the fact that one of the observers sent here by the United Nations announced Tuesday night that Caamano will talk about a cease-fire but that the junta, led by Gen. Antonio Imbert Barrera, will not.

There is very little talk now of Caamano's tie with the Communists here.

Col. Hector Lachapel, Caamano's military aide, said Tuesday in front of the rebel leader's downtown headquarters:

"Let me tell you reporters that we think we're going to win the war. But if we don't, we'll burn the city so that when the Yankees (and Imbert's troops) come in, all they will find is charred ruins and dead bodies."

1,000 Thwarted by Junta Guns
Appeal to U.S. Newsman for Help

May 31, 1965

SAN FRANCISCO DE MACORIS, Dominican Republic — An angry Dominican crowd of 1,000 or more, frustrated by its inability to stage a "constitutionalist" rally in the plaza here, Sunday was dispersed by junta police and army gunfire.

The only American reporter here at the time, I was ordered out of this city of 42,000 by junta police and soldiers who claimed that my car, with its "PRENSA" (press) sign helped create the disorder.

The 1,000 emotional and incensed people followed my car around town, chanting: "Constitucion! Constitucion!" before police shot bursts of fire into the ground and into the air near my car to disperse the angry demonstrators.

An hysterical woman begged that I stay in town ". . . or we'll all be massacred."

Ordered out, my driver Jose and I left town after pleading with the crowd to go home and avoid trouble.

On the last leg of a three-day survey of the provinces, I arrived at San Francisco de Macoris at about 9 a.m., about an hour before a rally planned by provincial rebel leaders was due to start. These leaders told me they were interested only in a return to constitutional government, and were not interested in communism, or Col. Francisco Caamano Deno, the Santo Domingo rebel chief.

The first thing we noticed was the empty plaza, with a cordon of grey-uniformed national police and khaki-uniformed soldiers around it.

I assumed they were there to keep order, as U.S. police keep order at political rallies.

My driver and I went across the street to the Macoris Hotel for breakfast. When they learned who I was, a group of young men swarmed to our table to tell us they would not be able to hold their rally.

They were mad, and started berating the police as ". . . worse than Trujillo henchmen."

I went across the street to talk to the police.

"We have orders not to let those agitators cause trouble in the plaza," a soldier told me.

Back in the restaurant, a local attorney, Dr. Jose Moreno Martinez, had arrived. He told me his friend, an attorney named Dr. Manuel Antonio Tapia, who with Moreno had invited me to the rally, "was in hiding."

"The police broke into the Esperanza Club (a social and cultural club, according to Moreno) at 4 a.m. Sunday and will not let us in," the agitated attorney said. "We were to meet at the club early today to coordinate the rally."

The crowd around our table began to grow . . . mostly young people, and the majority were university students.

Outside, men, women and children began leaving the church and heading for the plaza, where they thought there would be a rally.

The police ordered them to go home. There were angry words.

People Shoved

The police began to push and shove the people.

"I'm a Christian woman and a constitutionalist," shouted one young woman. "Why can't we hold our rally? This is worse than during the Trujillo days."

The woman was arrested, and was taken to the fortaleza, according to eyewitnesses. (The fortaleza is an old fortress, a military headquarters.)

"Why don't you go there and see what happens to that poor woman?" several in the crowd suggested.

Jose and I got in the car and started driving to the fortaleza. Most of the people near the plaza started following us on foot.

By the time we got to Caren St., six or seven blocks from the plaza, the crowd started growing and growing. I looked back and realized that about 1,000 angry, emotional, hysterical men, women and children were following us, and we inched our way toward the fortaleza.

Finally the police and army men stopped our car.

Tell the World

The chants of "Constitucion!" grew louder. People around the car shouted to me "Tell the world how we are treated." I got out of the car to tell the police and soldiers that I wanted to go to the fortaleza. Part of the crowd followed me.

Two young soldiers, who my driver said ". . . were as pale as you were with fright," fired several bursts of carbine fire into the ground. Bullets ricocheted within inches of where Jose and I were standing.

Some of the crowd ran for cover, but most of them started shouting even louder than ever.

The police asked us to leave, ". . . because your prensa car is exciting the people."

I shouted at the people that they must disperse and go home if I was to go to the cable office and write my story.

"They'll kill us if you leave," one man shouted.

But we left as ordered.

I don't know what happened after we left. Maybe they all went home, because there was a short, heavy thunderstorm minutes after we left town. Maybe there were more arrests. Maybe nothing happened.

Claim Doubted

But I had learned something—the people in the provinces are not as happy with their lot as is claimed by junta leader Gen. Imbert Barrera.

Maybe the Communists—Dr. Tapia is accused of being one, but I have no way of telling—were responsible for the disorder.

In the past I have covered "spontaneous" rallies which were nothing but carefully planned publicity stunts by clever press agents. I am acquainted with that type of gathering.

Couldn't Hold Rally

But what I saw Sunday was the most spontaneous thing I have ever witnessed.

The crowd had seen a foreign newspaperman, and they wanted to tell him their gripes. They were not allowed to. They were not allowed to hold their rally. In a complicated situation such as the currently developing situation in the Dominican Republic, it is unwise to make too many judgments. It is hard to tell who was responsible — Communists, or unruly hoodlums, or honest, frustrated citizens, or the police who pushed people when they gathered around our car.

Debate Continues

But as an American it is not hard to tell when people have no free speech. And the people in San Francisco de Macoris did not have free speech Sunday.

Meanwhile, the politicians continue to debate what sort of government can be set up to bring order and stability.

The people in the provinces are getting very restless. On the way to Santo Domingo, I saw scrawlings on a men's room wall which said: "Down with Imbert. Down with Caamano. Down with Communism. Down with the Yankees."

Then, in larger letters: "Long live myself."

Vietnam

A Big Pig, A Midget, An Angry Newsman

November 12, 1965

HUE, South Vietnam — Intrigue in this beautiful city by the River of Perfumes has unique aspects characteristic of the inscrutable East.

Take the other day, for instance. I heard a loud knock on my hotel door and found it to be the manager, a midget who has a huge white pig for a pet.

"Vietnamese monsieur looking for you," he said excitedly. I looked around and didn't see anyone except the midget hotel manager and his pet hog who was pushing his big snout against my half-opened door as if trying to gain entrance. I thanked the manager and closed the door.

Lunch on Terrace

A few minutes later I went across the street to the Cercle Sportif, a "private club" now opened to anyone with the Yankee dollar.

I sat down for lunch with another American correspondent on the terrace overlooking the river. Both of us were engrossed looking at colorful sampans when the "monsieur" the midget had mentioned earlier arrived.

One was a light, intense student with glasses and a Hitler-like hairdo and the other was an older peasant, a cigar-smoking man. Both of them had been following me for two days to tell me the story of their political party.

Story Filed Earlier

I had written a story in which I mentioned the party and something of its activities in this city just 75 miles south of North Vietnam. The story had been filed with the Vietnamese telegraph office before I went to the club.

I greeted the two men and asked them to join us. Their faces betrayed that something was wrong.

The older man started talking in fast Vietnamese and the younger man tried to translate. He began, "We wish to speak to you about a problem . . ."

Two Americans Arrive

At this moment the American consul general and a man from the U.S. Information Office arrived and joined us.

"I see you gentlemen have gotten together," said the consul. "They have been looking for you."

The young Vietnamese continued the translation in precise polite English.

"We are very happy that you have seen fit to mention in your journalistic dispatch . . ."

"Oh," I said. "You have read my dispatch already?"

Actually, this did not surprise me because everybody seems to have access to correspondents' dispatches in this country.

"We have many friends in the telegraph office," continued the young man. "They told us about your dispatch and we think it good and truthful, but we thought it would be filed from Saigon and not here."

Many Enemies in Here

"In Saigon it doesn't matter but here we have many enemies. Could you kindly file your dispatch from Saigon?"

I tried to be patient. The young man and his party colleagues had been extremely helpful since I had arrived. They had heard I was coming to Hue and had met me at the airport, settled me at a hotel, taken me out to dinner and even furnished me with "security guards" around the clock.

The security guards, intense young college students, had not let me out of sight for a second since I arrived. When an American correspondent colleague and I decided to stay overnight in a houseboat, recommended as a "delight" by the tourist office, two grim security guards had insisted on staying on the cold bow of the boat all night long.

"But you see," I now explained. "I have already filed my story with the Hue telegraph office. How can I file it in Saigon?"

"You filed at 11 o'clock and it is now siesta time so it hasn't gotten out yet," he said. "We could go to the telegraph office and my friends could give you back the dispatch."

"OK," I said wearily. "We'll do that." Then, almost, inadvertently, he took the story, which I had filed an hour before at the telegraph office, out of his pocket.

"Thank you, thank you," the man said. "Please file it in Saigon."

He must have noticed my rising anger after he pulled my story out of his pocket, and so the Vietnamese politico said sheepishly, "You care for some tea?"

"You lifted my story out of the telegraph office," I shouted. I looked at the American consul and the USIS man, who both gave me [their] this-is-the-far-East look and shrugged their shoulders.

"Please file it in Saigon and everything will be all right," the politico said trying to smile.

20 Bows of Apology

I grabbed the story from his hand and both Vietnamese men apologized profusely for making me angry and bowed Japanese-style at least 20 times. I dictated the story to Saigon by telephone, not an easy matter, and then went to my hotel room, weary of mind and body.

As I approached the door of my ground floor room I suddenly remembered that I had not closed the door and that it was half opened.

I walked in and gasped at what I saw. The midget's huge hog had entered my room and was blissfully by my bed. I sat down on the bed and had a good laugh.

Burial Rebuff Shakes Battlefront Buddies

May 31, 1966

BIEN HOA, South Vietnam—No one seemed to notice or care what color Pfc. Jimmy L. Williams, 19, was when he was hit by Viet Cong mortar fire in the jungle 30 miles southeast of Saigon.

His buddies, black and white, helped carry the wounded 173rd Airborne Brigade soldier to a medical evacuation helicopter where he died.

In Williams' hometown of Wetumpka, Ala., however, they knew that the dead soldier was Negro and so would not allow his parents to bury him there.

Because he was black. Williams had to be buried Monday in Andersonville National Cemetery—even though his parents would have preferred their son's permanent resting place be Wetumpka.

His buddies, black and white, still fighting the Viet Cong for, as one put it, the "advantage of even Wetumpka, Alabama," don't like "what they have done to Jimmy."

Reaction from Buddies

Three men, all Negroes who knew Williams, were interviewed at the dead man's company headquarters, Company B, 503rd Infantry, 173rd Airborne Brigade.

Most of Williams' other buddies are still in the jungle fighting the VC in an operation called Hardihood. The search-and-destroy operation has claimed 28 Viet Cong dead, by body count, and 30 other possible Communist dead.

Sgt. Dorris R. Resino, 27, of Los Angeles, told the *Times:* "Williams was a better than average soldier because he was a paratrooper. He deserved to be buried any place—even in the White House grounds. . . . That he was not permitted to be buried where his parents wanted him to be is going to bother me for a long time."

Tells Puzzlement

Then, his anger spent for the moment, Resino said with puzzled compassion:

"It seems to me that once a man is in the ground you don't know what color he is. . . . Why not bury him where his parents want him to be?"

Spec. 4 Herbert Mayo, 20, of Steubenville, Ohio, fondly remembers Williams as "a guy we used to tease because of the way he walked."

"You could tell from a mile away that it was Jimmy because of the way he walked," Mayo recalled. "He was not the type who liked to be in the armed forces but he did his job . . ."

Then in a more serious vein, Mayo said:

"When the firing started and he was hit, some of us went over and picked him up in a poncho . . . to take him to the Medivac helicopter. . . . I remember the last words he said were:"

"'Please wait. Please wait' . . . As we moved him toward the helicopter his pain got worse and he wanted us not to move him. . . . But we had to. . . . He died in the chopper . . ."

"I liked Jimmy. . . . I knew him since last September and he used to cut my hair. . . . He was a good barber . . ."

Then without rancor or anger, Mayo said:

"I think it's pretty bad that a man who gets killed fighting for his country cannot be buried in his home town. Jimmy used to talk about wanting to go back to Wetumpka. . . . He liked it there. . . . So why could he not be buried there? . . ."

Pfc. Freddie Connor, 20, of Detroit, remembered Williams as "a guy who missed the girls back home." Connor, who, like Resino and Mayo, is not particularly interested in the civil rights movement, said calmly:

"It seems to me that the people there (Wetumpka) could find a way to bury Jimmy in his home town. . . . He was fighting for the people back there, too . . ."

Carried Tape Recorder

Connor recalls that Williams often carried a tape recorder with him to tape music "over the radio or any place he heard music."

"He would often tell the guys, 'I've got a new tape of music, come over to my tent and listen to it,'" Connor said. "That was the kind of guy he was."

Then as if to himself, Connor said:

"If they (whites) don't want to bother with me I don't want to bother with them. . . . But what harm would have come for Jimmy to be buried where he wanted to be?"

Operation Hardihood, which started May 16, continued Monday. Jimmy Williams' platoon has suffered heavy casualties. All of Williams' buddies killed with him were resting this Memorial Day where their survivors wanted them to be.

All but Williams.

Mexico

Return of Diaz Body Stirs Row

November 6, 1966

MEXICO CITY — A political storm is brewing here over the earthly remains of Gen. Porfirio Diaz, a Mexican military hero turned ruthless dictator, who died in Paris in 1915.

With the blessing of President Gustavo Diaz Ordaz (no relation to Diaz), the family has been allowed to bring back the remains of the old general-dictator, who was exiled by the liberal revolution of 1910.

To political arch-conservatives, the decision spells justification of dictator Diaz, whom they view as the hero of Mexico's "Golden Age" — the 30 years in which Diaz kept the country at peace but under iron rule.

To the extreme liberals and "revolutionists," it means a "continuing trend toward the betrayal of the Mexican Revolution of 1910 and the opening of the doors to foreign capitalistic exploiters."

Family Affair

To President Diaz Ordaz, who recently participated in a ceremony honoring the memory of the dead dictator as a military hero, the return is simply a "family affair."

Actually the scheduled "return" of the dead dictator as such is not what is fanning the political ardors of Mexican leftists, moderates and rightists. Few, except the family, really care where the flamboyant old general is buried.

It's President Diaz Ordaz' participation in the affair which is kicking up a storm. After almost two years in office, President Diaz Ordaz, who

lacks the color of ex-President Adolfo Lopez Mateos, seems determined
to put a personal stamp on his administration.

Runs Own Show

The recent firings of five important public figures — the mayor of
Mexico City (who had served over 14 years under three presidents), the
chairman of the all-powerful Institutional Revolutionary Party, the rec-
tor of the University of Mexico, the director of the social security system and the governor of the state of Durango — indicate President
Diaz Ordaz wants to run his own show without leftovers from other
administrations.

What bothers politicians, from left to right, is what kind of show?

The planned "return" to Mexico of Gen. Diaz, symbol of pre-
revolutionary freewheeling days when large landowners and foreign in-
vestors were all powerful, has added spice to the annual debate — in the
press, congress and public speeches — on "How is the Revolution Going?" (The Revolution of 1910, which ousted Gen. Diaz and supposedly
made Mexico into a democratic country under a moderate left of center
system of government, is celebrated Nov. 20.)

Return to Past

That the extreme rightists are licking their chops in the belief that Diaz
Ordaz favors a return to Gen. Diaz' "Golden Age" and that the extreme
leftists are screeching "betrayal of the revolution" is of little importance.

President Diaz Ordaz is committed by law to the ideals of the revolution. It's his interpretation of what the revolution means at the moment that is important.

Within president Diaz Ordaz' party, the PRI, there is a constant
struggle between two groups:

— Those who think the revolution must mean suspicion of big foreign money, especially American, and continued "Mexicanization" of the
country's industry and natural resources.

— Those who think the revolution has matured enough so that Mexico can handle foreign investments without jeopardizing its sovereignty.

What Diaz Ordaz says publicly between now and the Nov. 20 celebra-
tion and next April 2, when the remains of Gen. Diaz are scheduled to
arrive in Mexico from Paris, will determine what "kind of show" Diaz
Ordaz intends to run and how different, if at all, it will be from that of
ex-President Lopez Mateo.

What happens within the PRI in the next few months, in the face of recent firings of elite PRI members, will determine how well the president is handling the dissident groups within his own party.

Mexico Indian Problem Still Defies Solution

April 13, 1967

GUELATAO, Oaxaca, Mex.—This is the time of year Mexicans are acutely aware of their great Indian heritage—when they celebrate the birthday of their only full-blooded Indian president, Benito Juarez.

Some more cynical Mexicans suggest that Juarez' birthday, which was March 21, is the only day in the year that Mexican officialdom concerns itself with the Indians who make up 30% of the Mexican population.

President Gustavo Diaz Ordaz made a pilgrimage this year to this tiny village (population 310) high in the Sierra of Oaxaca to pay homage to the Indian president who was born here in 1806.

Juarez would probably be pleased with material progress in his native village since he left as a boy to escape its crushing poverty.

Modern Facilities

Guelatao was spruced up for Diaz' visit. It now has electricity, a winding 35-mile paved road from Oaxaca, the capital, and a new monument to Benito Juarez.

This tiny community which Juarez left as a shepherd boy of 12, speaking only his native Zapotecan, to become the president of the "Reformation," is as colorful and quaint as any tourist could desire.

And that is what irks Indian-oriented Mexicans.

Though Juarez would undoubtedly approve some of the efforts the government is making to see that some of the conveniences of modern life are reaching the Indian villages, he would surely be saddened by the fact that Mexico's Indians are almost as isolated from the mainstream of Mexican life as they were when he was a boy.

Problem Outlined

In a recent interview, Mexico's director of the National Nuclear Energy Commission, Alfonso Leon de Garay, put the Indian problem, as many Mexican liberals see it, succinctly.

"It is time for (Mexican) Indians to be more than mere folklore, an inspiration to local popular art and object of tourist attraction. It's about time they were incorporated as part of the nation, with all the guarantees and rights of any Mexican."

"It is a lie that Indians suffer traumatic experiences when they are transported to another environment," Dr. De Garay continued. "On the contrary, they adapt quite easily."

It was this annual "temporary Juarez enthusiasm," as it is called here, that prompted the National Peasant Confederation (CNC) to charge that the National Indigenous Institute (INI) is using "obsolete, reactionary systems."

Amador Hernandez, director of the confederation, castigated INI for believing "that the Indians must remain an Indian always."

"He (the Indian) is used only to be photographed by tourists and to have fashion designers copy his clothing," Hernandez complained. He said that the Mexican Indians are used only as Mexican curios and called for a realistic program to solve the Indian's problem of becoming a first-class, contributing citizen of his fatherland.

The Indian problem is truly a national concern in Mexico.

Most of Mexico's 45 million people inherit the blood of the Zapotecs, Mayas, Toltecs, Tarascans, Mixtecs, Aztecs and an uncounted number of other ethnic subgroups which have battled for mastery in Mexico beyond recorded history.

Mestizo Defined

A Mexican, by definition, is a mestizo — a new nationality of mixed Indian and Spanish antecedents.

Even so, the Mexican Indians are as culturally isolated as they were in Juarez' day, or as Indians are in the United States, to a considerable extent.

The peasant confederation is not the only group to take notice of this. Last year, when charitable groups in the United States sought to aid the Tarahumaran Indians in the state of Chihuahua, the government refused entry to a 10-car train loaded with food, medical supplies and other aid for the Tarahumarans.

This shocked Americans, who could not comprehend why the Mexican government could not afford to have reports of such aid gain worldwide currency.

Rebuttal Offered

"Do you think," says a government official, "that the American government would allow England or Russia to send food to destitute American

Indians or Negroes while President Johnson is directing the war against poverty?"

Mexico, admittedly, has many problems, the government official continued, and noted that important among them "is the Indian problem, which we must solve ourselves because we're all Indian to a certain extent — but outside help can only make the problem worse."

Mexicans, aware of and disturbed by their Indian problem, nonetheless like to recall the time when an American reporter, shocked by Indian conditions in Mexico, asked the late Ambassador William O'Dwyer what he thought about the "frightful situation."

"Well," answered the colorful O'Dwyer, "the Mexican Indians are alive, which is more than we say for most of our Indians."

Quinn, Censors Cross Swords

September 17, 1967

MEXICO CITY — Anthony Quinn, who has recently become a bona fide Mexican, can't understand why he's having such a hard time making arrangements here to film "The Children of Sanchez."

The book, by American anthropologist Oscar Lewis, greatly offended official Mexico because it thought the study of a poor Mexican family gave a wrong image of the country.

When the book first came out in 1961, it caused such a furor among overly sensitive Mexicans that it was banned. Since, the ban has been lifted and anyone can now buy it, even in Spanish translation, in Mexico City.

Quinn, who has bought the movie rights for the work after other producers gave up making the picture here, still dreams of filming it in Mexico.

All right, say Mexico movie censors, but you've got to present a finished script first.

A finished script, figures Quinn, would cost between $100,000 and $200,000.

"What if the censor didn't like it — then where would I be?" asks the millionaire actor.

"I just don't understand censorship."

Born in Chihuahua, Mex., of Irish and Mexican parents, the 51-year-old movie star had never possessed a birth certificate until recently.

Here to film MGM's "Guns for San Sebastian," Quinn mentioned to important people that he lacked proof he was born in Mexico.

Chihuahua Gov. Praxedes Giner Duran took an interest and, after an investigation, ordered a Chihuahua birth certificate for Quinn.

"It seems to me," says Quinn with what Mexicans think is overly simplified logic, "that my Mexican birth certificate should prove that I would do nothing to denigrate Mexico."

Whatever the validity of Quinn's arguments, it is generally conceded here by foreign movie-makers that censorship is preventing Mexico from becoming a leader in international movie making.

"Mi dios," says Quinn. "I'm about to make a movie in Italy about a modern day Pope ('Shoes of the Fisherman') and the Pope has not asked to see a finished script."

Hiram Garcia Borja, the No. 2 man in the Mexican censorship office, has explained that "almost every country in the world has film censorship of some kind."

"We have our complexes, I don't deny that," continued Garcia. "We may have an exaggerated nationalism, but no more so than the French. All nations have complexes. Many North Americans have complexes about being North Americans, even though it's a great country."

According to Garcia, "Marriage on the Rocks," for which Frank Sinatra was barred from Mexico, "laughed at our constitution." The film was about quickie divorces on the border.

"I've never seen a movie that made fun of the United States Constitution. So by what right do they laugh at ours? It's just as honorable as theirs."

"The Children of Sanchez," however, contends Quinn, is a very serious work which "could hardly be called anti-Mexican."

"As a matter of fact it's pro-Mexican," said Quinn warming up to the subject. "It's not a documentary about Mexican poverty but actually about the sanctity of the family — something which is fast disappearing in other parts of the world."

Oscar Lewis, who subtitled his book "Autobiography of a Mexican Family," clearly states in the introduction to "The Children of Sanchez" that he is not making fun of or criticizing Mexico for its poverty. Writes Lewis:

"Even the best-intentioned governments of the underdeveloped countries face difficult obstacles because of what poverty has done to the poor. Certainly most of the characters in this volume are badly damaged human beings."

"Yet with all their inglorious defects and weaknesses, it is the poor who emerge as the true heroes of contemporary Mexico, for they are paying the cost of the industrial progress of the nation."

"Indeed, the political stability of Mexico is grim testimony to the great capacity for misery and suffering of the ordinary Mexican. But even the Mexican capacity for suffering has its limits, and unless ways are found to achieve a more equitable distribution of the growing national wealth and a greater equality of sacrifice during the difficult period of industrialization, we may expect social upheavals sooner or later."

As far as Mexican movie censors are concerned, however, poverty is a taboo subject. To them it is better to forget that half of the population of Mexico makes less than $200 a year. For instance, filming was recently stopped on a travelog until shoes could be found for barefoot peasants.

"I've got other movie commitments for a year and a half," says Quinn. "Maybe at the end of that period I can come to some understanding with the Mexican government about filming 'The Children of Sanchez.'"

"I sincerely think it would give Mexico a deserved image for respecting the truth."

Others, however, are less optimistic.

A Mexican director, who doesn't think "The Children of Sanchez" will ever be filmed honestly here, quotes [Octavio] Paz, Mexico's distinguished poet, essayist and diplomat, to prove his point.

Writes Paz in his "The Labyrinth of Solitude: Life and Thought in Mexico":

"The Mexican, whether young or old, general or laborer or lawyer, seems to me to be a person who shuts himself away to protect himself; his face is a mask. . . .

"He builds a wall of indifference and remoteness between reality and himself, a wall that is no less impenetrable for being invisible. The Mexican is always remote, from the world and from other people. And also from himself. . . ."

Quinn, however, being Irish, Mexican and American, hasn't given up yet.

Students Peril Mexico Image Before Olympics

August 18, 1968

MEXICO CITY — A student anti-government movement appears to be spreading throughout Mexico, threatening the image of stability so necessary for a country about to host the 1968 Summer Olympic Games.

Last Tuesday's impressive demonstration in front of the presidential palace was significant in that the 150,000 students, teachers, supporters and professional agitators took on the president himself.

"Diaz Ordaz, Diaz Ordaz, donde estas?" (where are you?) chanted the demonstrators at the historic Zocalo Plaza, site of the presidential palace and the national cathedral.

Tradition Broken

In taking their cause directly to President Gustavo Diaz Ordaz, the students and those who use them for good or ill, were breaking a tradition long held sacred in this "one-party democracy."

A Mexican, it is understood, can criticize everything except the president, who is a leader of the almost monolithic Institutional Revolutionary Party (PRI).

In the last two years there have been student uprisings in 13 of Mexico's 29 states as well as in the Federal District at the University of Mexico here.

In three cases, at the University of Morelia, at the University of Sonora and recently here, federal troops have had to be used to end the rebellions.

Though much was said about federal troops "violating the autonomy of Mexican universities," things quieted down once the president said he would personally look into the matter and correct it.

Asked for Peace

After the bloody July 29–30 student revolt here, in which students armed with Molotov cocktails battled tanks, troops, bazookas and club-wielding riot police, the president asked for serenity.

In an emotional speech after the latest student disturbances, President Diaz Ordaz said he "extended his hand" in the hope that it would be received by "millions of Mexican hands" who want to reestablish peace and tranquility.

The president said he hoped his outstretched hand would "not be left hanging in the air."

Last Tuesday the students in the mammoth demonstration below the president's balcony answered Diaz Ordaz' call.

The students waved crudely drawn pictures of the president with an outstretched hand — but in a Nazi salute. Swastikas were drawn on other pictures of Diaz Ordaz and other posters carried insulting messages to the president. Veteran observers were appalled.

"This sort of thing just doesn't happen in Mexico," said a foreign correspondent stationed here 20 years.

Anti-Diaz Ordaz

There were pictures and sayings of Che Guevara, too, but the demonstration was clearly anti-Diaz Ordaz. The second most surprising thing was that though the huge crowd marched eight miles from the Polytechnical Institute to the Zocalo, literally taking over downtown Mexico City at a peak traffic hour, there was not a uniformed policeman or soldier in sight.

It is generally conceded that if authorities had not allowed the demonstration to take place peacefully, a massacre would probably have resulted.

Meanwhile, students struck in four other states in support of the Mexico City movement.

Though the government blamed Communists for the disturbances, seasoned observers say it is too easy an explanation. Communists undoubtedly were involved, they say, but at least two other factors are more important:

1 — The low quality of Mexican university education and the lack of jobs for those who do finish their studies.

2 — A growing dissatisfaction within President Diaz Ordaz' Institutional Revolutionary Party (PRI).

In the 1966–67 school year, the University of Mexico operated at a deficit. This resulted in inadequate facilities such as laboratories, technical equipment and teaching resources, according to a recent survey.

Because of lack of professors, most classes at the university had 100 students enrolled. The survey said the classes to be effective should have no more than 40 students.

Out of a faculty of 7,000 only 145 were full-time professors in 1967. A total of 150 were half-time professors and the rest were professional people who contributed some time, when they could, to the university.

As to the PRI, there has been some serious dissension in the party since Diaz Ordaz took over three years ago. The dissatisfaction, not too surprising for a party that has controlled the political life of Mexico for 40 years, comes especially from politicians who think the PRI has lost all its "revolutionary" fervor and has become bureaucratically "institutionalized."

Carlo S. Madrazo, for example, former governor of the state of Tabasco who was fired as head of the PRI for proposing that open primaries be held in municipal elections, warns the PRI must change if it is to survive. He says youth must be given more opportunities within the PRI and out of it, pointing out that 31.6% of all Mexicans are between the ages of 15 and 34.

Warns of Crisis

Another wave-maker is Manuel Moreno Sanchez, former president of the completely PRI-dominated federal senate. He warns that the party is going through a crisis because even though there are 8 million registered members, very few are voting and youth is especially aware that this means the political life of the country is controlled by a handful of people.

The striking students claim they will continue their movement and that it will spread into the working classes much as it did in France last spring.

Few experts believe this possible, pointing out that the Mexican worker does not as yet have the political sophistication of the French worker. As for continuing the strike in Mexico City, which includes the university, the Polytechnic Institute and several high schools, many believe that the students "having shot off their mouths" will return to school if for no other reason than that the parents are getting impatient with too many demonstrations and not enough study.

Nevertheless, though the government will not admit it publicly, it is clearly worried because the student disturbances could not have come at a worse time.

The Olympic games are scheduled to open Oct. 12 and the students may choose to demonstrate against them.

They know that nothing could embarrass the government more. It could also affect attendance at the Olympics and hurt the country's much-needed tourist business.

Students Plan Massive Rally in Mexico City

August 25, 1968

MEXICO CITY — Striking students and their supporters plan a huge anti-government demonstration for Tuesday which could severely strain the current official "hands off" policy by police and the army.

Encouraged by their successful peaceful manifestation against President Gustavo Diaz Ordaz Aug. 13 in front of the National Palace, the students say they will now march against the Mexican Congress.

Last Tuesday, the students invited members of the rubber-stamped Mexican Congress for a debate in the university campus on student problems in particular and national problems in general. Congressmen and senators refused to attend.

It was then decided to demonstrate Tuesday.

Attracted 150,000

The unprecedented anti-Diaz Ordaz rally in the historic Zocalo Plaza attracted more than 150,000 people.

The student strike committee hopes to have 500,000 of this city's 6 million inhabitants participate in Tuesday's demonstration.

The strike would involve students from the National Polytechnical Institute, the University of Mexico, the National School of Agriculture and several high schools.

The trouble started as a minor free-for-all between students of two high schools July 23, which had to be stopped by riot police. It grew into a riot July 26, the anniversary of the start of the Cuban revolution, and mushroomed into open warfare between the students, riot police and the army July 29–30.

Students accused the police and army of brutality. They called for the firing of Mexico City's chief of police, disbanding of the riot police, release of "police prisoners" and revocation of laws dealing with political subversion.

No Intervention

Although the Aug. 13 demonstration was clearly against President Diaz Ordaz, an extremely rare event in Mexico where the president rules through the almost monolithic Institutional Revolutionary Party, not one policeman or soldier intervened.

The government obviously does not want another battle between students and the police and the army. This would further mar the image of stability which Mexico has enjoyed for years.

Officials also do not want further violence because of the thousands of foreign visitors scheduled to travel to Mexico for the summer Olympic Games which will start Oct. 12.

The government had apparently hoped that the peaceful Aug. 13 demonstration would prove its good faith and that negotiations could start to end the student movement.

Involve Workers

Since Aug. 13, however, the striking students have become more ambitious and now hope to involve the working class in the movement.

Since then, so-called "student brigades" have been canvassing working-class neighborhoods and the downtown area trying to recruit people for the Tuesday rally.

One of these "student brigades," for example, stopped traffic on busy downtown Juarez and Balderas Aves. during the lunch hour by having students stage a sit-down across the intersection.

While hundreds of honking cars waited for traffic to resume, students spoke into portable public address systems asking people to join the students' movement.

The police did not interfere.

Should the students be able to muster working-class support for Tuesday's demonstration, the situation would obviously become worse for the government.

But labor unions in Mexico are government-controlled and it's doubtful that union members will leave their jobs to join the demonstration. However, students hope to attract the "hundreds of thousands of unemployed Mexican workers," which militant students claim are on the verge of revolt.

In order to further embarrass the government, the striking students are concentrating more on attacking the Olympic Games.

Among the pamphlets being distributed, one says that while Mexico is going through a crisis of poverty, unemployment and social discontent, the reactionary government is committed to putting on an expensive Olympiad.

Another pamphlet shows bayonet-wielding and gas-masked troops dispersing students. It reads: "This is not Nazi Germany. It is Mexico of '68, home of the Olympics where the theme is peace."

Tuesday's planned demonstration is also calculated to influence President Diaz Ordaz' state of the union message which he is to deliver Sept. 1.

The most important problem for the government just now is how long it can afford to allow the students to demonstrate against the authorities without interfering.

Students, Army Troops Battle in Mexico City

October 3, 1968

MEXICO CITY — Mexican army troops battled students in downtown Mexico City Wednesday night in the bloodiest clash in more than two months of anti-government demonstrations. At least six persons were killed and hundreds were injured.

Although most of the casualties were taken to a military hospital, one doctor said three floors of the Red Cross hospital were filled with wounded and dead from the battle. Some sources said as many as 50 persons may have been killed.

Shooting between troops and student snipers broke out just after student leaders told a rally they were calling off a protest march against a campus of the National Polytechnic Institute still occupied by soldiers.

About 10,000 persons attended the anti-government rally at the plaza of the Three Cultures which is overlooked by the Foreign Ministry and the city's largest apartment complex, the Tlatelolco housing project.

Battles Erupt as Rally Ends

As the rally was ending the gun battles erupted between troops, surrounding the area in dozens of armored cars, and snipers in the apartment buildings. Troops opened up with machine guns on the snipers and persons in the square fled screaming for cover. The troops said the snipers opened fire first.

Six bodies were counted at the Colonial Church adjoining the square. It was not immediately known how many had been killed in the center of the square. Witnesses said the troops fired into the crowd.

Later gangs of youths roamed the streets shooting and throwing Molotov cocktails.

Gen. Marcelino Garcia Barragan, the defense secretary, said he had orders to crush the student uprising at any cost.

Garcia said there were many deaths on both sides but declined to say how many. He reported, however, that one army corporal was killed and 13 other army men wounded, including a general.

(The general was quoted by United Press International as saying the troops had acted to halt an illegal march.)

The housing project was the scene of another nightlong battle a week and a half ago when police and snipers fought after the army occupied the National University.

The new outbreak appeared almost certain to affect the success of the Olympic Games scheduled to start Oct. 12.

The men, women and children gathered at the square were ready to go home as ordered by strike leaders after cancelling plans to march on the Polytechnic campus at Casco de Santo Tomas.

Though federal troops have left the University of Mexico campus and the Zacatenco campus of the Polytechnic Institute, a small contingent of soldiers still holds the Casco de Santo Tomas campus.

This campus, located in a tough working-class neighborhood, was the scene of a previous bloody clash between students and the army.

The National Strike committee had said strikers and sympathizers would march from the Plaza of Three Cultures to Santo Tomas following the rally. But rain and the heavy concentration of military and police forces caused the leaders to change plans.

After the occupation by the army of the university and the institute Sept. 18, troops forbade any street marches.

The army was ordered out of the university last Sunday and strikers attempted their first march Monday, a successful "mother's march" which ended at the Chamber of Deputies building.

Though the Olympic Games start Oct. 12, striking students again dominate the University of Mexico campus where many of the events will be held.

(A high-ranking official of the International Olympic Committee, who declined to be identified for publication, said the renewed rioting could lead to cancellation of the forthcoming games, United Press International said.)

(He said that games organizers had a duty to guarantee the safety of the visiting athletes and officials. The Olympic Congress meets next Monday.)

The strike committee has promised not to attempt to sabotage the Olympics but reserved the right "to demonstrate if necessary during the games."

Striking students from the university, Polytechnic Institute, the national Agriculture School, several prep schools and high schools have said they will not end their movement until the government accedes to demands for reforms and the ouster of some officials.

The strike, involving some 150,000 students, started in late July.

Mexican Sniper Slain After Killing Passerby

October 5, 1968

MEXICO CITY—A sniper shot one passerby to death and wounded another Friday in a terrorist act that broke Mexico City's uneasy calm. An army marksman then killed the sniper with a bullet in the head.

The shootings occurred in front of the Tlatelolco housing project fronting on the Plaza of Three Cultures which was the scene of a bloody battle between soldiers, police and snipers Wednesday night which left at least 29 persons dead — including two soldiers — and scores injured.

The latest two fatalities brought to at least 31 the number of deaths resulting from the last few days of violence growing out of the anti-government student rebellion that began in July.

Even as sporadic cases of vandalism and sniper firing were reported in the city, a renewal of general violence was threatened by a self-styled "Constitutional National Liberation Army."

The "army" sent foreign correspondents and news agencies a printed statement saying it would wage guerrilla warfare against "the criminal government of President Gustavo Diaz Ordaz" and warning foreigners to stay away from Mexico.

The statement was dated Sept. 28 but distributed only on Friday, just eight days before the opening here of the 1968 Summer Olympic Games next Saturday. It was difficult to tell if it was the work of one man or an actual organization.

Thus, while organized rebellion against the government seemed to be under control for the time being, continuing random incidents and threats of this sort kept the city and government officials worried.

Meanwhile, police divided this city of 6 million people into four defense sectors, making city and state police responsible for different parts of the metropolis.

Troops still occupied the Tlatelolco housing project, where at least 50 families were evacuated either permanently or temporarily following Wednesday's fighting.

Soldiers also still occupied the Casco de Santo Tomas campus of the National Polytechnic Institute. At the University of Mexico, groups of students conferred quietly and vowed to continue the 2-month-old student strike.

They admitted, however, that rebel students are unable to use university buildings as strike headquarters as they did before and that the National Strike Committee now has to work in secret. One student said all members of the strike committee are dead, jailed or in hiding.

Wednesday's bloody battle between students and the army has for the present made anti-government marches, rallies and demonstrations "impossible," a striking student said.

"We've got to admit that after Wednesday a lot of us are scared," another said. "The army has guns and tanks, and we have nothing. Unfortunately, now that we cannot meet publicly to explain our cause, a few extremist youths who do have weapons will probably use them even though the strike committee is against this."

Wonderland of Color Welcomes Olympics

October 13, 1968

MEXICO CITY — With the start of the XIX Olympiad, this ancient Aztec capital has been transformed into a multicolored wonderland where the athlete is king and the visitor is welcomed with Latin warmth.

Only in the background are the sad reminders of the violence between students and police and soldiers that culminated in a bloody clash Oct. 2.

But nearly everywhere, the major theme is the 1968 Olympics.

In this 7,400-foot-high city where the atmosphere is so thin it literally takes away a man's breath, there is an air of carnival.

The airport terminal is inundated with huge balloons bearing the legend "Mexico 1968" and colorful concentric patterns.

Pretty girl guides in psychedelic miniskirts in gaily-painted kiosks on the wide, tree-shaded Paseo de la Reforma give visitors information and steer them to their taxis and hotels.

On the pereferico, or freeway, Olympic cyclists pedal with earnestness and smile at motorists who politely give them the slow lane in a city not noted for driving courtesy.

All over Mexico City there are billboards saying, "Everything is possible in peace," in most of the world's languages.

The city is sparkling clean for the historic event, for this is the first time the Olympic games are being held in Latin America and in a "developing" country. And all of Mexico is proud of the honor.

The city's striking students are generally friendly to the athletes from all over the world, all dressed in distinctive blazers with their country's shield on their breast pocket. At the University of Mexico some militant students whistle derisively at athletes in training. But many others applaud politely.

The National Strike Committee has long said it had nothing against the Olympics. But it had insisted that it reserved the right to continue its anti-government struggle during the games even if it embarrassed the regime.

However, members of the student strike leadership pledged Friday they would not hold any public demonstrations for the duration of the games — apparently ending any threat that might mar what is supposed to be an international gathering of goodwill.

Everywhere the visitor goes he is sure to see the symbolic white peace dove. It is on banners, painted on windows and placed on car stickers. A close look shows that on some of the snow-white doves a bleeding heart has been painted in red.

While policemen looked the other way, striking students and their sympathizers have made the alterations. The gesture is a sad tribute to the men, women and children who have been killed during the recent clashes with the army and police.

On street corner newsstands the visitor, if he knows Spanish, can read big black headlines saying the student war is over. The headlines seem to be contradicted by picture magazines like *Por Que?* whose cover shows the body of an 11-year-old boy killed by army or sniper fire in the Oct. 2 clash.

Inside the magazine are grisly photographs of dead youths with the caption: "Assassinated Youths Representative of Mexico's Hope for the Future."

Yet, the visitor goes his way, enjoying the freshly planted flowers along the Paseo de la Reforma and looking up with awe as the sun hits the "golden angel" statue across from the fashionable Maria Isabel Hotel.

Wherever the visitor looks all is color. Near the Olympic village, close to the ultramodern University of Mexico, are slums like the ones Oscar Lewis so eloquently describes in his "Children of Sanchez." Even these are gay for the moment.

The adobe facades of the slum buildings have been painted with shocking pink, purple and yellow — temporarily hiding the misery.

Along the freeway are abstract sculptures, indefinable save for the inevitable peace doves executed by artists of many countries visiting Mexico for the Olympics.

Special white buses race toward downtown, carrying athletes, tourists and sports enthusiasts to their destinations. They all get there, but it takes at least half an hour longer than it did before the world's most famous sports event clogged Mexico City streets with what one wit called "bumper-to-bumper traffic to ulcer-to-ulcer traffic."

But there are compensations. At night a drive from Chapultepec Park to downtown along the Paseo de la Reforma is an adventure in lights and sounds.

A million light bulbs have been used for the multicolored illumination of streets, public structures and private buildings. But they don't just decorate. The lights have been arranged in different colors, showing the way to each Olympic event.

There are also elaborate figures, symbols, inscriptions, sports themes and garlands, outlined in many-colored electric bulbs — some displays utilizing as many as 11,000 lights.

Turning right from the Paseo de la Reforma into narrow Juarez Avenue and the grandly illuminated white marble Palace of Fine Arts, the visitor enters colonial Mexico on Madero Avenue. The narrow street seems suddenly to explode into a vast, colorfully lighted plaza, the Zocalo with the National Cathedral, Presidential Palace and Supreme Court all trimmed in glittering lights.

On nearby 20th of November Avenue is a huge lighted Mayan sports scoreboard, covering 384 square meters.

The plaza is so charged with light, color and sound that the visitor feels he knows how Cortez must have felt when he first saw Mexico City, then called Tenochtitlan.

Now it is Olympic City, filled with gaiety, the wine of sportsmanship and a bit of sadness.

FOUR

THE CHICANO MOVEMENT, 1969-1970

Los Angeles Times

Militants Fight to Retain Spanish as Their Language

January 14, 1969

EL PASO — The Spanish language, spoken in the Southwest long before Plymouth Bay and Jamestown were settled, is under fire in some quarters as being detrimental to Americanism.

The result is that militant Mexican-Americans, who prefer to call themselves Chicanos, are fighting back with a rising chauvinism which had begun to blur after years of conditioning by U.S. society.

Throughout the Southwest, and especially along the Mexican border, the old controversy of whether Mexican-American students should speak Spanish in school and on the playground is stirring racial sensitivities.

In the lower Rio Grande Valley, more than half of 150 high school students demonstrating against a rule that prohibited the use of Spanish on the playground were recently arrested.

Students Threaten Walkout

In El Paso, students threatened a massive walkout at Bowie High School, composed of about 95% Mexican-Americans, over a rule against students speaking Spanish. The rule was enforced with detention for any violations.

In both cases the defenders won the day — the lower Rio Grande Valley students were exonerated and the contested rule at Bowie was rescinded. Nevertheless, the issue, long an explosive one in the Southwest, is again out in the open with its complicated implications.

Shortly after the Rio Grande Valley and the El Paso incidents, Mexican-American high school students at Uvalde — the Texas hometown of the late Vice President John N. Garner* — staged a "Chicano happening."

---

*John Nance Garner served as vice president of the United States between 1933 and 1936 under Franklin Delano Roosevelt.

Attending the year-end school dance, which is the semester's big affair, Mexican-American students showed up in Mexican ponchos, while
the rest of the students came dressed in conventional dark suits and long
dresses. The Mexican-Americans then segregated themselves from the
rest of the crowd and started making tacos with tortillas, chili and meat
which the girls had brought in containers.

It caused a stir, not only among Anglo students, parents and teachers,
but also among Mexican-American parents who couldn't understand
why their children were "disgracing" themselves after they (the parents)
had worked so hard to give them clothes like the ones the other students wore.

Puzzled by Youth

Mike Gonzales, an attorney and controversial Mexican-American leader
in Del Rio, said: "Anglos and older Mexican-Americans just don't seem
to know what is happening. Mexican-American kids are in the throes of
self-identification."

Use of the Spanish language, say other leaders, is one thing that
Mexican-Americans have over other students and they tend to exploit it.

The controversy centers on two arguments:

Mexican-American students should concentrate on English because
speaking Spanish too much hurts their proficiency in the "national language," English. Besides, said a school psychologist, children growing
up in a bicultural environment are more prone than others to neurosis
and mental disorders.

Mexicans are indigenous to the Southwest, and so the Spanish language is part of their culture which should not be tampered with. Having colonized the Southwest, Spanish-speaking people refuse to abandon their traditions because of the advent of Anglo-American culture.

The controversy is not one of whether Spanish, or any other foreign
language, should be taught in school. All educators agree that a person
is better off speaking two or more languages. But some school officials
object to Mexican-American students speaking Spanish in school and on
the playground not only on the basis of it being detrimental to their
English but because it irks other students who don't speak Spanish.

In south Texas, a teacher, commenting on the controversial issue,
wrote a pamphlet which reads in part:

"They are good people. Their only handicap is the bag full of superstitions and silly notions they inherited from Mexico. When they get rid

of these superstitions, they will be good Americans. Their schools help more than anything else."

Change Foreseen

"In time, the Latin will think and act like Americans. A lot depends on whether we can get them to switch from Spanish to English. When they speak English at home like the rest of us, they will be part of the American way of life. I just don't understand why they are so insistent about using Spanish. They should realize that it's not the American tongue."

This approach infuriates the growing number of militant Mexican-American leaders, many of whom now insist that meetings held to discuss the problems of this ethnic group should be conducted in Spanish.

Some education experts say that what is needed in the Southwest is for non-Mexican-Americans to become "Mexicanized" — not the other way around. Asked how the Mexican-American can find his way into U.S. society, Dr. Jack D. Forbes, research program director of UC Berkeley's Far West Laboratory for Educational Research and Development, recently told the U.S. Civil Rights Commission:

"The Anglo-American, quite obviously, is the new-comer." It is the Anglo-American, he said, who should learn more about the Mexican-American, his heritage and his culture. No one, he continued, can truly call himself a Southwesterner "unless he is a Mexicanized person to a considerable degree."

Not Enough

To the extremist Mexican-American leaders not even this is enough. What these leaders want for the 5 million Mexican-Americans in the five Southwestern states — California, Arizona, Colorado, New Mexico, Texas — is separatism not a "Mexicanized" society.

The controversial New Mexico Spanish-speaking leader, Reies Lopez Tijerina, who preaches to his followers that they should speak Spanish as often as possible, is a prime advocate of a separate — but equal — state for Mexican-Americans.*

Though few take the separatist movement seriously, educators in the Southwest worry about Mexican-Americans retreating into a "Mexican shell." Not only are many Mexican-American students affecting Mexican

---

*Beginning in 1963, Reies López Tijerina organized the Alianza Federal de Mercedes in New Mexico to renew claims to land grants stolen from Mexican Americans as a result of the conquest and annexation of New Mexico by the United States in 1848.

rural dress but many have posters in their bedrooms depicting such Mexican revolutionary heroes as Emiliano Zapata and slogans reading "Primero la Raza" (the Mexican race first).

"Attempts to prohibit the use of the Spanish language, no matter how lofty the reasons, will only make things worse," says an El Paso teacher.

Those who would try to abolish the use of Spanish in informal situations in school and on the playground are guilty of the "cowboy-and-Indian viewpoint," says Harold Howe II, former U.S. Commissioner of Education.

Mexican-Americans Threaten Action for Movie, TV Jobs

January 17, 1969

The militant Mexican-American Political Assn. Thursday threatened to instigate picketing, boycotts and legal action against the movie-television industry despite new efforts to establish a better relationship between the industry and the nation's 5 million Spanish-speaking people.

Abe Tapia, MAPA president, said the recent formation of the Latin American Performing Arts Foundation "does not change the fact that the industry's management is bigoted against Mexican-Americans."

The foundation was formed to seek an improved image of Latin Americans in motion pictures and television and to find employment for them. One founder was Al Ortega, a Mexican-American representative of Mayor Sam Yorty and a member of the Board of Public Works.

Ortega said the foundation will work in the "same pattern" the NAACP has used to promote jobs for Negroes in the movie and television industry and to improve the image of the Negro in the entertainment world.

A spokesman for the Assn. of Motion Picture and Television Producers said the industry's relations with the NAACP are "very good" and that, as a result, more Negroes are working in the industry than ever before.

The spokesman said the industry hopes it can work through the newly formed foundation to iron out employment problems between the industry and Mexican-Americans. He said meetings with MAPA representatives "have been disastrous" and punctuated with personal insults "which the industry does not have to take."

Celes King, president of the Los Angeles central branch of the NAACP, agreed that Negroes are getting good jobs in the industry but said his branch had to use tactics — such as MAPA now threatens — to get results.

Ray Martel, a television and movie actor who heads the MAPA committee dealing with the industry, said meetings with movie and television executives have failed because the "industry is run by Jews who themselves have been persecuted but still fail to understand the problems of the Mexican-Americans."

MAPA contends that Mexican-Americans are stereotyped by the industry "as serape and sombrero clad, stupid, shiftless, immoral bandidos."

In the meetings with the producers association and the writers guild, MAPA has demanded, among other things, that Mexican-Americans be depicted in all walks of life — lawyers, doctors, engineers, teachers, etc. — that they get "full and equitable employment across the board" and that the industry "immediately cease portraying Mexican people in a derogatory and abusive" manner.

MAPA charges that the movie and television industry is "violating Federal Communications Commission regulations in its unfair treatment of Mexican-Americans" and said their organization will prosecute if necessary.

A spokesman for the producers association released a report showing that 442 Mexican-Americans were employed in motion pictures, television film productions and television film pilots during the quarter period ending Oct. 30, 1968, as compared to 362 Negroes employed during the same period.

Employers' Group Warned Minorities Must Have Jobs

January 30, 1969

Mexican-American leaders and members of unemployment-ridden barrios have personally warned management representatives that to avoid "economic decay" they must provide good jobs for racial minorities instead of just finding means to sell them color television sets and new cars.

In a two-day Southern California Employers' Conference on Mexican-American Employment which ended Wednesday, industry and business representatives were taken to task by members of such militant Spanish-speaking organizations as the Brown Berets, the League of United Citizens to Help Addicts (LUCHA) and ALMA (Soul).

At conference workshops at Whittier College, confrontations between Mexican-Americans and employers led to heated discussions which ranged from alleged prejudice by management against how Mexican-Americans dress to charges that business and industry training programs are inadequate.

Tells of Frustration

Jose Avila of the East Los Angeles Labor Community Action Committee summed up what he described as the "frustration faced by Mexican-Americans trying to find employment."

Speaking to representatives of the oil industry, public utilities, large department stores and communications media, Avila said:

"You say you can't find qualified Mexican-Americans. How in hell can you find them if you won't appreciate the fact that Spanish-speaking people must struggle to get jobs, educate themselves and fight old prejudices all at the same time."

"Industry and business must readjust their thinking and training programs to suit these special problems just like they have designed their sales campaign to attract racial minorities."

Avila also hit the education Mexican-Americans receive in schools saying that "many Mexican-Americans are out in the streets who learned how to make ash trays in school craft shops but did not learn any skills which would help them get jobs."

Vincent T. Ximenes, chairman of the cabinet-level Inter-Agency Committee on Mexican-American Affairs, was the conference's luncheon speaker Wednesday.

He said that by 1990 there will be 18 million Spanish surnamed Americans in the United States and noted that "it remains for the government to lead the way to a better educated American populace."

He said that Mexican-Americans are now "dropping out of school at a rate double the national average and getting only about eight years of schooling compared to 12 years for the average Anglo-American youngster.

"We all know the reasons. . . . A Spanish-speaking child goes to school and finds a teacher who expects to teach him English. His confidence is further whittled away when he is left without part of his bicultural heritage to which he has a right. . . . He has a right to know that the early Mexican-Americans contributed much to governmental organization; he has a right to know that they were as brave and resourceful as the New England colonists."

Mexican-American Community Groups Plan 'Neglect' Protest

February 11, 1969

Representatives of Mexican-American community welfare groups plan to formally complain to the Board of Supervisors today about alleged neglect by the County Department of Public Services in dealing with East Los Angeles residents.

The move will follow charges by Mrs. Alice Escalante, head of the Los Angeles Welfare Rights Organization, that Ellis P. Murphy, director of the county's social services, walked out of a meeting Monday with East Los Angeles community leaders before they had an opportunity to air their grievances.

Steve Monroe, a spokesman for the county's social services, said Murphy left the meeting after a county social worker, who admitted he had been prohibited from attending the meeting, defied Murphy's "suggestion that he go back to work."

Mrs. Escalante heads an East Los Angeles group which has been at odds with Murphy since his department refused to allow her to speak at a social workers union meeting held in county social service facilities.

Union meetings were then banned at the county facilities and 43 social workers were suspended for breaking the ban.

Pickets later paraded in front of the East Los Angeles county office. The protesters belonged to the AFL-CIO Social Workers Local 535, the Brown Berets and Mrs. Escalante's Welfare Rights Organization.

Mrs. Escalante said her group will not only complain to the Board of Supervisors about "Murphy's lack of courtesy and concern" but will also present the board with a copy of 43 demands by East Los Angeles welfare recipients and social workers.

The demands include a public apology to the East Los Angeles community, transfer of Fred Gustafson, head of the social services office in East Los Angeles, and the naming of Mexican-Americans to posts of deputy directors in the East Los Angeles and Belvedere social services centers.

Latins Fail to Get Apology, Walk Out of County Hearing

February 12, 1969

Mexican-American militants walked out of a Board of Supervisors hearing Tuesday after they demanded and did not get a public apology to the

East Los Angeles community from Ellis P. Murphy, director of the county's social services.

Tension rose at the verbally explosive meeting when members of the Brown Berets quietly walked to the side of Mrs. Alicia Escalante, head of a welfare group demanding the apology, as she was being ordered by a deputy sheriff to leave the speaking stand and sit down.

Mrs. Escalante, chairman of the Los Angeles Welfare Rights Organization, at first refused to budge but then decided to walk away, followed by four Brown Berets, thus avoiding a possible confrontation.

Under Attack Earlier

Earlier, Murphy had been under attack by East Los Angeles organization spokesmen for allegedly walking out of a meeting with them Monday as they tried to discuss their problems with the official.

Murphy contends that he left the meeting because he had ordered a county social worker to leave the meeting but that the worker, technically an employee of Murphy, refused to do so.

Board of Supervisors' chairman Ernest Debs backed Murphy, saying the social worker was "insubordinate," but ordered Murphy to again meet with a small group headed by Mrs. Escalante. Debs said no county social worker could attend this meeting.

After Mrs. Escalante led an exodus of about 50 representatives of various East Los Angeles organizations, she told the *Times* that her group would not meet with Murphy unless Supervisor Debs, whose district includes East Los Angeles, is present.

Debs ordered his field representative, Arnold Martinez, to arrange a meeting between Mrs. Escalante's group and Murphy but it was not clear whether Debs would attend.

Mrs. Escalante claimed at the board meeting that Murphy has "insulted Los Angeles publicly three times." She said Murphy showed his "lack of concern for East Los Angeles" when his department refused to allow her to speak to social workers in a county facility when he walked out of the Monday meeting.

Murphy, who was present at the Board of Supervisors meeting, told the group he would meet with them any time. He was booed and called names from the audience.

Supervisors Debs, Warren Dorn and Kenneth Hahn publicly praised Murphy and condemned the hecklers as rude and undemocratic.

Appearing with Murphy was Armando Torrez, a Mexican-American

Public Social Services advisory commissioner, who defended Murphy's action Monday. The militants shouted "Tio Taco" (Mexican Uncle Tom) and "vendido" (sellout).

Ex-Dope User Tries to Help Mexican-American Addicts

February 18, 1969

Joe Ortiz hopes that it's true that "you can't go home again."

An ex-drug addict fighting desperately to resist the temptations of easily available heroin, Ortiz often visits a fetid slum area known as Hicks Camp where he started using drugs 18 years ago.

He goes to Hicks Camp as a volunteer worker for the League of United Citizens to Help Addicts (LUCHA). Ortiz knows that the difference between attempting to help "junkies" and falling back into the drug world is sometimes a sliver of self-control.

On this particular morning, as Ortiz entered Hicks Camp, he spotted an old "carnal" (soul brother) with whom he had in the past shared the bliss and misery which all addicts experience.

Ortiz' friend looked as if he would collapse into a nervous breakdown any moment. Ortiz recognized the state: dope withdrawal symptoms.

"I'm with LUCHA now," Ortiz told his friend. "If you want to 'dry out' we'll help you."

"Maybe if things get really bad I'll call you," said the suffering man. Another man approached and Ortiz' friend started to leave with him.

Ortiz quickly jotted down LUCHA's telephone number and handed it to his friend. He took it with trembling hands and then walked down a bush ravine with his other friend.

"They're going down there to shoot heroin," Ortiz said. "Maybe someday he'll call me."

Called Spiritual Vacuum

A 20-acre island of misery, unpaved streets and crumbling shacks, Hicks Camp is surrounded by a neat El Monte residential area, the El Monte Airport and an industrial district.

In its isolation in the midst of plenty, Hicks Camp is symbolic of the spiritual and material vacuum surrounding many Mexican-Americans who live in barrio pockets throughout Southern California.

Hicks Camp is a depressing refuge for Mexican-American families who can't or won't cope with the outside "Anglo world." County officials say that health and housing regulations are difficult to enforce in the privately owned camp unless formal complaints are made by "interested persons."

According to Ortiz, Hicks Camp people are "too uneducated, too scared or too apathetic to make complaints."

"When you're trapped by circumstances as these people are, you get to accept it and try to forget it by leaving reality," says Ortiz, who in his 33 years has spent 11 years and 7 months in prisons.

While living in Hicks Camp, Ortiz found school was a "drag" because the teachers tried to "teach me as if I was just another gabacho (Anglo) kid."

He says he also noted early that even those who "sweated out school" never got good jobs.

(According to the National Advisory Committee on Mexican-American Education, a recent study in California showed that in some schools more than 50% of Mexican-American high school students drop out between grades 10 and 11 and that Mexican-Americans account for more than 40% of the so-called "mentally handicapped" in California . . .)

("These facts give tragic evidence of our failure to provide genuine educational opportunity to Mexican-American youth," says the committee, which was created to advise the U.S. commissioner of education, "and today there are nearly 2 million of these children between the ages of 13 and 18.")

As a kid, Ortiz' hero was his brother who hung around the "Pachucos," Mexican-American rebels who battled with U.S. sailors in the early 1940's East Los Angeles racial riots.

By the time Ortiz was 13 he was using marijuana and at 14 he took his first shot of heroin at Hicks Camp. Says Ortiz:

"I was sure my brother was using heroin so I thought it would be all right if I used it, since I wanted to be just like him and I wanted my brother to accept me."

When Ortiz' brother was sent to San Quentin, Ortiz felt a pang of envy. "There it was—my brother being sent to San Quentin and the thing that came to my mind was that some day I would be with him there," says Ortiz. "That became my goal."

After a series of arrests and convictions for robberies and narcotics addiction, Ortiz, at the age of 20, was picked up for possession of heroin.

He was sent to San Quentin where he shared a cell with his brother for two years. After Quentin, Ortiz decided his goal needed a drastic change.

Back to Camp

That change had led back to Hicks Camp, where by now a cluster of "batos locos" (crazy guys) had gathered at the "plaza," a cement slab once part of a shack which burned down years ago.

They milled about aimlessly, talking in low voices. A middle-age wino, whom police say is handed the junkies' hypodermic needles when Hicks is raided, sat by a tree.

From time to time a "bato loco," the young elite of Hicks Camp, headed down the ravine to shoot heroin while another kept watch by the railroad tracks. It was only 11 o'clock in the morning.

"At nights, nobody ever bothers to hide," Ortiz said.

Ortiz gave some of his old buddies LUCHA's telephone number and tried to explain to them that his organization works much like Alcoholics Anonymous — that if they call the number they'll be helped by people who understand ex-dope addicts.

Self-Help Plan

"LUCHA does not accept funds from city, county or federal government agencies," says Ortiz. "That money always has strings attached to it. We try to help ourselves by working at odd jobs and any private contributions that might come our way."

Hicks Camp was originally part of the domain of a giant ranch in the pioneer days of Southern California. In 1917 it was sold to a family by the name of Hicks and since then has changed hands several times. At first a shantytown for agricultural workers, Hicks Camp has been shrunk through the years by growing El Monte and industrial zoning. It undoubtedly will disappear completely in the next few years.

Nevertheless, it is still a microcosm of much of the Mexican-American condition in the Southwest, according to mounting studies.

The serious narcotics problem among Mexican-Americans, say experts, is to a large extent symptomatic of this ethnic group's social and cultural isolation.

Many Mexican-Americans, say these experts, feel neither Mexican nor American. They feel especially "out of it" in a society where to be white English-speaking is of the utmost importance, adds Ortiz.

Before leaving Hicks Camp, Ortiz knocked on a few doors to renew old acquaintances. At one shack, an old, toothless man appeared at the door and Ortiz asked for an old friend, "Chuy."

'Nothing can be done'

"Oh, he's been in jail for the past two years," said the man, who turned out to be Chuy's father. The man had lived in Hicks Camp for 25 years when he paid $3 a month rent. Now he pays $45.

"Nothing can be done here," he said in answer to a question as to whether conditions could be improved in Hicks Camp. "It's too late."

At another shack, a "three-bedroom home," a young mother of seven invited Ortiz in. She spoke in a combination of English and Spanish, common with many Chicanos.

Her problems tumbled out as if discussing personal misfortunes were as easy to her as gossip is to other women. Her brother, a narcotics violator, had just been arrested and her husband was out of a job.

("The lowest income per capita, the lowest sub-standard housing, the lowest educational achievement, the highest high school dropout rate, the highest narcotics rate for youths, the lowest level of job classification and the least amount of government or private resource assistance is in the Mexican-American community and not . . . in Watts . . ." So said Richard S. Amador, executive director of Community and Human Resources Agency, to a recent Southern California Employers Conference on Mexican-American Employment.)

Family Grows

"My husband is too proud to go on welfare," the woman continued, "but I'm not so worried about that as about my brother. Why can't the police leave him alone?"

Ortiz then went to visit his mother, who lives in a neat, well-furnished home just outside Hicks Camp. After telling her not to worry about him, that he's staying "clean," Ortiz got in the car, relieved at leaving Hicks Camp.

Chicanos Hold 5-State Event in Colorado

March 30, 1969

DENVER — Chicano youths from the five Southwestern states — where Mexican-Americans are asserting themselves politically — are meeting here in an attempt to focus their potential power.

They hitchhiked, drove and flew from California, Arizona, New Mexico, Texas and other parts of Colorado to discuss what is "bugging" them: society's alleged neglect.

About 1,000 of these youths, bilingual, angry and energetic, have congregated in the former Calvary Baptist Church, now the headquarters of the Mexican-American Crusade for Justice organization, to articulate their frustrations.

Long-Haired Boys

The boys wear brown berets, Zapata moustaches and long hair. The girls sport miniskirts and Mexican serapes. To "belong" in this group one must speak Spanish. The few black and Anglo youths present stay in the background.

The guru of this Chicano youth conference is Rodolfo (Corky) Gonzales, a former prizefighter, who has just won an important victory from the Denver superintendent of schools.

Last week, students at West High School, whose enrollment is about half Mexican-American, walked out in protest against what Chicanos felt were anti-Mexican-American school policies.

Victory Claimed

The three-day walkout, which produced nasty police-student confrontations, ended after Gonzales announced that the superintendent had acceded to most of the Chicano demands.

A teacher accused of racism was transferred, walkout leaders were exonerated and Mexican-American studies were expanded.

Ethnic nationalism, the unofficial theme of the conference, was dramatized Friday when Chicano youths lowered an American flag in front of the State Legislature and hoisted a Mexican flag.

Of the 1,000 Chicano youths attending the conference, more than 100 are from the Los Angeles area, representing such organizations as the United Mexican-American Students (UMAS), the Brown Berets and Alma (Soul).

Papers to Guide

The meeting, which ends Monday, will produce "position papers" which will try to guide the Chicano youth movement.

The interim steering committee of the revolutionary caucus has already released a statement which claims Mexican-Americans "for 144 years have been trying to peacefully coexist yet no peace has come to our communities."

"Revolution is the only means available to us," continues the statement. "We owe no allegiance, no respect, to any of the laws of this racist country. Our liberation struggle is a war of survival."*

Chicano Conferees Plan 5-State School Walkout

April 1, 1969

DENVER — About 1,500 youths attending the Chicano Youth Liberation Conference Monday committed themselves to work for a massive school walkout in the five southwestern states on Sept. 16, Mexican Independence Day.

Chicano nationalism was preached throughout the five-day conference which Monday projected the walkouts as a first step toward "liberating" Mexican-American youths from "Anglo concepts."

At the final session of the revolutionary-rhetoric-filled conference the plan of Aztlan was read to the cheering youths from California, Arizona, Texas, New Mexico and Colorado.

Aztlan is the Indian word for northern Mexico. The plan says that Chicano youths do not recognize the "Anglo conquest of the Southwest" and that as indigenous people of that area they are loyal only to Chicanoism.

Victory for Leader

It was a victory for Rodolfo (Corky) Gonzales, leader of the Denver-based Crusade for Justice, a civil rights organization, who contends that ethnic nationalism must be the ideology of the Chicano movement.

The conference was in danger of breaking up at times over such issues as whether Chicano youths should form coalitions with the Negro youth groups and whether the movement should start "internationalizing" itself by making contacts with the rebel youths of other countries.

Gonzales was able to sell the conference the idea that such issues can wait until the Chicano youth movement is powerful enough to "deal from a strong base and not one which we have to ask for favors."

Though Gonzales did not say it, it was obvious to the observer of the

---

*The National Chicano Youth Conference is best known for its proclamation of the Plan de Aztlán, a Chicano "declaration of independence" that articulated the theme of ethnic and cultural nationalism as the guiding ideology of the Chicano movement.

present Mexican-American movement that when he talks of "liberation" he is in effect calling for independence from Mexican-American leaders who get their financial support from the government and who have ties with the "establishment."

Ex-Prize Fighter

Gonzales, 40, a former prize fighter, left the war-on-poverty program which he headed in the Denver Mexican-American community and resigned from the Democratic Party after running unsuccessfully for public office.

Since then he has been calling not only for nationalism but also self-reliance to the Mexican-American community.

"The Chicano must do his thing by himself and for himself," says Gonzales, who feuded with the black leadership during the Poor Peoples' March on Washington.

Rebel youths at conference workshops spoke glowingly of Ernesto (Che) Guevara, Fidel Castro, Pancho Villa and Emiliano Zapata. But when it came to identifying their leaders in the Southwest, only Corky Gonzales and Reies Lopez Tijerina, the New Mexican land-grants crusader, were mentioned.

Pomona Student

Says Jorge Licon, 19, a Pomona College student:

"The young people are turned on by 'Corky,' not only because he talks of revolution but because he is beholden to no one. We young people are sick of the old established so-called Mexican-American leaders who talk but don't act, Corky acts."

Licon was referring to Gonzales' leadership in a recent walkout by West High School, located in the Mexican-American community. According to Gonzales the Chicano students won most of the demands made by the walkout leaders, including the transferring of a teacher accused of racism, the serving of Mexican-American food in the school cafeteria and the expansion of a Mexican-American studies program.

Should Gonzales have some success in leading a Southwest school walkout on Sept. 16, he will become the most important leader among the Chicano youth movement.

So far, most of the Mexican-American civil rights activities have been funnelled through war-on-poverty programs and through such organizations as the Ford Foundation.

Many of the youths who returned home Monday will be preaching Chicano nationalism, liberation and "Corky" Gonzales to their fellow students.

Chancellor Says He Agrees with Thrust but Not Specifics

April 5, 1969

UCLA Chancellor Charles E. Young agreed Friday with the "thrust" but not the specifics of seven demands made by the United Mexican-American Students [UMAS], among them the enlargement of the campus Chicano enrollment to at least 12% of the student body.

UMAS said this does not satisfy the organization and set Monday as a deadline for Young to answer the demands specifically.

The university says there are about 700 Mexican-Americans in an enrollment of 35,000 but UMAS claims the "true figure is less than 300."

Not from the U.S.

More than half of the students the university calls Mexican-Americans, according to UMAS, are actually Latin Americans from outside the country and not Southwest Chicanos.

Young told newsmen that "my intent is not to answer the proposal point by point, but to take the thrust of what their proposals say and respond favorably to the thrust, rather than the specifics."

In referring to the deadline, UMAS, which calls the demands "non-negotiable," said it has the backing of the Mexican-American community.

"We have contacted the relevant organizations in the Mexican-American community and they are behind us," a UMAS spokesman said.

There are about 100 UMAS members at UCLA.

The demands were originally made on March 12 with the following introduction:

Special Entry Program

"It is a primary goal of UCLA United Mexican-American Students that within five years the proportion of Mexican-American student population at UCLA minimally match the proportion of Mexican-American population of the local area predominantly served by UCLA, that this proportion be maintained thereafter, and that the education offered the Mexican-American at UCLA be relevant — in terms of what is taught, who teaches, what degrees and certificates are offered, what research and special programs are fostered and by whom — to the problems, other concerns and interests of the Mexican-American community."

The demands include the appointment of four Mexican-Americans to positions paralleling existing posts and the establishment this fall of a permanent special entry program for Mexican-Americans modeled on the experimental High Potential program.

One proposal, setting up a Mexican-American Urban Center, was satisfied Wednesday with the official opening of the center in East Los Angeles, Young said.

UMAS also wanted the appointment of a Chicano "as assistant to the dean of graduate admissions to help assure the greater recruitment and financial aiding of the Chicano into the graduate division" and the "assigning of a central campus building to house the special entry program . . ."

While noting the significance of the proposals, Young said "some of the requests are not capable of a positive response by anyone because the response would be illegal — to the extent they're asking for, separate programs, if that's what's really meant."

UMAS responded that the organization "along with the rest of the Mexican-American community, of which we students are only a part, insist that our goal is just and that the specifics of our presentation are feasible."

UMAS to Be Reinstated at Roosevelt High

April 23, 1969

Roosevelt High School has agreed to reinstate the United Mexican-American Students (UMAS) provided a teacher who has publicly denounced the organization is named its faculty co-sponsor.

UMAS President Mario Esparza said Tuesday the school's suggestion was "an insult" because "an enemy of UMAS is being named as faculty sponsor so she can control our organization and destroy it."

UMAS was suspended for one month by Principal Thomas Dyer, who said the organization has violated its own constitution by working in conjunction with other UMAS chapters, by sponsoring a sit-in when it said it would favor a speak-in instead, and by failing to keep "outsiders" off campus.

Faculty sponsors Antonio Ortiz, Miss Alice Sandoval and Fred Sanchez contend that the alleged violations were made by individuals and not UMAS as an organization and that the suspension was unfair.

This was the first time an activist student organization has been suspended in the Los Angeles school district.

Under a proposal made by Roosevelt's administration staff, UMAS was reinstated as of Monday under certain conditions, among them being that Mrs. Carmen Terrazas be appointed co-sponsor along with Ortiz.

Miss Sandoval and Sanchez would be dropped as faculty sponsors. Ortiz said he has told Dyer he will resign as sponsor.

Mrs. Terrazas, a teacher and chairman of the school's scholarship committee, recently wrote *The Times* a letter highly critical of UMAS. Published last Saturday, the letter implied that UMAS "perpetuates racism."

Unpublished Portion

In a portion of the letter not published, Mrs. Terrazas said, "A sampling of teachers indicates that the majority of teachers at Roosevelt feel strongly that UMAS disrupts the educational process at the school . . ."

Asked by *The Times* why she agreed to be co-sponsor of UMAS considering her feelings about the organization, Mrs. Terrazas said she did not care to comment now.

UMAS President Esparza told *The Times* that he and "most of the members of UMAS" would have agreed to have Mrs. Terrazas as co-sponsor but that her letter to *The Times* "ended all that."

Union Marchers to Hold Rally, Woo Mexican Farm Workers

May 13, 1969

MEXICALI — Juan Gomez, 24, a farm worker, gets up at 1 a.m. in Mexico to work in the Coachella Valley across the border.

He takes the bus to the international line and crosses the border after showing his immigration green card.

His green card says that Gomez is a legal alien resident of the United States — an immigrant.

But because he prefers to live in Mexico, one of the reasons being that it is cheaper there, Gomez commutes to the fields of Imperial and Coachella valleys.

On the American side of the border he and many like him are picked up by labor contractors' trucks who charge them $2 a piece for the ride to the farms.

Gomez is usually up five hours before he even begins to work. But he is not unhappy. Gomez, father of four children, is making $1.69 an hour, much more than he could ever make working in the fields of Mexicali Valley.

A group of farm workers, belonging to Cesar Chavez' grape striking farm workers union, is marching to the border to tell Gomez and his fellow commuters that they should join the union.

On the Mexican side, some officials of the Confederation of Mexican Workers (CTM) are helping to plan the event.

On Monday the marchers, who started from Indio Saturday in weather of up to 106 degrees, were camped at Salt Creek by the Salton Sea. They hope to reach Calexico by next Sunday where they plan an "international solidarity of farm workers rally" at the border.

Chavez' people, many of whom are green-card holders themselves but live on the American side, plan to tell the commuters that if they join the union they can force the growers to pay for their transportation to work and that their pay and benefits will improve as union members.

The grape harvest at Coachella Valley is due to begin at the end of this month and union officials claim the workers are ready for a strike.

But they also know that, as in 1968, the growers were able to replace striking workers with commuters from Mexico.

A survey made by the U.S. Immigration Department indicates that there are fewer than 50,000 commuters who work on the American side and live on the Mexican side along the 1,800-mile U.S.–Mexico border.

The AFL-CIO, however, claims the figure is closer to 150,000.

According to a report prepared by the U.S. Commission on Civil Rights, there is also, but to a smaller extent, commuter traffic across the American-Canadian border.

However, the report says, "Canadian commuters do not depress local economic conditions, as do Mexican commuters, because they live in a substantially identical cost-of-living economy, work in highly unionized occupations and are highly unionized themselves.

"Being well assimilated into the labor force, they offer no undue competition to American labor."

Encouraged by the demise of the bracero program, which brought hundreds of thousands of Mexican national farm workers to American farms under a U.S.–Mexico agreement, unions have been trying to find ways to end the commuter system.

The marchers, whose number varies from 100 to 500 depending on how hot the weather is, are in effect conceding that the commuter system is probably here to stay and that the only way the commuters can stop them being "strike breakers" is to unionize them.

The march is due to reach the more populated areas in Brawley, El Centro and Calexico this weekend and so increase in number, according to its planners.

Jim Drake, an official of Chavez' union, said the feeling among union members now is not to fight the commuter system as such but to sympathize with the commuter's problem and help them by inviting them to join the union.

Brown Berets Hail 'La Raza' and Scorn the Establishment

June 16, 1969

David Sanchez, prime minister of the Brown Berets, was at the East Los Angeles Free Clinic when he learned two of his top aides, along with eight other people, had been indicted for involvement in disturbances and fires set in the Biltmore April 24.

The fires in several floors of the hotel were started just before Gov. Reagan was to address a Mexican-American educator's conference. The disturbances occurred during the governor's speech.

Authorities say a rookie policeman who had infiltrated the militant Chicano organization tipped off police and firemen in advance, which probably prevented a catastrophe.

"It looks bad all right," Sanchez said about the indictments, "but La Raza (the race) will understand. La Raza knows it's just another maneuver by The Man to destroy us."

Sanchez, voicing the unanimous sentiment of Brown Beret leadership, says he doesn't care what "the white establishment or press" thinks of the organization.

But, he adds, if it is true that his ministers of information and discipline were involved in arson "they did it as individuals and not as Brown Berets."

The East Los Angeles Free Clinic at 5106 E. Whittier Blvd. was opened by the Brown Berets May 31 with financial help from the Ford Foundation.

Sanchez says the sparsely furnished facility was modeled after the Fairfax Free Clinic in Hollywood and is offering free medical, social and psychological services to Mexican-Americans with volunteer help of professionals.

Indicted himself for his part in the East Los Angeles High School walkouts last year, Sanchez, 20, looks like a clean-cut Mexican-American boy.

But he's much more complicated than that. He heads a tightly knit, quasi-military organization of about 60 disciplined youths which the police consider dangerous.

Besides Los Angeles, the Brown Berets claim to have chapters in 27 other cities including Fresno, San Francisco, Sacramento, Berkeley, Oxnard, Denver, Albuquerque and San Antonio. The members range in age from 14 to 35.

At a recent Chicano youth liberation conference in Denver, at which many Brown Berets participated mostly as security guards, about 1,500 Chicano youths from the five Southwestern states adopted a statement of beliefs which condemned the "brutal gringo invasion of our territories."

Brown Berets look up to the leadership of Reies Lopez Tijerina, the New Mexico land grants crusader, and Rodolfo (Corky) Gonzales, leader of the Denver-based civil rights organization, the Crusade for Justice. Both men preach ethnic nationalism and separatism.

Admirers of Cesar Chavez

"We especially admire Cesar Chavez (the farm labor leader) for his advocacy of nonviolence," Sanchez says.

The Brown Beret manual, however, indicates the organization does not entirely condemn violence as does Chavez.

The manual says: "If those Anglos in power are willing to (give Chicanos their rights) in a peaceful and orderly process, then we will be only too happy to accept this way. Otherwise, we will be forced to other alternatives."

The manual also points out that there are three ways to apply pressure: by direct communication with persons or agencies "you wish to change," by "demonstrations or pickets" or "by any and all means necessary."

As if remembering the rule in the Brown Beret manual which says, "The problem is not a problem, it is a situation that must be dealt with," Sanchez perked up.

Legal Defense Needed

"Our job now is to get adequate legal defense," Sanchez said. The phone rang often and Sanchez would usually answer. "Raise the money for bail," Sanchez said into the phone several times.

In the clinic's outer office were Rona Fields, an instructor of educational psychology and sociology at San Fernando Valley State College, and her husband, Charles Fox, a political science teacher at Cal State Los Angeles.

Without commenting on the indictments, Miss Fields, who goes by her maiden name for professional reasons, agreed with Sanchez that the authorities are out to destroy the Brown Berets.

"In the context of East Los Angeles, the Brown Berets can be compared to the Israeli youth underground," Miss Fields said.

Miss Fields Tells Views

A wiry Jewish woman with intense light eyes, Miss Fields, who hopes to write her Ph.D. dissertation on the Brown Berets, has written:

"As an organization the Brown Berets are continually confronted with the established institutions in a social matrix which rigidifies structures and becomes irrelevant through antiquation before new institutions can be enacted.

"The consequent frustration would apparently provide only two alternatives for the Chicano youth — acquiescence to the established order, which would include acceptance of assimilation, or violence, either revolutionary style or delinquency.

"The Brown Berets are trying to develop a third alternative. This third alternative is embodied in the East Los Angeles Free Clinic. This alternative is to create new institutions which are devised to be flexible, to be continually responsive to the community and which grow out of and for the needs of the community as the community sees them."

There is no doubt that the Brown Berets have rejected the first alternative Miss Fields talks about — assimilation. "There are very few Gabachos (Anglos) who don't turn me off," says Sanchez. "To the Anglo, justice means just us."

In the Brown Beret manual, written by Sanchez, when he was in jail for disturbing the peace, appears a statement which must be memorized by every Brown Beret.

"For over 120 years the Mexican-American has suffered at the hands of the Anglo establishment. He is discriminated against in schooling, housing, employment and in every other phase of life. Because of this situation, the Mexican-American has become the lowest achiever of any minority group in the entire Southwest."

It's when you discuss the second alternative that the Brown Berets are vague.

"We're not a violent or a nonviolent organization," says Sanchez, "we are an emergency organization."

What does that mean?

"Well, if we see a cop beating up a Chicano we move in and stop the cop," Sanchez says. "We try to be ready for every emergency."

But the testimony to the county grand jury by the undercover policeman Fernando Sumaya would indicate the Chicano militant organization is definitely violence-oriented.

Sumaya's Account

Sumaya, 23, told the grand jury that the day of the Biltmore fires, he attended a meeting at East Los Angeles College with the Brown Berets and friends where guerrilla warfare tactics and civil disobedience were discussed.

According to Sumaya, Carlos Montez, 21, the Brown Berets' minister of information, interrupted the meeting, saying the group shouldn't just sit around talking about guerrilla warfare tactics but should put them into practice.

Sumaya said Montez urged the group to begin that night at the Biltmore, when Gov. Reagan was to speak.

Indicted with Montez and eight non-Brown Berets was Ralph Ramirez, 19, the Berets' minister of discipline.

Original Leaders

Sanchez, Montez and Ramirez are the original leadership of an organization which began in 1967 as Young Citizens for Community Action. As it became militant, the organization's name evolved into the Young Chicanos for Community Action and then the Brown Berets.

Sanchez, who was president of Mayor Sam Yorty's Advisory Commission on Youth in 1967, still lives with his parents in a neat, well-furnished home (including a color TV set) in East Los Angeles.

On the wall of the living room is one of those silk souvenir banners service men buy for their mothers or sweethearts. This one was sent to Sanchez' mother by her other son, Michael, 23, who recently returned from fighting in Vietnam.

Well-Kept Home

The well-kept lower middle-class home is in sharp contrast to the Brown Beret headquarters at 4715 E. Olympic Blvd. where Sanchez spends much of his time after attending classes at Cal State Los Angeles.

The headquarters windows are boarded up and revolutionary posters pasted on them. Inside, the walls are covered with murals depicting Mexican-Indian civilizations.

On one wall is the startling legend in large black letters "Por mi raza mato." (For my race, I kill.) The organization was recently given an eviction notice by the landlord. The previous Brown Beret headquarters on Soto St. was bombed last Christmas Eve.

Montez Background

Montez, who tends to be the organization's visionary, used to work as an assistant Teen Post director, lives near Sanchez' home and is a native of Mexico. A lean, intense young man who often sports a Zapata moustache, Montez is noted for his articulateness on the Chicano movement and his wit.

Ramirez, a beefy and laconic young tough, often travels to New Mexico from where his family came and likes to identify with the Indian as well as the Chicano.

"We try to bring about changes to help our people by working through conventional channels, including war on poverty programs," says Sanchez. "But we soon found out the insensitivity and corruption of establishment bureaucracy and left in disgust."

Open Coffee Shop

Changing their organization's name to Young Chicano Youths for Community Action, Sanchez, Montez and Ramirez opened up a coffee house, La Piranya, in late 1967 with the help of an interfaith church organization.

By now the Young Chicano Youths for Community Action had taken on an ethnic nationalism image and were openly feuding with the Sheriffs Department and the police.

The coffee house served as an office and meeting hall. Reies Tijerina, Cesar Chavez and black militants H. Rap Brown, Stokely Carmichael and Ron Karenga met there with the group which by now had adopted its present name, the Brown Berets.

Plagued by inadequate licensing, curfew violations, insufficient funds and "police harassment," La Piranya closed on March 3, 1968, three days before the East Los Angeles High School walkouts.

At the time of the walkouts, Sanchez denied that the Brown Berets were, as the police charged, among the "outside agitators" who helped cause the student disturbances.

"The Chicano students were the main action group," Sanchez says. "The Brown Berets were at the walkouts to protect our younger people. When they (law officers) started hitting with sticks, we went in, did our business, and got out."

The "business" Sanchez explains, means that "we put ourselves between the police and the kids, and took the beating."

Shock Troops

Sanchez says the Brown Berets, which could be called the shock troops of the Chicano movement, think and feel so alike that "we need few words to communicate with each other."

Most of the members were once "batos locos," literally barrio gang toughs, successors to the zootsuiters of the 1940s.

"The Brown Berets recruit from the rebels without a cause and make them rebels with a cause," says Sanchez.

The Brown Beret Manual stresses personal cleanliness, strict discipline, prohibition of drugs and excessive drinking and strict attendance at "all meetings, all demonstrations and drills."

"I wear the Brown Beret," says the organization's pledge, "because it signifies my dignity and pride in the color of my skin and race."

Because of the presumed close-knit makeup of the Brown Berets, it came as quite a shock to them that they had been infiltrated by the police.

On May 10, before the Biltmore fires, Sumaya, the police infiltrator, and three others who Sanchez says were trying to become Brown Berets but were not, were arrested following a fire at an East Los Angeles Safeway store.

Sumaya said he tipped off the police but allowed himself to be arrested for security reasons. The other three have been indicted by the grand jury.

As for Sumaya, Sanchez says "his mind has been messed with — the poor guy is trying to be a white Anglo."

"I was in jail when he joined the Brown Berets last December," Sanchez said. "It is a clear case of entrapment. It is obvious that he designed and manufactured the events that led to the indictments."

"The day after the fires he told me how it was he who removed the battery from the Biltmore elevator to stop it. He said he was afraid the hotel manager might have seen him but he really bragged about his part."

Sanchez said he started suspecting Sumaya early "because he would never be with me by himself. He always had someone with him."

The Brown Beret leader said he then had someone call Sumaya's old school in Calexico. Posing as a potential employer, the Brown Beret asked where Sumaya's school transcripts had been sent.

The school said they had been mailed to an Alhambra adult school. Using the same ruse, the Brown Berets learned Sumaya's transcripts were then sent to the Los Angeles Police Department.

One day, a Brown Beret called Sumaya's home and asked whether S-257, Sumaya's code name, was there, according to Sanchez. Told that he was, the Beret instructed the officer to report to Hollenbeck Police Station. When Sumaya reported there, the Brown Berets were sure they had been infiltrated.

Other Infiltration

At a recent news conference at the Greater Los Angeles Press Club, Sanchez claimed two other law-enforcement officers infiltrated the Brown Berets. The Mexican-American Legal Defense Fund, financed by the Ford Foundation, says it is interested in looking into the Brown Berets' charge of entrapment.

Asked whether the Brown Berets would retaliate against Sumaya if they could, Sanchez said: "No, he's got a wife and a family and he was doing what he thought was his job. Besides, we don't do things which will be used by the press merely for the entertainment of the white middle class."

On the issue of anti-Anglo sentiment, the Brown Beret leadership is unequivocal. They say they don't care what the "white establishment or press" thinks of the organization. "Our only concern is Chicanos," said Sanchez.

Dangerous Aspect

This extreme ethnic nationalism, say some concerned observers, is what could be the most dangerous aspect of the Brown Berets. Admired by activists and high school students, the Brown Berets are working hard to polarize "Chicano youth."

In a study by social scientists Fields and Fox it is pointed out that "the militancy of the Brown Berets is not much different from that of the Students for Democratic Society (SDS), Students Nonviolent Coordinating Committee (SNCC) and the earlier Israeli Youth in Palmach."

"As for the group (Brown Berets) as it is currently constituted, its main concern is to achieve an interfactional unity which would, through presenting a united front, give Chicanos a modicum of political power at least comparable to the current Negro condition . . . ," the study said.

UC Mexican-American Adviser Quits in Anger

July 31, 1969

The University of California's top adviser on Mexican-Americans has resigned, calling the university program for Chicano students "totally inadequate," *The Times* learned Wednesday.

Paul Sanchez, special adviser on Mexican-American affairs to UC President Charles Hitch, quit after serving six months. In a letter to Hitch, Sanchez charged that he found "pervasive elements of racism exist with most people I met (in the university system) from chancellors on down."

He said his "evaluation" after six months is that the university's efforts in Mexican-American student recruitment, employment, curriculum development, studies and research "are so negligible as to stand as an indictment of the institution's meager commitment to the largest minority population in the state."

Sanchez said his letter, dated June 30, has not been answered by Hitch. He said he has accepted the directorship of San Jose State College's graduate department of social work.

Plans Meeting

In a telephone interview from Berkeley, Hitch told *The Times* he declined comment on Sanchez' letter but said he was "very concerned and very disappointed that there are so few Chicanos at the university in all levels."

"I don't know why this is so," Hitch said, "but I am determined to do something about it. I will soon meet with a group of concerned Chicano faculty members and administrators to discuss the problem."

Asked whether there was any question about Sanchez' competency prior to his resignation, Hitch said no. He would not comment on why he has not answered Sanchez' letter, saying only that he plans to meet with "concerned Chicano faculty members and administrators."

Sanchez, who holds a master of arts degree in social science from the University of Colorado, was a member of the Santa Clara County Social Planning Council before joining the UC staff.

In his letter, Sanchez said that with rare exceptions he found "the university staff completely lacks a sensitivity and commitment to Chicano needs."

"The (Mexican-American) exclusion processes have been solidly institutionalized, and administrators are clearly ignorant of the nature of these processes," Sanchez continued.

"The pervasive elements of racism exist with most people I met from chancellors on down . . ."

Sanchez charged that this alleged racism "is not only tolerated but abetted by responsible people." The University, he asserted, "is not marshalling its resources or rearranging its priorities to deal with the needs of Chicanos in any kind of equitable or realistic manner, which is clear evidence to me of the failure to face up to these university-wide problems."

Sanchez said that of the 600 persons employed at University Hall, the administration headquarters of the 100,000-student university system, there were only "two Chicanos on significant positions" (himself and another one) and "about half a dozen secretaries."

"This is typical of the situation which does not even approach the reprehensible level of a token effort," Sanchez said.

University officials said there is no way of accurately telling how many Mexican-American students are enrolled at the university campuses, but Hitch said that "whatever the number there are too few."

Local Control Held Key to Chicanos' Struggle

September 9, 1969

Stanford's new assistant dean of students for Mexican-American relations thinks community control of schools, the police force and hospitals is essential if California Chicanos are to catch up with Negroes in the struggle for equality of opportunity.

Felix Gutierrez, 26, former public information officer for the Los Angeles Economic and Youth Opportunities Agency, became Stanford's first Mexican-American assistant dean of students Sept. 1.

In a telephone interview, Gutierrez said that "when a situation demands militancy, Chicano and black students can well join forces to achieve mutual goals."

"But in the long run," Gutierrez said, "Chicanos must work apart from the blacks because of national and language differences and also work apart from the white community because of the apparently unbridgeable gulf of prejudice and hostility of the Anglo population."

Community control, especially in places like East Los Angeles, Gutierrez said, is especially important because "outsiders who don't know or care about the community's needs" control the schools, the economy, the police force and the hospitals.

"Chicanos should be able to control their present and future as does the establishment," Gutierrez asserted.

Stanford has increased its enrollment of Chicano students from last year's 57 to about 200, Gutierrez said.

Gutierrez, who was student body president of Cal State Los Angeles and that college's adviser to the United Mexican-American Students, said he expects there will be some special problems among new Chicano students at Stanford because of the university's "upper middle-class white orientation."

He said, however, that private institutions "do not bow to backlash as readily as do public ones."

Gutierrez expressed surprise at Stanford's "far-flung efforts to recruit Chicano students," noting that the neighboring San Jose area has one of the largest Mexican-American populations in the state.

Stanford plans a series of seminars on the Mexican-American community in early October.

Black and Chicano Ties Worsen After Walkout at Santa Barbara

September 15, 1969

Relations between Mexican-American and black activists in California colleges and universities — which are cool at best — have deteriorated as a result of a Chicano walkout during an educational opportunity workshop at UC Santa Barbara.

Chicano students and administrators stalked out of the private conference after black participants refused to support a resolution which in effect emphasized that there are more Mexican-Americans than there are Negroes in California.

Black and Chicano students and administrators — representing most California colleges and universities — met August 13–15 in the Francisco Torres Conference Center to discuss problems faced by Educational Opportunity Programs throughout the state.

In a report of the closed conference just released, however, it was revealed that much of the conference time was used "to bring into the open underlying hostilities between the Chicanos and black participants."

The report said the Chicano caucus charged at the conference that:

— "The black, because of his national push, has gotten the lion's share of the 'goodies.'"

— "In California and the Southwest he (the black) is using the Chicano to get funds but utilizing these funds only for his own people." (This meant, a Chicano caucus spokesman said later, that Negro officials receive money to help "minorities" and help only blacks.)

— "All major positions opening up are filled by black faces," especially on campuses, "with the result that Chicano kids are not entering colleges at the rate they should be."

Chicanos told the conference that it is the blacks who are "pushing" for a "coalition" but that when such a coalition is formed the blacks try to control it.

"Blacks say that blacks and browns are fighting over the white man's bone, but that isn't so," the report said. "The black man has the white man's bone and is fighting to keep the Chicano away from it."

Chicanos walked out of the conference, the Chicano caucus said, after the blacks refused to support a resolution which said in part:

"Each institution of higher education must reflect in its student body, representation of Chicanos proportional to the Chicano population of its immediate service area or to the Chicano population statewide, whichever is higher."

Had the blacks supported this resolution, it would have meant in effect that blacks approved the Chicano demand that Chicanos be given preference in California colleges on the basis that Spanish-speaking people are the largest minority in California.

The argument, plus the continuing shortage of money, had earlier threatened the Educational Opportunity Program at San Jose State College. There, Chicanos demanded and got a larger share of this year's EOP students.

San Jose Figures

At first, there were to have been 275 new Chicano students at San Jose State and 225 blacks. After bitter protests by Chicanos, the figures were changed to 350 for Chicanos and 250 for blacks.

The Chicanos won this victory by pointing out that in the San Jose area there are 50,000 to 60,000 Mexican-Americans and only about 4,000 or 5,000 Negroes.

Chicanos complain that national exposure of Negro problems has clouded the fact that in California and throughout the Southwest, Mexican-Americans outnumber Negroes.

Latest U.S. Census Bureau figures show there are about 22 million Negroes in the United States. Figures for Mexican-Americans are much more difficult to determine because Spanish-surname people are counted as "whites."

After pressuring from the U.S. Inter-Agency Committee on Mexican-American Affairs and many Mexican-American organizations in the Southwest, the U.S. Census had committed itself to a comprehensive count of Spanish-surname people in the United States during the 1970 census.

Mexican-American organizations contend there are from 8 to 10 million Spanish-surname Americans. In California, the Mexican-American Opportunity Foundation says that information obtained from the census bureau shows that Mexican-Americans comprised 53.1% of the state's minority population, while the Negroes number 32.9% of the minority population.

Request to Blacks

When the Chicanos at the Santa Barbara conference asked the blacks to back the resolution demanding representation of Chicanos in California colleges proportional to the Chicano population, the Chicanos were asking that the blacks admit publicly Mexican-Americans' greater numbers in California and in the Southwest.

The blacks caucused for about an hour and a half and then returned to the conference to report that the blacks voted not to support the resolution because they were not representative of all black people.

The blacks said, however, that they would ask the Black Educators Conference in Atlanta Aug. 21–24 for consideration of the Chicano demand.

At this point the Chicanos accused the blacks of "copping out" and walked out of the conference.

Ernie Clark, black EOP director at Cal State Long Beach, said the Black Educators Conference voted to cooperate with Chicanos but that it did not back the resolution.

"The black educators at the Atlanta conference felt supporting the Chicano resolution might enhance blacks to Chicanos in California but would be unrealistic in other parts of the country," he said.

Judge's Latin Slurs Bring Call for Removal

October 2, 1969

SAN JOSE — Demands mounted here Wednesday for the resignation of a Superior Court judge who made anti-Mexican remarks from the bench and said "maybe Hitler was right" about destroying the "animals in our society."

A court transcript shows that Judge Gerald S. Chargin in sentencing a 17-year-old Mexican-American boy for incest said:

". . . Mexican people, after 13 years of age, think it is perfectly all right to go out and act like an animal . . . we ought to send you out of the country — send you back to Mexico. You belong in prison for the rest of your life for doing things of this kind. You ought to commit suicide . . ."

The judge then went on to say that "maybe Hitler was right. The animals in our society probably ought to be destroyed because they have no right to live among human beings . . ."

Wednesday about 200 members of Mexican-American organizations and civil rights groups picketed the Superior Court building in downtown San Jose. This city of 450,000 people has the largest Spanish surname population in urban Northern California.

A meeting between community representatives and presiding judge Joseph Kelley was unproductive, according to Paul Sanchez, chairman of the graduate school of social welfare at San Jose State College.

"Judge Kelley informed about 30 leaders of the Mexican-American community that he could do nothing," Sanchez said.

"He rightfully informed us that he has no jurisdiction in getting Judge Chargin off the bench. However, what shocked us is that Judge Kelley was not sufficiently morally shocked by Judge Chargin's behavior to support us even philosophically."

Sanchez said that the community is in a very volatile mood and that "anything could happen."

Chargin, 65, member of an old San Jose family of ranchers, told newsmen that "juvenile court proceedings are private for the protection of the minor and the family involved."

"Only those persons directly concerned are allowed to be present. For this reason it is difficult to comment as fully and freely as otherwise might be the case."

Excerpts from the transcript which showed what Chargin said were distributed by the California Rural Legal Assistance and the Community

Service Organization, a Mexican-American group. The names of the juveniles involved were not disclosed in the excerpts distributed.

The Mexican-American boy was charged with incest with his 15-year-old sister, who is mentally retarded. The boy claims he is innocent and that he pleaded guilty only because attorneys advised him to do so in order that the case would not go to trial.

The boy was arrested after the County Welfare Department learned about the girl's pregnancy.

Chargin placed the boy on probation.

Because of the controversy and because juvenile cases are usually dealt with in private, it could not be confirmed that attorneys advised the young defendant to plead guilty.

However, Al Pinon, head of the San Jose Community Organization, said this aspect of the case "is of much interest to the community and we are going to insist that it be explored."

Pinon, a San Jose real estate man, said he had "good information" that the youth had been told to plead guilty.

"Not only was the whole Mexican-American community insulted," Pinon said, "but apparently our people are also forced, you might say, to plead guilty to crimes they have not committed."

Don Kates of the California Rural Legal Assistance said he understands the youth was advised to plead guilty but that "this is strictly what the boy said and I have nothing to back it up right now."

Kates said that if the case had gone to trial and the boy had been found guilty, he could have received up to 20 years in prison.

Judge 'Goes Along'

The court transcript shows that Judge Chargin decided to "go along with the [Juvenile Probation Department's] recommendation" and placed the boy on probation.

The San Jose Human Relations Commission, in a meeting marked with emotional protests from the Mexican-American community, voted unanimously Tuesday to ask that Judge Chargin be disbarred "if it is true that he said what the transcript says he said."

Judge Chargin has not denied the authenticity of the transcript made available to the public.

Speaking about the remarks that he made in court, Chargin told newsmen that the distribution of the excerpts was "not only a disservice to the youth and family involved but may involve a violation of the law."

The California Rural Legal Assistance said no law has been violated because the names of the minors were not divulged.

The group confirmed that it has complained to the State Judicial Qualifications Commission which has been asked to remove Chargin from the bench.

The judge told newsmen that "I am compelled to set the record straight in this regard. The case involved the admitted unnatural crime of incest between a 17-year-old boy and his 15-year-old sister, who is now pregnant. Without revealing more of the facts, it was a situation which was so revolting it offended my sense of morality and conscience."

Chargin said that he is not prejudiced against any ethnic group.

"I am pleased to say that my entire adult life, both in the law and on the Superior Court bench, has been an effort and a striving for justice for all."

"The most recent example of this is my nomination of the only Mexican-American individual presently serving on the County Grand Jury."

Pinon told newsmen that Chargin's remarks were "racist, bigoted, biased and defamatory to all individuals of Mexican ancestry and we cannot in good conscience, remain silent . . ."

According to the court transcript, right after Chargin made his remarks about the Mexican people, animals and Hitler, the boy's attorney, Fred Lucero, interrupted:

"Your honor, I don't think I can sit here and listen to that sort of thing."

The judge answered, "You're going to have to listen to it because I consider this a very vulgar rotten human being."

Later, Lucero said, "What appalls me is that the court is saying that Hitler was right in genocide."

To that the judge answered:

"What are we going to do with mad dogs in our society? Either we have to kill them or send them to an institution or place them out of the hands of good people because that's the theory — one theory of punishment is that they get to the position that they want to act like mad dogs, then we have to separate them from society."

In his statement to the press, Chargin said that the reason he made those statements was that "it is an accepted fact that these lectures (in court) are stated in harsh terms to impress upon the minds of the youth the seriousness of the situation in which they find themselves."

"Sometimes, the words of the lecture are purposely accentuated and exaggerated. However, it is to the ultimate disposition of this case that one must look."

"In this case, the youth was returned to his grandmother, as a ward of the court under supervision of the Juvenile Probation Department, which followed the recommendation of the Juvenile Probation Department."

"Suffice it to say, much harsher alternative dispositions were available to me."

The U.S. Commission on Civil Rights said that it would investigate the matter.

Meanwhile, leaders of the Mexican-American community in San Jose said they were having trouble keeping militants from taking drastic steps.

Pinon said the Mexican-American community would be satisfied only with the removal of Chargin from the bench. He said that although it is true that Judge Kelley cannot remove Chargin, he does have the authority to transfer him from the juvenile court.

"But Judge Kelley is not willing to do even that," Pinon said. "It seems to us that Judge Kelley has a moral responsibility here as far as the Mexican-American community is concerned to at least side with us philosophically. We cannot have this sort of man (Chargin) on the bench."*

800 Supporters of Sal Castro March on School Board

October 7, 1969

About 800 supporters of controversial teacher Sal Castro marched Monday from the Old Plaza near Olvera St. to the Board of Education to protest the proposed transfer of the East Los Angeles Chicano teacher.

Led by a mariachi band the peaceful marchers held a rally in the board building's patio while representatives of the group spoke before the board.

Castro, under indictment for alleged conspiracy in last year's eastside high school walkouts had been transferred from Lincoln High School but later was reinstated by the board.

Before the summer vacation this year, Principal George Ingles again asked for the transfer of Castro, charging that the teacher had violated school rules, including tardiness.

---

*Judge Gerald S. Chargin was not removed from the bench but was instead transferred to a nonjuvenile court.

At the beginning of the current semester Castro was assigned temporarily as a translator in the administration offices downtown pending a ruling by a board of review.

The Rev. Vahac Madirosian, chairman of the board-created Mexican-American Education Commission, charged at Monday's board meeting that in assigning Castro to a downtown job while the board of review was studying the case, a board rule had been violated.

The rule was adopted after Castro was transferred last time to protect teachers from being transferred until they had hearings.

Board president Arthur Gardner told the meeting the rule did not apply in this case and later addressed the unfriendly crowd in the patio.

Gardner explained that since a review board will start deliberations on the Castro case Oct. 15, the board cannot return Castro to Lincoln High School now, as the crowd demanded.*

Bilingual Texas Public School Gains Support

October 13, 1969

LAREDO, Tex. — When the children at Nye Elementary School here pledge allegiance to the Flag, they do it in English and in Spanish. These children are participating in what is probably the only truly bilingual public school educational program in the United States.

In Los Angeles and other parts of the Southwest with large Mexican-American populations, limited bilingual programs are geared to helping Spanish-speaking students make the transition into English instruction as soon as possible.

Spanish is used as a tool only until the children are proficient enough in English to use it exclusively in classes. No attempt is made to improve the quality of the children's Spanish, much less make Spanish an educational tool for the whole community.

At Nye, where the students are roughly half Anglo and half Mexican-American, the teachers and school administrators believe the Southwest's bicultural and bilingual traditions should be expanded instead of "phased-out."

Nye is one of three grammar schools in the rural United Consolidated School District of Webb County, Tex., which borders on Mexico.

The children from grade one to five not only pay their respects to the

---

*By late 1969 Sal Castro was reinstated to his former teaching post at Lincoln High School. He continues to teach in the East Los Angeles schools.

Flag in both languages but are taught all their classes, reading, writing and arithmetic, in English and in Spanish concurrently.

At a recent second grade reading class, a blond, blue-eyed boy went to the blackboard to take dictation from the teacher, Mrs. Rosario Garcia.

Yo tengo un libro rojo, the Anglo boy wrote as the teacher dictated. A Mexican-American boy was then called to translate the sentence into English. The Spanish-speaking student wrote, "I have a book red." "What is wrong with that sentence?" the teacher asked the class.

An Anglo boy made the correction on the board. "I have a red book." The adjective in English, unlike in Spanish comes before the noun and not after it, the boy explained in simple English all could understand.

"This time the English-speaking student helped the Spanish-speaking one correct his English," Mrs. Garcia told a visitor. "Sometimes it's the other way around. The result is that both learn English and Spanish at the same time. Communication among kids is fantastic."

After much experimentation, the district has decided to work on this theory: As long as there are Anglos and Mexican-Americans attending school together the language of both should be used to the advantage of both.

Bilingual education in most areas is conducted in classes totally Mexican-American because the idea is to use Spanish only until English is learned.

"This is not truly bilingual education," says Mrs. Dolores Alvarado Earles, chairman of the district's program. "This is just a way of helping the Spanish-speaking student rid himself of what is considered a hindrance, the Spanish language."

"We believe the knowledge of Spanish is a blessing which should be developed by the Mexican-American child and shared with his Anglo fellow student."

The district's superintendent, Harold C. Brantley, has made a national reputation for expounding this philosophy in the pedagogic world where bilingual education is still a vaguely defined concept.

Brantley, as Texas as Lyndon B. Johnson, on the surface seems an unlikely exponent of bilingualism, especially in a state where in parts "Mexican" is still a dirty word.

The 60-year-old educator has the demeanor of a no-nonsense Texan, wears a diamond in his Rotary pin and has no sympathy for school militants, whether they be Chicano, black or Anglo.

This "conservative" appearance is deceiving. On the wall of his office, decorated with student art work, is a sign which reads, "If a child lives with ridicule, he learns to be shy. If he lives with approval, he learns to like himself."

To him, terms such as "culturally deprived" or "disadvantaged" when used to describe children make no sense at all.

No fuzzy-brained idealist, Brantley makes it clear that helping the Mexican-American child "enter the mainstream of the dominant culture and the dominant language of the country is very important."

Provide Opportunity

"We try to do this," says Brantley. "But we also try to stress to that child who comes from this other culture, speaking this other language, that we want to provide him with the opportunity to improve upon his knowledge of his culture and his ability to function in his own vernacular."

"We try to create an atmosphere in the classroom where the children who come to us from the dominant culture, speaking the dominant language recognize that the Mexican-American kid has something that he, the Anglo child, doesn't have and that Anglo kids ought to be interested in getting what this other little kid can teach him."

The Rev. Theodore M. Hesburgh, president of Notre Dame University and chairman of the U.S. Commission on Civil Rights, has said Brantley's program has "cut the Gordian knot," because it has "taken what seems to many people to be a problem and made it a great education advantage."

For years, educators in the Southwest have tried to sell the idea that both Anglos and Mexican-Americans could benefit from bilingual education.

Resistance to this idea has been constant since the end of the Mexican-American War in 1848, when Mexico lost half of its territory to the United States. The general attitude of the Anglo establishment has been that the English language and Anglo culture should be stressed exclusively.

Historians say that one of the reasons New Mexico and Arizona were admitted to the union so late was legislators' resistance to a bilingual and bicultural people.

Differing View

Some educators feel the plan is utopian at best and that bilingual education should confine itself to helping the Mexican-American child make the all important transition into the mainstream of our dominant English language and Anglo culture.

Armando Rodriguez, chief of the Mexican-American affairs unit of the U.S. Office of Education, disagrees:

"We must use the Mexican-American cultural heritage to rich advantage in our educational system," he says. "This country has assumed the monocultural and monolingual role for generations. We have always stripped our immigrants of their language and culture and expected them to conform to our customs and traditions . . . to the American way of life."

"We must recognize the contribution of other cultures to the American heritage and must stop trying to blot out differences."

The scarcity of bilingual teachers, of course, prevents most school districts from adopting such a successful bilingual program.

One of the reasons for this is that Texas has a better record than California in the enrollment of and graduating of college students of Spanish surnames who would presumably become bilingual teachers.

In the 1968–69 school year, for instance, figures from the Department of Health, Education and Welfare for the Inter-Agency Committee on Mexican-American Affairs show that while University of Texas enrolled 852 Mexican-American students, UCLA enrolled only 325 (UCLA says the figure should be closer to 500).

The figures show that of the 852 Mexican-American students enrolled at the University of Texas, 208 graduated. Figures for UCLA's graduating Mexican-Americans for this year are not available.

The figures also show that Arizona and New Mexico were ahead of UCLA in the number of enrolled and graduating Mexican-Americans.

In Los Angeles, which has the largest Mexican-American population in the country, the school district has not as yet defined its bilingual education programs as clearly as has Supt. Brantley in Laredo.

The Malabar project, for instance, Los Angeles' best-known bilingual program, almost lost its federal funds because, according to the U.S. Office of Education:

"The foundation for the program rests almost exclusively . . . in [a proposal] concerned entirely with English-as-a-second-language instruction, rather than a bilingual approach. Nowhere is there any indication that the child's mother tongue will be used as a tool of instruction in grades one through three."

The Malabar project, highly praised by those educators who do not feel the district is ready to define bilingual education, at least until more bilingual teachers are available, was saved through the pressure applied by the California congressional delegation.

Latins' Image in Advertising Held 'Inferior'

October 20, 1969

Some mass media advertisers are depicting Mexican-Americans in a prejudiced, stereotyped fashion, according to a Stanford University sociologist.

In a study called "Advertising and Racism: The Case of the Mexican-American," Thomas M. Martinez, director of Stanford's Mexican-American Seminars, asserted that "racist thinking" is behind many T.V. magazine and newspaper ads depicting Spanish-speaking people.

The study, researched with the help of sociology students, is being widely distributed among educators and Mexican-American organizations.

Presented at Stanford's first seminar on Mexican-Americans, now in progress, the study asserts that this advertising trend "symbolically reaffirms the inferior social status of Mexicans" in the eyes of viewers and readers of the mass media.

The "Frito Bandido" corn chip TV commercial, which has been fought by the Mexican-American Anti-Defamation Committee throughout the country, is given special attention in the study.

'Frito' Cartoon Character

"Seldom a day goes by in the United States without at least one young Mexican-American being called, 'Frito Bandido,'" it says. "Indeed, this cartoon caricature of a short, mustached, two-gunned thief is very effective . . . in terms of making the out-group appear inferior and the in-group superior."

"The Mexican-American children are paying the price in loss of self-esteem for the Frito-Lay Corp.'s successful advertising attempt at product association."

A student of Martinez' racial and cultural minorities course, who wrote the company complaining about the Frito Bandido commercial, got the following answer from the corporation's director of advertising:

". . . We did not and never have had any racist intentions in presenting the Frito Bandido cartoon character. It was meant to be a single character which is intended to make you laugh, in turn we hope that this laughter will leave our trademark implanted in your memory . . ."

"Tell this to the Mexican-American kids," said Martinez. "They have the Frito-Lay Corp. to thank for adding another racial stereotype to our language."

As for the corporation's explanation that Frito Bandido was created "to make you laugh," Martinez asked, "Is humor less harmful . . . than outright verbal statements expressing deeply held racial prejudice?"

The Stanford sociologist said that "Freud believed that humor was a reflection of unconscious, repressed feelings."

"Many of the same people who claim not to be prejudiced easily laugh at ethnocentric jokes and are amused by stereotyped characters. Does our laughter betray us? It most certainly does," Martinez said.

To find nothing objectionable or distasteful about advertising's image of Mexicans and Mexican-Americans suggests tacit agreement with the image, he added.

Martinez cited nine major advertisers, which the study charges with slurring Mexican-Americans.

For example, he told about the TV commercial that shows "a band of horse-riding, ferocious looking Mexican bandidos emerging from a cloud of dust." The band is called to a halt by the sombrero-covered, thick-mustached, fat-bellied leader, who, upon stopping, reaches with the utmost care for a small object from his saddlebags.

He picks up the object, lifts up his arm and smiles slyly—to spray Arid deodorant.

An American Midwestern voice is then heard over the television saying "If it works for him, it will work for you."

"The message," says Martinez, "is that Mexicans stink the most."

Others Mentioned

Other mass media advertisements in this same vein mentioned by the study include those of Granny Goose Potato Chips, Liggett & Meyers, A. J. Reynolds, Camel Cigarets, General Motors, Philco-Ford and Frigidaire.

"Not only are advertisers exhibiting racist thinking at the expense of everyone of Mexican descent," the study says, "but they are also creating, in many cases, unfavorable racial and cultural stereotypes in minds that previously did not harbor them."

Latins Form Distinct Class, U.S. Aide Says

October 23, 1969

A spokesman for the federal government Wednesday told a Superior Court hearing on the makeup of the County Grand Jury that Mexican-Americans are a "separate and distinct" class of people.

Phillip Montez, western regional director of the U.S. Commission on Civil Rights, made the assertion at a hearing on a motion to quash the indictment of a Brown Beret and five others on the grounds that the grand jury is "illegally constituted."

The hearing is of special significance to a group which in the past has been identified as "Caucasian."

DA's Position

Because of this, the district attorney has argued that since there are Caucasians on the grand jury, Mexican-Americans are represented.

Oscar Z. Acosta of the Mexican-American Legal Defense and Education Fund told the hearing that before he can prove Mexican-Americans have been systematically excluded from grand jury service, it must be acknowledged that this ethnic group constitutes a "class" of people.*

To this, Judge Adolph Alexander commented: "Does anyone deny that Mexican-Americans are a definable group?"

"The district attorney does," answered Acosta. Dep. Dist. Atty. Bruce Campbell did not object.

Biltmore Incident

The motion was filed on behalf of Carlos Montez, Brown Beret information minister, and five other Mexican-American activists involved in disturbances April 24 at the Biltmore where Gov. Reagan addressed a Mexican-American education conference.

A similar motion was denied last year in the case of an Eastside high school walkout leader Salvador Castro after the district attorney contended that Mexican-Americans cannot be considered a separate class. This case is on appeal.

Attorneys for Carlos Montez and the five other defendants contend they were wrongfully indicted by the grand jury "in that there has been, and to the present still exists, an unconstitutional underrepresentation of the defendant's peer group of American citizens of Spanish surname on [grand juries], all in violation of the due process and equal protection clauses" of the U.S. Constitution.

---

*Oscar Zeta Acosta was a writer as well as a militant Chicano attorney. His first book, *The Autobiography of a Brown Buffalo* (New York: Vintage Books, 1989; orig. pub. 1972), was followed by *The Revolt of the Cockroach People* (New York: Vintage Books, 1989; orig. pub. 1973). In the mid-1970s, Acosta vanished during a trip to Acapulco. His disappearance has never been explained.

Judges Subpoenaed

Seventy of the 150 Superior Court judges already have been subpoenaed to testify in the hearing, which is expected to last a month.

Acosta says he intends to ask the judges, among other things, the race, ethnic origin, wealth and education of the judges' nominees to the grand jury to determine the class or classes exclusively considered for nomination.

Attorneys Acosta and Hugh Manes presented lists of grand jurors which show that only 1.7% of the ultimately selected persons over the past 11 years have been of Spanish-surname ethnic minority even though this "class" represents about 13% of the county's population.

Judge Alexander told the attorneys he would at first only hear testimony concerning the 1969 grand jury.

The present grand jury has no Mexican-Americans on it. Sitting on the jury, however, are two Negroes, one Chinese and one Filipino.

All, according to Acosta, voted against the indictments.

In 1970, Salazar became the news director at KMEX, the Spanish-language television station in Los Angeles, and started writing a weekly column for the Times *on Chicano issues.*

Who Is a Chicano? And What Is It the Chicanos Want?

February 6, 1970

A Chicano is a Mexican-American with a non-Anglo image of himself.

He resents being told Columbus "discovered" America when the Chicano's ancestors, the Mayans and the Aztecs, founded highly sophisticated civilizations centuries before Spain financed the Italian explorer's trip to the "New World."

Chicanos resent also Anglo pronouncements that Chicanos are "culturally deprived" or that the fact that they speak Spanish is a "problem."

Chicanos will tell you that their culture predates that of the Pilgrims and that Spanish was spoken in America before English and so the "problem" is not theirs but the Anglos' who don't speak Spanish.

Having told you that, the Chicano will then contend that Anglos are Spanish-oriented at the expense of Mexicans.

They will complain that when the governor dressed up as a Spanish nobleman for the Santa Barbara Fiesta he's insulting Mexicans because the Spanish conquered and exploited the Mexicans.

It's as if the governor dressed like an English Redcoat for a Fourth of July parade, Chicanos say.

When you think you know what Chicanos are getting at, a Mexican-American will tell you that Chicano is an insulting term and may even quote the Spanish Academy to prove that Chicano derives from chicanery.

A Chicano will scoff at this and say that such Mexican-Americans have been brainwashed by Anglos and that they're Tio Tacos (Uncle Toms). This type of Mexican-American, Chicanos will argue, don't like the word Chicano because it's abrasive to their Anglo-oriented minds.

These poor people are brown Anglos, Chicanos will smirk.

What, then, is a Chicano? Chicanos say that if you have to ask you'll never understand, much less become, a Chicano.

Actually, the word Chicano is as difficult to define as "soul."

For those who like simplistic answers, Chicano can be defined as short for Mexicano. For those who prefer complicated answers, it has been suggested that Chicano may have come from the word Chihuahua — the name of a Mexican state bordering on the United States. Getting trickier, this version then contends that Mexicans who migrated to Texas call themselves Chicanos because having crossed into the United States from Chihuahua they adopted the first three letters of that state, Chi, and then added cano, for the latter part of Texano.

Such explanations, however, tend to miss the whole point as to why Mexican-American activists call themselves Chicanos.

Mexican-Americans, the second largest minority in the country and the largest in the Southwestern states (California, Texas, Arizona, New Mexico and Colorado), have always had difficulty making up their minds what to call themselves.

In New Mexico, they call themselves Spanish-Americans. In other parts of the Southwest they call themselves Americans of Mexican descent, people with Spanish surnames or Hispanos.

Why, ask some Mexican-Americans, can't we just call ourselves Americans?

Chicanos are trying to explain why not. Mexican-Americans, though indigenous to the Southwest, are on the lowest rung scholastically, economically, socially and politically. Chicanos feel cheated. They want to effect change. Now.

Mexican-Americans average eight years of schooling compared to the Negroes' 10 years. Farm workers, most of whom are Mexican-American in the Southwest, are excluded from the National Labor Relations Act, unlike other workers. Also, Mexican-Americans often have to compete for low-paying jobs with their Mexican brothers from across the border who are willing to work for even less. Mexican-Americans have to live with the stinging fact that the word Mexican is the synonym for inferior in many parts of the Southwest.

That is why Mexican-American activists flaunt the barrio word Chicano — as an act of defiance and a badge of honor. Mexican-Americans, though large in numbers, are so politically impotent that in Los Angeles, where the country's largest single concentration of Spanish-speaking live, they have no one of their own on the City Council. This, in a city politically sophisticated enough to have three Negro councilmen.

Chicanos, then, are merely fighting to become "Americans." Yes, but with a Chicano outlook.

A Mexican-American Hyphen

February 13, 1970

The U.S.–Mexican border, or la frontera, is an 1,800-mile-long, virtually imaginary line of barbed wire fencing, an undergrowth of mesquite or chaparral and an easily forded river.

Orators, both American and Mexican, like to describe the border separating their countries as one of the two only such unfortified frontiers in the world, the other being the U.S.–Canadian border.

To many Americans living in the Southwest and to many Mexicans living in northern Mexico, however, the border is symbolic of the negative differences between the two nations.

Americans who know only the shady aspects of the border towns think of Mexico as a place where they can enjoy doing what is not allowed at home — but would be shocked, the morning after, if such goings on were allowed in "America."

Mexicans not lucky enough to be among the Latin affluent think of the American border towns as gold mines where nuggets can be picked off the streets. And when they discover this is not true, they blast the Americans as exploiters, unmindful that they had created their own false image of the United States.

These superficial and inaccurate concepts of both countries help only to widen the understanding gap between two peoples who are so close geographically and in many other ways so far apart.

That may help explain why Mexican-Americans can feel a deep and agonizing ambivalence about themselves.

They can love the United States for reasons Mexicans cannot understand, while loving Mexico for reasons Americans can understand.

Being a Mexican-American, a wag once said, can leave you with only the hyphen.

On the United States' other border there are no such esoteric considerations.

Canadians may conceivably feel bitter about the fact that the British Empire lost the 13 colonies but this chauvinism is tempered by knowing that, after all, Canadians and Americans communicate easily and enjoy more or less the same material goods.

Chauvinistic Mexicans, however, are very cognizant of the fact that Mexico lost what is now the American Southwest to the United States in the Mexican-American War which even Gen. Ulysses S. Grant called "unfair."

Mexicans like to argue that if the United States had not "stolen" half of Mexico's territory, Mexico would be as rich as the United States is now. This historical controversy, now for the most part taken lightly, might have disappeared altogether by now, it is said, if Mexicans and Americans spoke the same language on both sides of the border and so understood each other better.

Yet, many Mexican-Americans in the Southwest, who speak both languages and admire both countries, feel strangely foreign in their own land.

Members of other minorities — Italians, Irish, Poles, etc. — often wonder why Mexican-Americans have not been able to assimilate as well as they have.

They tend to forget that Italy, Ireland, Poland, etc., are oceans away from the United States while Mexico is very much in evidence to the Southwest's eight million or so Mexican-Americans.

This makes it difficult for the Mexican-Americans to think of Mexico in the abstract as, for instance, Irish-Americans might think of Ireland.

The problems of Mexico are and will remain relevant to the Mexican-American. Relations between Mexico and the United States can affect the Mexican-American in the Southwest materially and emotionally.

In the border areas, for instance, the large number of Mexicans crossing the international line everyday to work in the United States can directly affect the economic lives of Mexican-Americans, who must compete with this cheap labor.

Projects such as Operation Intercept, a crackdown on dope smuggling across the Mexican border, hurt the pride of southwest Mexican-

Americans who feel the United States is trying to blame Mexicans for a problem which is to a large extent uniquely "Anglo."

The border may indeed be unfortified, but it separates two people who created the Mexican-American — a person many times tormented by the pull of two distinct cultures.

Chicanos Would Find Identity Before Coalition with Blacks

February 20, 1970

Mexicans and Negroes are learning that they must know each other better if their differences are not to help those who would like to kill the civil rights movement.

This necessary lesson is not easy to come by.

Blacks, scarred by the bitter and sometimes bloody struggle for equality, consider Mexican-Americans or Chicanos as Johnnies-come-lately who should follow black leadership until the Chicanos earn their spurs.

Chicanos, not untouched by bigotry and wary of the more sophisticated black leadership, insist on going their own way because, as they put it, "our problems are different from those of the Negroes."

Despite the loud mouthings of radicals, most blacks and Chicanos want the same thing: a fair chance to enter the mainstream of American society without abandoning their culture and uniqueness.

Much has been made of late of the growing rift between Negroes and Mexican-Americans. Chicanos complain that blacks get most of the government help in the fight against racism, while Negroes scoff that Mexican-Americans have not carried their share of the burden in the civil rights movement.

Leaders of both communities throw up their arms in despair, saying that the blacks and browns are fighting over peanuts and that political coalitions must be formed to make a real impact on the establishment.

Blacks and browns have always been cast together by the forces of history and the needs of these two peoples.

Los Angeles, for instance, was founded not by Spanish caballeros, as romantics would have it, but by blacks and browns.

Historian H. Bancroft points out that Los Angeles was founded on Sept. 4, 1781, with 12 settlers and their families, 46 persons in all, "whose blood was a strange mixture of Indian (Mexican) and Negro with here and there a trace of Spanish."

C. D. Willard, another historian, adds that "cataloguing this extraordinary collection of adults by nationality or color, we have two Spaniards, one mestizo, two Negroes, eight mulattoes and nine [Mexican] Indians."

The children of the settlers, continues Willard, were even more mixed, as follows: Spanish-Indian, four; Spanish-Negro, five; Negro-Indian, eight; Spanish-Negro-Indian, eight; Spanish-Negro-Indian, three; Indian, two.

Since then, Mexicans and Negroes have more or less followed their own separate destinies, due partly to their cultural and language differences but also because of the racist strain in American society.

Mexican-Americans have a saying about Negroes that goes, "Juntos pero no revueltos" — together but not mixed. Negroes, on the other hand, tend to think of Mexican-Americans — as do many Anglos — as "quaint and foreign."

One hundred and eighty years after the small group of black and brown people settled in what became Los Angeles, however, six Mexican-American children and six Negro children are involved in a Superior Court ruling in which Judge Alfred Gitelson ordered the Los Angeles school district desegregated.

When the Los Angeles school district is finally integrated, history will again have thrown the blacks and the browns together again.

To understand why Mexicans and Negroes are having their differences now, one must look at it in the light of the black revolution.

The revolution exploded partly from a condition which had been known all along but which became the basis for a black-white confrontation: the color of one's skin is all too important in America. White is good, Black is bad.

Faced with an identity crisis, many Mexican-Americans — especially the young who were excited by black militancy — decided they had been misled by the Mexican establishment into apathetic confusion.

It came as a shock at first: Mexican-Americans felt caught between the white and the black. Though counted as "white" by the Bureau of Census, Mexican-Americans were never really thought of as such.

The ambivalence felt vaguely and in silence for so long seemed to crystallize in the wake of the black revolution. A Mexican-American was neither white nor black.

One of the reasons for the growing distrust between Mexicans and Negroes is that the Chicano is still searching for his identity.

As yet, most Mexican-Americans seem not to identify with any one single overriding problem as Americans. Though they know they're somehow different, many still cling to the idea that Mexican-Americans are Caucasian, thus white, thus "one of the boys."

Many prove it: By looking and living like white Americans, by obtaining and keeping good jobs and by intermarrying with Anglos who never think of it as a "mixed marriage."

Many others, however, feel they have for too long been cheated by tacitly agreeing to be Caucasian in name only. These Mexican-Americans, especially the young Chicanos, feel that the coalition with the Anglos has failed.

And they're not about ready to form a new coalition — this time with the blacks — until they, the Chicanos, find their own identity in their own way.

Mexican-American's Dilemma: He's Unfit in Either Language

February 27, 1970

". . . A Los Angeles Police Department officer was beating a Spanish-speaking motorist, calling him a dirty Mexican. Occupants in the motorist's car yelled out to the police officer that the person he was beating was not a Mexican, but that he was a Nicaraguan."

"At that moment the officer stopped beating him and obtained medical help for him."

So testified a psychiatric social worker at a hearing before the U.S. Commission on Civil Rights in December of 1968.

The testimony gives some insight into the complicated subject of the differences among the Spanish-speaking people in the United States.

Mexican-Americans, about 8 million of the 10 million Spanish-speaking people in the country, are, ironically, among the most abused of this minority simply because they're Americans. This holds true for Puerto Ricans who are also Americans.

Non-American Spanish-speaking people, like Nicaraguans, Argentineans and Colombians, are as the police officer knew instantly, treated with more respect.

The reason may be that Americans, originally immigrants to this country, show more consideration for other immigrants than they do for indigenous people like Mexican-Americans and Indians.

Because of the civil rights movement, there has been an intense search for Spanish-speaking teachers, journalists, social workers, salesmen, etc.

Invariably, when found, these specialists turn out to be non-American Spanish-speaking people — Cubans, Central Americans, South Americans and native Mexicans.

The reason is simple. Non-American Spanish-speaking people have a better education — and so speak good Spanish — and assimilate well into Anglo society because they came here expressly to do this.

The Mexican-American, meanwhile, many of whom speak neither good Spanish nor good English, are victims of an educational system which purports to "Americanize" them while downgrading their ethnic background.

For instance, the first truly bilingual education program in this country was set up not for Mexican-Americans but for Cubans in the wake of the Cuban crisis. Bilingual education was made available to Cuban refugees at Florida's Dade County schools in 1963.

Yet, as late as December 1966, educators testified before the U.S. Commission on Civil Rights that Mexican-American children were being punished for speaking Spanish on school grounds in other parts of the country.

Cubans today, then, have a better chance of obtaining jobs requiring bilingual people — now that Spanish has been discovered as an asset instead of a liability — than do Mexican-Americans.

Belated bilingual education programs for Mexican-Americans are geared toward using the Spanish language as a tool only until the Chicano kid has learned enough English to overcome the "problem" of speaking Spanish. These are not truly bilingual programs, which should be the teaching of both languages on an equal basis.

The truth of the matter is that despite our talk in the Southwest about "our great Spanish heritage" and the naming of our towns and streets in Spanish, the Spanish language has never been taken seriously by American educators even in areas where both languages could be learned together and correctly.

Too often the difference between a Mexican-American and a non-American Spanish-speaking person is that the non-American can speak better Spanish than the Mexican-American — and so is more qualified for the emerging bilingual job.

And the difference between the Mexican-American and the Anglo-American is that the Anglo speaks better English than the Mexican-American and so is better equipped for the more conventional jobs.

The pattern could change when the American educational system is as considerate of Mexican-Americans as it was of Cubans in 1963.

Chicanos vs. Traditionalists

March 6, 1970

Last Saturday's Chicano Moratorium and the activities of the Catolicos por La Raza dramatize the gulf which exists between the traditional-minded Mexican-Americans and the young activists.

Unless this is understood, observers can fall easily into the simplistic conclusions that the traditionalists are Tio Tacos (Uncle Toms) or that the activists are irresponsible punks.

Either conclusion misses the essence of the present Mexican-American condition.

Traditional-minded Mexican-Americans blush at the mention of the word Chicano. They blanch at the thought of being called brown people. The reason for this, outside of personal views, is the psychological makeup of the Mexican in general.

Octavio Paz, the Mexican poet-essayist-diplomat, has tried to explain it this way: "The Mexican, whether young or old, white or brown, general or lawyer, seems to me to be a person who shuts himself away to protect himself. . . . He is jealous of his own privacy and that of others. . . . He passes through life like a man who has been flayed; everything can hurt him, including words and the very suspicion of words. . . ."

The Mexican, says Paz, "builds a wall of indifference and remoteness between reality and himself, a wall that is no less impenetrable for being invisible. The Mexican is always remote, from the world and from other people. And also from himself."

Is it any wonder, then, that the more conservative Mexican-Americans — and there are many of them — are embarrassed and angered at Chicanos (suspicious word) who say they don't want to fight the war in Vietnam and Catolicos who are questioning the church and the world about them?

The Mexican, says Paz, wears his face as a mask and believes "that opening oneself up is a weakness or a betrayal."

The Chicano activists are trying to rid themselves of their masks and to open themselves to themselves and to others. It is significant that in doing this they should pick as a means the Vietnam war and the Catholic Church.

That more than 3,000 people braved torrential rains last Saturday to participate in the Chicano Moratorium is important not because so many people showed a distaste for the war — Anglos have done this in a bigger way — but because it was Mexican-Americans who did it.

Mexican-Americans, who include a disproportionate number of Medal of Honor winners and who, like the blacks, are suffering a disproportionate number of deaths in Vietnam, had up to now fought our wars without question.

It was part of the "machismo" traditions. When called to war, Mexican-Americans showed everyone how "macho" or manly they were and never questioned the justification for the war.

Mexicans, says Paz, judge manliness according to their "invulnerability to enemy arms or the impacts of the outside world. Stoicism is the most exalted of (Mexicans') military and political attributes."

The Chicano Moratorium strove to end this stoicism, which is hardly a democratic attribute.

"We weren't shedding our machismo," said a young marcher. "We were proving our machismo by asking the establishment the tough question: 'Why are we dying overseas when the real struggle is at home?'"

When the Catolicos por La Raza demonstrated during a midnight Christmas mass last year, they were also breaking with tradition and asking tough questions at the cost of going through the ordeal of being tried for disturbing the peace.

A San Antonio teacher, testifying before the U.S. Commission on Civil Rights last year, said he has noted that the difference between Anglo and Mexican-American students is that when "some situation befalls the Mexican-Americans," the Mexican-American tends to leave things up to God while the Anglo tries to solve it on his own.

Catolicos por La Raza, who greatly embarrassed the traditional-minded Mexican-Americans by their questioning of the Catholic Church's relevance to present society, were breaking with this concept.

Chicanos and traditional-minded Mexican-Americans are suffering from the ever-present communications gap. Traditionalists, more concerned with the, to them, chafing terms like Chicano, are not really listening to what the activists are saying. And the activists forget that tradition is hard to kill.

Latin Newsmen, Police Chief Eat . . . but Fail to Meet

March 13, 1970

The Los Angeles Latin press corps took Police Chief Ed Davis out to dinner the other night. The enchiladas were good but the conversation left both sides hungry for understanding.

The dinner had been planned for some time but it was the chief's bad luck that it came on a night when Roosevelt High School was still much in the minds of the Latin newsmen.

It had been a week in which Spanish-speaking reporters had seen policemen drag teenage girls by the hair on the Roosevelt campus, a predominantly Mexican-American school. It had been a week in which a police captain tried to prevent a cameraman from a Spanish-language television station from filming a student disturbance by putting his hand in front of the camera's lens.

It had been a week in which a Mexican-American editor with 25 years of service in the Spanish-speaking community was denied entrance to the Roosevelt campus because he had a sheriffs press card and not a police press card. And it had been a week in which a policeman had yelled at the manager of a Spanish-language television station: "You ought to be ashamed of yourself for filming this!" (a student walkout).

The Latin newsmen who had invited Chief Davis to dinner were not Chicano underground press types. On the contrary, many were more businessmen than newsmen and far more conservative than the average Anglo newsman.

Yet, on that night the Latin newsmen, while waiting for the chief to arrive, talked about the growing disrespect between the police department and the Spanish-speaking community and voiced the opinion that they now understood [what is meant by] a "police riot."

It was the first time in memory that a Los Angeles police chief had publicly gotten together with a significant number of Spanish-speaking reporters and the newsmen were anxious to get to the guts of the agenda: finding ways to attain mutual respect between the Spanish-language press and the police department so that this respect can be reflected in the community.

It didn't go well.

The chief started by talking about a trip he made recently to Mexico and his great admiration for the country and its pyramids. After a while, the chairman interrupted apologetically and said, "Chief, we know all about Mexico and the pyramids. . . . Could we get on with the business at hand . . ."

Some of the newsmen insisted that the chief appoint a Spanish-speaking lieutenant for liaison between the Latin media and the police department. The chief explained patiently that this would be impossible because of budget problems but said he might assign a patrolman to the job.

One of the newsmen became indignant, as only touchy Latins can, and said that perhaps they would have to go to Washington or the Latin embassies to get what they needed.

The chief scored a point by saying that he ran the police department and not President Nixon or anyone else and informed the newsmen that the chief had just written the President telling him off. This would have been a pretty good lesson in democracy except that the chief chose to go further.

Telling the President off could not be done in Mexico, the chief told the Latin newsmen, because Mexico had a "Napoleonic" style of justice which to Americans smacked of "tyranny and dictatorship."

This went over like a dead pinata especially with the newsmen who work for Mexico City newspapers.

It was decided that another meeting be held between Latin newsmen and the chief to further explore their problems. Both sides left feeling frustrated — but not too unhappy over the possibility that a line of communication might be opening. After all, when you eat enchiladas together, it's a beginning.

Police-Community Rift

April 3, 1970

Los Angeles police sergeant Robert J. Thoms, formerly a "community relations" officer, has gone into the intelligence business and has testified before a U.S. Senate subcommittee about what he considers subversive and violent organizations.

As a community relations officer from March 26, 1967, to Feb. 11, 1968, Sgt. Thoms worked with many of the barrio and ghetto organizations which, if nothing else, understand the problems of people who do not relate to, much less participate in, the mainstream of American life.

Thoms gained the confidence of leaders in the barrios and ghettos who felt there was still hope for at least a working relationship between frustrated and disadvantaged communities and the equally frustrated but relatively powerful police force.

After working for a year in this sensitive area, Sgt. Thoms was transferred by the police department to intelligence work.

The next time the communities, which had known Sgt. Thoms as a community relations officer, heard from him was as an intelligence officer testifying before a U.S. Senate subcommittee investigating subversive and violent organizations.

Sgt. Thoms told the subcommittee chaired by Sen. Thomas J. Dodd that "the organizations in Los Angeles that are considered to be violent or subversive in nature are: Ron Karenga's US, the Black Congress, the Black Panther Party, the Friends of the Panthers, and the Brown Berets."

In the 59-page report, however, Sgt. Thoms also touches upon such diverse organizations as the Ford Foundation, the League of United Citizens to Help Addicts, the Episcopal Diocese of Los Angeles, the UCLA Industrial Relations Commission and the East Los Angeles Community Union.

Nowhere does Sgt. Thoms say that these organizations are subversive or violent but he leaves the clear impression that they are somehow un- savory. J. G. Sourwine, the subcommittee's chief counsel, asked Thoms, for example, why the sergeant had mentioned the East Los Angeles Community Union.

"Is the organization a violent one?" Sourwine asked.

"No, sir," answered Thoms.

"Perhaps I do not follow you," pressed Sourwine. "Why is it brought out here?"

To this Sgt. Thoms answered: "Just as an example of the umbrella organizations we deal with which will contain some good intentioned organizations to give it an air of respectability."

On page 22, Sgt. Thoms tells the subcommittee that "Next I would like to deal with the federal funding of various organizations in the Los Angeles area."

Sourwine: "Funding subversive and violent organizations?"

Thoms: "Yes, sir."

Sourwine: "Go ahead."

Thoms: "One program known as the educational opportunities pro- gram (EOP) for the California State College of Los Angeles, was funded in 1968 in the amount of $250,000 for 124 students."

After explaining that the money was used to give minority students "a monthly stipend for attending school and also used for books and a place to live," Sgt. Thoms said: "I can document that there are 43 stu- dents [of the 124 students receiving EOP funds, presumably] attending Cal State College at Los Angeles that belong to militant organizations in Los Angeles."

Perhaps the most revealing part of the Thoms testimony is when Chief Counsel Sourwine asks Thoms whether his information was gath- ered from a reliable source. Yes, answers Thoms, "the report was made public in May in Chicago."

Who put the report out? asks Sourwine. "I made the report to a convention of the International Security Conference."

Retorts Sourwine: "When I asked you if it came from a source you believed to be reliable I am not surprised you said, 'Yes.'"

Thoms' report should be read by all Americans concerned with the problem of the credibility gap.

Reason in Washington, Passion in Denver—What Will Work?

April 10, 1970

WASHINGTON — If Daniel Moynihan speaks of "benign neglect" for the black, what is in store for the Chicano?

This was in the minds of some of us who came here at the invitation of the Urban Coalition to discuss the image of the Spanish-speaking people in the mass media.

It was not long before the chilling truth overcame us. Image? Hell. Washington doesn't even know the Chicano exists, so how can we talk about image?

But we did. The 15 of us—Chicano newsmen, educators, consultants—went through the motions of telling the attentive Urban Coalition people how the news media and the advertising, television and motion picture industries hurt the sensibilities of Spanish-speaking people.

The Coalition set up a meeting for us with members of the Federal Communications Commission—including rebel commissioner Nicholas Johnson. During that meeting it suddenly dawned on me how quaint the Chicano group must seem to Washington bureaucrats.

I got the strong impression that the FCC is not really a regulatory agency in that it does not sit in Washington as a judge ready to correct, for instance, any inequities perpetrated on the Chicano by radio or television.

"The FCC is not only gutless in this respect, but also impotent when it tries to do something on its own," I was told by an FCC staffman.

The FCC, however, is responsive to community or political pressure, I was assured.

Power, Chicano. Power. That's what Washington understands.

This obvious conclusion is sometimes hard to come by for those of us who are conditioned to think that reason, information and patience will eventually triumph.

At least one of us, though, seemed to understand Washington instinctively better than most of us. He was a young Chicano from Texas who wore a bush jacket and a badge with Chicano Power printed on it.

After two days of deliberation and exchange of ideas in the plush Mayflower Hotel and in the ultramodern Urban Coalition building, the young Chicano concluded:

"About the only thing accomplished these two days was that the Xerox machine worked overtime."

He then took a plane to Denver to attend Corky Gonzales' Chicano Youth Liberation Conference.

In Denver, Gonzales, an ex-prize fighter and poet, told a crowd of 3,000 young Chicanos, like the ones who left Washington in disgust, that growing Chicano militancy "has turned a spark into fire." With clenched fists in the air, the young Chicanos screamed "Chicano power!" Then, without the help of Xerox machines, they started the job of uniting for "la causa."

In these days of "benign neglect," one wonders how much good such a meeting as the one we had with the Urban Coalition does. And come to think of it, what came out of the dozens of meetings and conferences we've attended throughout the years?

After two days in Washington, the melancholy thought arises that representatives of the Denver Chicanos would have more of an impact on Washington than our carefully prepared papers which probably moved no one except the Xerox machine.

Maligned Word: Mexican

April 17, 1970

Mexican. That good name has been vilified for so long that even in the Southwest, where Mexicans are as plentiful as Yankees in New England, the word is used cautiously.

Most Mexican-Americans have experienced the wary questions from an Anglo: "You're Spanish aren't you?" or "Are you Latin?" Rarely will the Anglo venture: "You're Mexican aren't you?"

The reason is that the word Mexican has been dragged through the mud of racism since the Anglos arrived in the Southwest. History tells us that when King Fisher, the famous Texas gunman, was asked how many notches he had on his gun, he answered: "Thirty-seven not counting Mexicans."

"Remember the Alamo!" is still used as an anti-Mexican insult where "Remember Pearl Harbor" has been forgotten.

Carey McWilliams in his enlightening "North from Mexico"* notes
that the word "greaser" was well-known in early California and that it
was defined as "Mexican: an opprobrious term." He also reports that
"greaser" is "California slang for a mixed race of Mexican and Indians."
"Greaser," McWilliams points out, is defined in the Century Dictio-
nary as "a native Mexican . . . originally applied contemptuously by the
Americans of the Southwestern United States to Mexicans."

All this, and more, has contributed to the psychological crippling of
the Mexican-American when it comes to the word Mexican. He is un-
consciously ashamed of it.

State Sen. Jose Bernal of Texas told the U.S. Commission on Civil
Rights last year that the "schools have not given us any reason to be
proud" of being Mexican. People running the schools "have tried to take
away our language," the senator continued, and so Mexican-American
children very early are embarrassed by the Spanish language and by being Mexican.

One of the reasons for this, Bernal told the commission, is that "it has
been inculcated" in the minds of grammar school children that the Mexican "is no good" by means of, for instance, overly and distortedly em-
phasizing the Battle of the Alamo and ignoring all contributions made
by Mexicans in the Southwest.

Unfortunately, California Superior Judge Gerald S. Chargin has
dragged the word Mexican to a new low. In sentencing a 17-year-old
Mexican-American boy for incest in San Jose last Sept. 2, Judge Chargin
looked down from the bench and told this American citizen that "we
ought to send you out of the country—send you back to Mexico . . .
You ought to commit suicide. That's what I think of people of this kind.
You are lower than animals and haven't the right to live in organized
society—just miserable, lousy, rotten people."

Is it any wonder, then, that the Mexican-American community is bitterly disappointed in that the California Commission on Judicial Qualifications recommended that the Supreme Court publicly censure Judge
Chargin instead of recommending that he be removed from the bench?

The commission, in making its recommendation, calls Chargin's re-

*Carey McWilliams was a journalist, writer, and editor who, beginning in the 1930s,
wrote exposés of the exploitation of immigrant workers in California agriculture, including
Mexicans. He became a defender of Mexican American civil rights. His 1948 book North
from Mexico: The Spanish-speaking People of the United States (New York: Greenwood Press,
1968) represented the first significant history of Mexicans in the United States. It was re-
discovered in the late 1960s during the period of the Chicano movement, and it influenced
the development of Chicano historiography.

marks "improper and inexcusable" and says, they "constituted conduct prejudicial to the administration of justice that brings the judicial office into disrepute."

The commission goes on to say, however, that "there is no evidence of bias or prejudice by (the judge) except for the incident of Sept. 2, 1969. There is evidence," concludes the commission, "that apart from this (the judge) has been a tolerant and compassionate judge with a background of understanding and interest in the problems of the underprivileged and ethnic minorities."

The Mexican-American community seems not to buy that. The general feeling seems to be that if Judge Harold Carswell* was denied a seat in the Supreme Court for, among other reasons, making a racist speech in his youth, Judge Chargin should be removed from the bench for making anti-Mexican remarks, on record, from the bench.

This, the community seems to feel, would help cleanse the much maligned word Mexican.

The 'Wetback' Problem Has More Than Just One Side

April 24, 1970

When *la migra* calls, the Mexican trembles.

La migra is Chicano slang for the U.S. Immigration Service which, with the Border Patrol, plays an important and sometimes terrifying role in the lives of thousands of Mexicans, Mexican-Americans and other Latins in the Southwest.

A recent crackdown by the immigration department against illegal entrants in the Los Angeles area has again dramatized the human tragedy which can occur when a poor country, Mexico, borders on a rich country, the United States.

The fact that at least one American citizen, a mentally retarded Mexican-American boy, was mistakenly deported in the immigration service dragnet indicates the vulnerability of the underprivileged Chicano to la migra's power.

Wetbacks and Chicanos look alike to the border patrolman.†

---

*Judge Harold Carswell, nominated in 1970 by President Richard Nixon to a seat on the Supreme Court, was rejected by the U.S. Senate.

† "Wetback" is a derogatory term for undocumented Mexican immigrants. In the 1950s and early 1960s, the term was widely used even by some Mexican Americans, including Salazar, although not necessarily in a derogatory fashion.

The problem of illegal entrants to the United States can be looked at very coldly. It is illegal to enter the United States without the proper papers, so, from time to time, these people must be rounded up and deported.

A closer look at why Los Angeles has become the wetback capital of the world, however, shows why it's unfair to blame only the illegal entrant for the breakdown of the law.

Why is it that it is estimated that at certain times of the year there are at least 80,000 wetbacks working in California? Because employers are willing to hire them.

A wetback lives in constant fear. Fear that he will be discovered. Fear of what might happen to him once la migra finds him. Fear that he will not be paid before being deported.

The wetback employers know no such fear. There is no law against hiring wetbacks. There is only a law against being a wetback.

A sweat shop employer of low-paid wetbacks has only one small worry—the temporary stoppage of production between the time his wetbacks are discovered in his plant and the time the next wave of wetbacks arrives.

When the wetback is caught he is jailed and deported. Nothing, however, happens to the employer. As a matter of fact, the employer can gain from the wetback raid on his plant because he can easily get away without paying the wetbacks' salaries due at the time of the arrests.

State Sen. Lewis Sherman, a Republican from Alameda County, would like to change this. He feels the employer should bear some of the responsibility for the wetback situation. He has introduced a bill (S.B. 1091) which would make it a misdemeanor to knowingly hire wetbacks. Under the proposed law, the employer could be fined as much as $500 for each wetback he hires. Sen. Sherman contends that with "reasonable care" employers could detect wetbacks from legal workers.

Most people concerned with the problem feel this would help immensely.

But it would probably not solve the basic reason for the wetback problem: poor Mexicans willing to take a chance at arrest for what they think will be a good job and the employers willing to take a chance at getting caught because they want cheap labor.

Bert Corona, a leader in the Mexican-American Political Assn., claims that the immigration service, in its dragnets, is "conducting a reign of terror and exploitation against the Mexican people" and that among the 1,600 recently deported there were persons born in the United States who did not have their papers with them, Mexicans with valid tourist visas, persons separated from their families.

The policeman, this time the immigration and border patrol man, is invariably accused of "brutality" when enforcing the law and undoubtedly they have made mistakes.

But anyone who has seen the fetid shacks in which potential wetbacks live on the Mexican side of the border can better understand why these people become wetbacks. In comparison, the detention center for wetbacks in El Centro — called a "concentration camp" by Chicano activists — looks like a luxury hotel.

The point is that Mexico has a grave poverty problem which is growing alarmingly. Mexico, with its limited resources, has grown from a nation of 15 million in 1910 to an estimated 44 million in 1966. In another 10 years some Mexican demographers estimate an increase to 61 million people and by 1980, to 72 million. Many, many of these will be potential wetbacks.

Though Sen. Sherman's proposed bill should help alleviate the wetback problem, it is obvious that the United States and Mexico must talk and plan on the highest level to forestall an even more serious wetback explosion in the future.

Consecration of Bishop Flores Shows the Strength of an Idea

May 8, 1970

The consecration of Patricio Flores, a former Texas migrant farm worker, as a bishop of the Catholic Church indicated once more the church's growing sensitivity to the Chicano community.

The mass of consecration held Tuesday in San Antonio on the Mexican holiday Cinco de Mayo was unusual in many ways. The ceremony was conducted in English, Spanish and Latin and televised in Los Angeles, San Antonio and Mexico City.

Instead of holding the rite in an august cathedral, it was held in an informal convention center to accommodate large numbers of *la raza* who applauded enthusiastically — unheard of in such ceremonies.

The music came not from a serious choir or majestic organ but from a joyful *mariachi* band.

Among the special guests of the 41-year-old cleric, who became the first Mexican-American to be raised to the hierarchy of the church, were Cesar Chavez, Bishop Sergio Mendez Arceo of Cuernavaca, Mexico, and Jose Angel Gutierrez, leader of the activist Chicano organization MAYO.*

The guest list alone showed how involved Bishop Flores is in the problems of the Mexican-American, the farm worker, the young.

Chavez, who read one of the epistles at the mass of consecration, had already been recognized by the church as an important leader when the church's Bishops Committee announced in Los Angeles April 1 that the "breakthrough" agreement between Chavez' grape strikers and the California grape growers had been reached with the help of the Catholic Church.

It was a bitter defeat for those who claimed Chavez was not the true leader of the grape strikers. The defeat for growers wanting to discredit Chavez became more poignant when Archbishop Timothy Manning of Los Angeles told a press conference that he hoped the agreement between Chavez and a small number of growers "will be but the beginning of a chain of such contracts."

The fact that Bishop Mendez Arceo of Cuernavaca was present at the consecration of Bishop Flores publicly revealed the new bishop's affinity to the church's liberal wing. Bishop Mendez Arceo, a maverick in the Mexican conservative hierarchy, has many times proclaimed himself a staunch *Zapatista*. Emiliano Zapata, a Mexican revolutionary and a land reformer, is a hero of the Chicano movement.†

Bishop Mendez in 1968 was the only Mexican bishop who refused to sign a declaration in support of the Pope's new ban on artificial contraception and was the only member of the Mexican hierarchy to condemn the Mexican government's repressive acts against students in the riots at the University of Mexico.

The invitation of Gutierrez, MAYO leader, who also read an epistle at the Flores consecration, probably shocked the Texas establishment because Gutierrez is known as one of the most militant Chicano youth

---

*The Mexican American Youth Organization (MAYO) was founded in 1967 by José Angel Gutiérrez and other Mexican American college students in San Antonio. It concentrated on civil rights and political activity. In the period 1967–1969, it played a leading role in various school walkouts. MAYO took the initiative in the formation of La Raza Unida party in Texas, an independent Chicano political party that functioned in the Southwest during the late 1960s and early 1970s.

† Emiliano Zapata (1879–1919) was one of the leading figures of the Mexican Revolution of 1910. Fighting in his home state of Morelos, Zapata stressed agrarian reform for *campesinos* (peasants). Perceived as too radical for the more moderate forces who gained control of the revolution, Zapata was assassinated in 1919. In search of historical role models of rebellion against oppression, the Chicano movement of the 1960s and 1970s appropriated the figure of Zapata as an "authentic" Chicano hero.

leaders in the Southwest. Unlike Chavez, who is softspoken and dislikes Chicano militant talk, Gutierrez is a forceful speaker on what he considers "Anglo crimes" ranging from the Vietnam war and the draft to bad Mexican-American education and the "suppression" of Mexican culture in the United States.

Bishop Flores, who with his parents and eight brothers and sisters migrated from farm job to farm job in his youth, believes communication between the church and the so-called militants must remain open.

Bishop Flores' consecration was a remarkable spectacle: guitar-playing *mariachis* mingling with miter-wearing bishops and *barrio* Chicanos mixing it up with plume-hatted and white-tie-and-tailed Knights of Columbus.

It gave one hope that an ideal, like the Catholic Church, can still bring people together.

Mexican-Americans Come Out 2nd Best in High School Course

May 15, 1970

"The young Mexican-American husband must show his male acquaintances that he has more sexual energy than his wife can accommodate. To prove his prowess, he often continues the sexual hunt of his premarital days. He may demonstrate his physical and financial resources by visiting (a house of prostitution) with drinking companions after an evening in a tavern. The most convincing way of proving *machismo* and financial ability is to keep a mistress in a second household known as a *casa chica*."

A quote from a racist or pornographic tract? No, it's from a paper until recently used in a Pomona high school sophomore class to teach Mexican-American culture.

Before the instructional material was ordered removed by the board of education, Victor Sherreitt, principal of Ganesha High School, tried to defend the paper in this manner:

"At the beginning of each semester, every teacher looks across his class at inquiring students. In their eyes you see one question formed — 'Are you, Mr. Teacher, a phony? Are you going to tell it the way it is?'"

"The course, cultural anthropology, offered in the 10th grade, is a study of man and his society. In an attempt to have students gain a broader knowledge of the diverse nature of American society, this essay was incorporated into the unit on family and society."

One wonders if Sherreitt would agree, then, that high school sophomores learning about Anglo culture should be taught about Anglo martini-guzzling, pill-popping, wife-swapping suburbanites?

Sherreitt and the social science teachers who incorporated the paper in the course do not seem to realize that the material contains blatant stereotyping.

One of the reasons Mexican-Americans object to the Frito Bandido television commercial is that it stereotypes Mexican-Americans as ridiculous, sleazy bandit types. This can badly damage the self-image of young, impressionable Mexican-American minds and feed prejudice to young, impressionable Anglo minds.

The Ganesha High School paper stereotypes the Mexican-Americans in many ways but tends to emphasize sexual stereotyping. In a section called Marital Conflict, the paper says in part:

"Sexual promiscuity on the part of the wife is a heinous crime. So fragile is a woman's purity, according to Mexican-American belief, that one sexual indiscretion inevitably leads to a life of complete sexual abandon. No Mexican-American man would remain with a promiscuous wife unless he is already so abused that nothing matters. . . ."

Then the paper gives an example. Reynaldo's "excessive drinking interferes with the employment he needs to provide money for liquor. Quenching his thirst is more important to him than sex or respectability so he allows his wife, Flora, to have a generous Anglo lover. Flora maintains this illicit relationship partly to punish Reynaldo for his failings. Her shame about her promiscuity leads her to give her husband most of the money she receives from her lover. . . ."

Though the paper is no longer used in the course on Mexican-American culture, its very existence and Principal Sherreitt's written defense of it have left a deep wound in Pomona's Mexican-American community.

Sherreitt stoutly defends his social science department and says the controversial paper was "misinterpreted or taken out of context."

Mrs. Ascension Garcia, a school employee who prompted the protest to the board of education, thinks the paper has polarized Pomona's minority population.

"Suddenly we realized that though Mexican-Americans and Negroes comprise 40% of the 90,000 Pomona population there is not one Mexican-American or Negro school principal or even vice principal," says Mrs. Garcia.

"So we Mexican-Americans and Negroes have decided to form a coalition to fight the school district's lack of sensitivity."

Chicano's Long Love Affair with Democratic Party Ends

May 29, 1970

Covering Mexican-American candidates in Tuesday's primary election, a reporter can get the impression that they are more interested in gaining independence from the Democratic Party than they are in getting elected.

The Chicano candidate looks back in bitterness at the Democratic Party and casts a cynically hopeful eye at the Republican Party.

With the assassination of Bobby Kennedy, who publicly thanked the Chicano vote for its significant help in winning the California primary, the Mexican-American politician ended his long love affair with the Democratic Party.

"Actually," says a Chicano party worker, "we discovered that it wasn't a love affair at all but really a kept woman situation. The party took us for granted and gave little in return."

This bitterness stems from the reapportionment of California's political districts in 1962 by a Democratic Assembly under Jess Unruh.*

"Those were hopeful days for the Chicano community," recalls Bert Corona, a longtime Mexican-American activist. "We thought we could get at least four 'safe' Chicano districts. After all, the reapportionment committee was made up of so-called liberal members and who had been more loyal to the party than the Mexican-Americans."

"Instead, we got nothing."

"Why do you think Ed Roybal can not afford to be a truly Chicano congressman?" asks Enrique (Hank) Lopez, another longtime Mexican-American activist. "Because the district he ended up with has more blacks and Anglos than Chicanos."

Lopez, who ran for California secretary of state as the Democratic candidate 12 years ago, recalls his campaign with anger.

"The party gave me a piddling $1,500 to run a difficult statewide campaign and Pat Brown refused to appear on the same platform with me," says Lopez. "Hell, the party wouldn't even let me use a float in a parade."

Lopez, who is now a New York attorney and author but is presently teaching a Chicano course at UC Riverside, feels strongly that one of the reasons blacks have been more successful politically than Chicanos is that they don't allow either party to take them for granted.

---

*Jess Unruh was Speaker of the House in a Democrat-controlled assembly in the California State Legislature during the 1960s and 1970s.

"Blacks have learned to work within both parties and have not been blinded by unrealistic party loyalty as have Chicanos," says Lopez.

Chicano politicians think that as a result of the treatment they have received from the Democratic Party, Mexican-Americans are becoming politically sophisticated enough to ignore their differences for the sake of eventually electing Chicano candidates.

The trend in the *barrios* right now is Chicanos first, party second. And the emphasis is on organization more than election.

Herman Sillas, who is running for state controller, is the only Mexican-American candidate officially endorsed by such Democratic bigwigs as Jess Unruh and Sen. Alan Cranston as well as the Mexican-American Unity Congress and the Mexican-American Political Assn.

The two Chicano organizations, however, have refused to endorse Unruh in the primary as they would have automatically in the past. Instead, they are supporting Richard Romo, a Peace and Freedom party candidate for governor, if for nothing else because he's a Chicano.

At the Mexican-American Political Assn. endorsing convention in Fresno, MAPA president Abe Tapia, a candidate for the 45th assembly district, urged Chicanos not to support "traditional liberal Anglo candidates, merely because they are 'friends,' unless they declare themselves as being in full support of all Mexican-American candidates as well as in full support of the farm workers and the grape boycott."

In the barrios at least, Tapia, who has been endorsed by Cesar Chavez, seems to be getting the message through.

As for the Republicans, Chicano politicians feel Mexican-Americans will fare better when a presumed Republican-dominated Assembly will reapportion political districts in 1972.

"In wanting to strengthen their own districts, the Republicans will tend to isolate the Chicano districts the Democrats should have given us and never did," say MAPA strategists.

Narrowly a Candidate Lost

June 2, 1970

When you're as politically impotent as are Mexican-Americans, the extent of the latest election defeat takes on an exaggerated significance.

With characteristic resignation, the Chicano candidate on election night watches for future trends more than immediate victories.

Perhaps the "best defeat" for the Chicano in Tuesday's election was that of Abe Tapia, candidate in the 45th Assembly District. Looking over the election returns, Tapia was realistically jubilant.

"I got 29% of the vote and the district is about 30% Chicano," Tapia said. "I went out for the Chicano vote and that is what I got. Why should I complain?"

President of the Mexican-American Political Assn., Tapia conducted a strictly Chicano campaign: no Anglo advisers, no emphasis on party labels, no compromises.

The advice he did take was from Cesar Chavez who told him to organize the barrios and not to worry about immediate results. Tapia lost the election but won the Chicanos. He's not too sure what it all means right now but he smiles happily when he talks about all those Chicanos who went to the polls for the first time in their lives.

Another Chicano who had an impressive loss was Oscar Z. Acosta, a militant attorney who received more than 100,000 votes for sheriff. During the campaign, he defended establishment-shaking Catolicos por La Raza,* spent a couple of days in jail for contempt of court and vowed if elected to do away with the sheriff's department as it is now constituted.

Acosta, easily recognized in court by his loud ties and flowered attache case with a Chicano Power sticker, didn't come close to Sheriff Pitchess' 1,300,000 votes but did beat Everett Holladay, Monterey Park chief of police.

A poet of sorts, Acosta complains about a society which prefers "the soft lights to the glare of nakedness" and castigates "people too weak in character to raise the necessary issues."

Looking back at his campaign, which was confined mostly to self-dramatization, Acosta is most proud of running as a Chicano who "stuck to my guns and never copped out to a thing."

Why he got 100,000 votes for sheriff will have to be analyzed by political pundits. But in the Chicano community Acosta's impressive loss was an enigmatic ray of sunshine.

Then there were the Mexican-American candidates who tried to win by more conventional means. The best known, of course, was Dr. Julian Nava who ran for the "non-partisan" office of superintendent of public instruction.†

---

*Catolicos por La Raza was organized in 1969 in Los Angeles by some Chicano Catholics who believed that the Catholic church in Los Angeles was not sensitive to the conditions of Chicanos.

†Julian Nava was elected to the Los Angeles School Board in 1967. He was the first Mexican American to serve on the school board since the nineteenth century. In 1980, Nava was appointed U.S. Ambassador to Mexico. See García, *Memories of Chicano History,* 229–231.

He got 300,000 votes to Max Rafferty's 2 million votes and Wilson Riles' one million plus votes. The fact that Nava, a Mexican-American, and Riles, a Negro, ran against each other strained black-brown relationships — unavoidable in the minorities' desperate scramble for meaningful participation in our society.

To the Chicano, despite many valid arguments to the contrary, Riles' victory means simply that blacks receive more support and understanding by California in general than do Chicanos.

Jess Unruh tried to salve this situation by publicly supporting a Mexican-American for controller, Herman Sillas, but apparently it was too late. Sillas lost to fellow Democrat Ronald Cameron and Chicanos, whether fairly or not, blame the Democratic Party. The party, they complain, never goes all out for a Chicano candidate.

The Chicano candidate who may have made his last "impressive loss" and will be missed is Richard Calderon who lost the nomination in the 29th Congressional District to State Sen. George E. Danielson by about 2,000 votes.

This is Calderon's fourth defeat in politics, the last two by very small margins.

Commenting on Tuesday's results, Rep. Ed Roybal, the only Mexican-American California congressman, lamented that Calderon could have won if he had gotten the votes another Mexican-American, Isaac Ruiz Jr., received in the race. Calderon lost by 2,000 votes and Ruiz received 2,000 votes.

Ah, Chicanos.

Don't Make the 'Bato Loco' Go the Way of the Zoot Suiter

June 19, 1970

A *bato loco* is a zoot suiter with a social conscience.

He may be an ex-con, a marijuana smoker and dangerously defiant. But the difference between the zoot suiter or *pachuco* of the early 40s and a present bato loco, literally a crazy guy, is that the bato loco is experiencing a social revolution and so is learning and liking political power.

The difference is so important that unless we understand it we can contribute toward reverting the bato loco to an anarchistic zoot suiter.

An anarchistic zoot suiter, as we learned just before World War II, can be easily driven to violence. A bato loco, though impossible to convert into an Eagle Scout, can be dealt with on a political basis.

Because of the civil rights revolution, the so-called Establishment had deemed it necessary to accept innovations ranging from Head Start to Chicano Studies.

A countering "silent majority" revolution, however, is trying to reverse this acceptance and the trend today is to junk social innovations because, it is felt, they only "pamper" militants.

What we must realize is that it is easier to open a Pandora's box than to close it.

The economy slowdown, the lingering Vietnam War and surging "hard hat" militancy are beginning to strip the bato loco of his newly gained social conscience.

"The *gabacho* (white man) never really changes," a bato loco said recently. "He gives you an inch and takes away a yard."

It is easy to understand the silent majority's frustration with high taxes, disrespectful militancy and seemingly unending social innovations. But to the bato loco in the barrio this frustration is a luxury which he cannot afford and does not understand.

All the bato loco knows is that things were looking up for a while and that unlike his zoot-suiter predecessor he could get involved in such projects as the Neighborhood Adult Participation Project. Now he knows the heat is on and that such projects are being condemned by political and law-and-order leaders as subversive and money-wasting.

Stripped of his potential political power — and that, after all is what barrio and ghetto social innovations produce — the bato loco has no way to go but to the dangerous shell of an anarchistic zoot suiter.

Recently, a front-page story appeared, in of all places, the *Wall Street Journal,* which warns of possible violence in the Southwest's Chicano barrios.

According to the newspaper, Jose Angel Gutierrez, a Texas Chicano activist who holds a master's degree in political science, said that "It's too late for the gringo to make amends. Violence has got to come."

This may sound scandalously alarming but the mood in the barrios seems to back it up.

This mood is not being helped by our political and law-and-order leaders who are trying to discredit militants in the barrios as subversive or criminal.

In the traditionally quiet town of Pomona, for instance, a crowd of Mexican-American parents, not known for their civic participation, recently applauded Brown Beret speakers.

The importance of this is that a year ago it would be impossible to find Mexican-American parents hob-nobbing with Brown Berets. Police chiefs, mayors and other leaders must learn that they can no longer discredit a movement by just pointing out that the Brown Berets, or any other militant group, are involved.

In other words, whether we like it or not, Brown Berets are gaining the respect of barrio people at the expense of traditional mores.

But perhaps more importantly, the Mexican-American establishment is finding it more difficult every day to communicate with barrio Chicanos.

Before we scrap all the social innovations which gave the bato loco hope we should probe the probable consequences.

Mexican-American School Walkout Focused on Problem

June 26, 1970

During the massive East Los Angeles high school walkouts in 1968, board of education member Dr. Julian Nava turned to their school superintendent Jack Crowther and said, "Jack, this is BC and AD. The schools will not be the same again."

"Yes," said Crowther, "I know."

Actually, as Nava and Crowther must have suspected, more than the schools were changing. What was happening was that a significant portion of the Mexican-American community, in supporting the walkouts and their symbolic leader, teacher Sal Castro, was asserting itself.

Few will deny that the walkouts marked a new direction for the traditionally apathetic Mexican-American community. Behind the school disorders, an unusual unity was forming which since then has solidified.

The recent decision by Dist. Atty. Evelle J. Younger to refile felony complaints in the walkout and Biltmore disturbance cases necessitates focusing some issues which could be lost in the rhetoric-filled courtroom drama sure to follow.

First, there seems to be a tendency to refer to the incidents as the "Brown Beret cases" — especially by a local wire service which called them that in its dispatches last Monday and Tuesday. Much more than the activities of a small militant group are at stake.

Brown Berets were involved in the walkouts and in the disturbances and fires at the Biltmore during a speech by Gov. Reagan April 24, 1969. But it is important to know, not from a legal but from an overall point of view, that the cases stem from a genuine concern over the quality of education Mexican-Americans are receiving.

Sal Castro, who was indicted by the grand jury on felony conspiracy charges in the school walkout case, has repeatedly been defended, putting aside the indictment, which is a legal matter, by many Mexican-American organizations and such public figures as Dr. Nava, Congressman Ed Roybal and George Brown and Dr. Miguel Montes, former member of the state board of education.

Nava went so far as to tell a news conference July 31, 1969, that Castro "has been singled out for harassment and persecution" for his "telling criticism and disclosures of the ineffectiveness of Los Angeles schools."

Castro, by the way, was called a Brown Beret by a local newspaper (not *The Times*) and the controversial teacher carries a printed retraction by the paper.

In the Biltmore case, fires allegedly set by Brown Beret types beclouded the fact that many of those arrested, since exonerated of any crime, merely had wanted to tell Gov. Reagan, if somewhat impolitely, what they thought of our schools.

The very reason why the district attorney decided to refile charges against Castro and 12 others involved in the walkouts and against five persons in the Biltmore case opens important questions.

For some time now the cases have been bogged down in appellate court where the defendants contended that the grand jury indictments were illegal because persons with Spanish surnames are systematically excluded from Los Angeles County grand juries.

Dep. Dist. Atty. Richard Hecht told this column that a decision by the appellate court did not seem forthcoming and that in the interest of a speedy trial for the defendants, the district attorney's office had decided to ask that the present cases on appeal be dismissed. This way, he continued, new charges would be processed by way of preliminary hearings, rather than the grand jury.

Predictably, Castro's attorney, Herman Sillas, takes issue with the district attorney. He says the new move will deny an opportunity to the Mexican-American community to hear what an appellate court has to say about the composition of the grand jury.

Retorts Hecht: "We're as anxious as anyone else to learn whether our grand juries are illegally constituted — which we do not think so — but a ruling from the appellate court does not seem to be in sight."

Hecht also pointed out that there is a Sirhan Sirhan appeal in the State Supreme Court involving his claim that Los Angeles grand juries are not representative and that a ruling in that case could clear the air on the matter.*

---

*Sirhan Sirhan was convicted of murdering Senator Robert Kennedy on the evening of Kennedy's victory in the 1968 California Democratic presidential primary.

The fact remains, however, that according to the U.S. Commission on Civil Rights, in Los Angeles County, with almost 500,000 eligible Spanish surname residents, only four served as grand jurors during a 12-year period studied.

Sillas also wonders why if Castro is being charged with felonious conspiracy in the school walkouts, no teacher was so charged during the recent teacher's strike.

Hecht answers that in the first place there is some evidence of violence in the East Los Angeles walkouts — which is denied by the participants — and that besides, the teachers' strike involved a union. "Union activities have a greater degree of protection under the First Amendment than do other activities," Hecht said.

The point is that whatever one may think of the merits of either side in these cases, grassroot movements such as the school walkouts bring out these important overall issues. And that is what democracy is about.

Why Does Standard July Fourth Oratory Bug Most Chicanos?

July 10, 1970

A small group of Chicanos sat before a TV the Fourth of July to watch Honor America Day for the explicit reason of trying to determine why such events bug them.

How could a show honoring the Flag, God and country offend any American? The Chicanos knew they had tackled a tough one and that any answer to the nagging question could be easily misinterpreted.

But being that they were merely indulging in mental and emotional calisthenics they tackled the job with alacrity.

The trouble with such patriotic bashes as Honor America Day, the Chicanos decided, is that they tend to dehumanize the Flag, monopolize God and abuse the word America.

For too long the American Flag, the Chicanos agreed, has been the symbol of those who insist that property rights are more important than human rights.

Fourth of July oratory, the Chicanos noted, tends to paint God as a super American who has blessed this country with its great wealth and power because right thinking people — like those who attend Honor America Day celebrations and wave the Flag vigorously — run the place.

But the thing that bugged the Chicanos the most was that the United States is called America, as if that name belonged exclusively to Anglo United States.

All this spelled one thing to the Chicanos: our system insists on Anglicization.

Most Anglos, the Chicanos decided, are unconscious of this and so cannot comprehend why Honor America Day could offend any "good American."

After watching Honor America Day and making their comments the small group of Chicanos unwound and had a good Fourth of July, just like many other Americans.

The thing to remember, however, is that this small group of Chicanos voiced the thinking of a significant part of the Chicano movement. Chicanos are resisting Anglicization.

UCLA's Mexican-American Cultural Center has just released the first issue of a "Chicano Journal of the Social Sciences and the Arts." The journal is called Aztlan for the Mexican Indian word which describes the Southwestern part of this continent which includes the five U.S. Southwestern states and Northern Mexico.

Chicanos explain that they are indigenous to Aztlan and do not relate, at least intellectually and emotionally, to the Anglo United States.

The journal, written by Chicano university scholars, starts off with the "Spiritual Plan of Aztlan" which was adopted by the Chicano Youth Liberation Conference held in Denver in March, 1969.

The wording of the "plan" may shed some light for those wishing to understand the Chicano movement:

"In the spirit of a new people that is conscious not only of its proud historical heritage, but also of the brutal 'gringo' invasion of our territories, we, the Chicano inhabitants and civilizers of the northern land of Aztlan, from whence came our forefathers, reclaiming the land of their birth and consecrating the determination of our people of the sun, declare that the call of our blood is our power, our responsibility, and our inevitable destiny."

"We are free and sovereign to determine these tasks which are justly called for by our house, our land, the sweat of our brows and by our hearts, Aztlan belongs to those that plant the seeds, water the fields, and gather the crops, and not to the foreign Europeans. We do not recognize capricious frontiers on the bronze continent."

"Brotherhood unites us, and love for our brothers makes us a people whose time has come and who struggles against the foreigner 'gabacho' (white) who exploits our riches and destroys our culture. With our heart in our hands and our hands in the soil, we declare the independence of our mestizo nation. We are a bronze people with a bronze culture. Before the world, before all of North America, before all our brothers in the bronze continent, we are a nation, we are a union of free pueblos, we are Aztlan."

Whether we like it or not Fourth of July Americanism is in disrepute among minorities because they can't seem to relate to it.

Singer Joan Baez, who is part Chicana, recently said that the defense of country, as used in Fourth of July oratory, "has absolutely nothing to do with the defense of people." She continued:

"Once we get rid of the obsession with defending one's country, we will be defending life. . . . That's why I hate flags. I despise any flag, not just the American Flag. It's a symbol of a piece of land that's considered more important than the human lives on it. . . ."

Whether we agree or not, it behooves us to revamp our Fourth of July oratory to relate to people instead of to fixed ideas that apparently are not working.

The Mexican-Americans NEDA Much Better School System

August 28, 1970

A week ago today Vice President Agnew stood in a sea of television lights at the Century Plaza Hotel to announce the formation of a new national organization to promote business development among the nation's 10 million Spanish-speaking citizens.

Agnew said the undertaking would help ensure that "Americans of Hispanic descent get a fair chance at the starting line."

By the end of the day, thanks to the great coverage the Vice President gets from the news media, the whole nation knew of the formation of the National Economic Development Assn. or NEDA.

In the barrios Chicanos immediately started calling NEDA NADA, which in Spanish spells "nothing."

Why this rude put-down about an organization which undoubtedly will help some worthy, energetic Spanish-speaking entrepreneurs?

The bitterness stems from the distortion of priorities in this country.

Just two days before Agnew made his announcement, Sen. Mike Mansfield complained that too much attention was being given to the ABMs and the SSTs* and not enough to the ABCs.

NEDA, started with a grant from the Small Business Administration, will initiate business development for the Spanish-speaking through

* Acronyms for nuclear missiles.

public and private sources, it was announced. Fine. Great. Long overdue.

But is it accurate for the Vice President to say that NEDA will ensure that "Americans of Hispanic descent get a fair chance at the starting line"?

NEDA, as good a concept as it is, will invariably help only those who have already made it — those who are in business or ready to go into business. This is hardly the "starting line" for the Mexican-American in this country.

The following has been said and written many times but it has yet to effectively penetrate the minds of our national leaders: The Mexican-American has the lowest educational level, below either black or Anglo; the highest dropout rate; and the highest illiteracy rate.

Yet, bilingual education was one of the items President Nixon vetoed in the educational bill. The veto was overridden but the veto indicates a strange definition the Administration has about where the "starting line" is.

Martin G. Castillo, chairman of the Nixon Administration's Cabinet Committee on Opportunity for the Spanish Speaking, said during the NEDA press conference that the Vice President had recently donated $10,000 to the Salesian Boys Club from proceeds of the sale of Spiro Agnew watches.

Castillo complained that this gesture typifying the "other side of the Vice President" got little mention in the news media.

That may be. But something besides the Vice President's Spiro Agnew watch gesture was being ignored by the news media.

On the same day that Agnew was getting nationwide publicity over the formation of NEDA, the U.S. Senate's Select Committee on Equal Educational Opportunity was winding up a two-day hearing on minority educational problems. The Vice President and NEDA got the lion's share of the publicity.

Complained Sen. Walter Mondale, chairman of the committee: "We found that the best way to get television cameras out of this room and reporters to leave is to hold a hearing on Mexican-American education. There doesn't seem to be any interest. Yet this is the second largest minority in America."

Mario Obledo, director of the Mexican-American Legal Defense and Educational Fund, told the senators that it was a "tragedy on the part" of federal and state government to ignore the educational problems of Mexican-Americans.

"How do you bring this to the attention of the American public?" asked Obledo. "Does it require some overt act of violence to bring it forth, or can it be handled in a manner that is conducive with the American way of life?"

Father Henry J. Casso, also of the Mexican-American Defense Fund, asked Sen. Mondale: "How long would you and I continue to do business with a lawyer who lost eight out of 10 cases; a doctor who lost eight of every 10 of his patients? Being a religionist, what would my bishop do if I lost eight of 10 parishioners?"

"Yet, the institutions, including government, have remained mute to see eight out of every 10 Mexican-American children drop out, kicked out and pushed out of the educational institutions of this country. No one has asked an accounting for the vast sums of public money that have been wasted. But the young are demanding an accounting and I stand with them."

Dr. Hector Garcia, a Texas physician and former member of the U.S. Commission on Civil Rights who was dumped from the commission by the Nixon Administration, testified that 80% of Mexican-American students in Texas never get past the sixth grade.*

". . . the system has not worked for us," Dr. Garcia said. "I am here as a capitalist. I am one of the few Mexicano capitalists. They say, 'Dr. Garcia, why do you criticize?' I say, I only criticize because I want more Mexicano capitalists, educated, in college . . ."

NEDA, then, will mean little until the government is serious about creating more Chicano capitalists — through good schools.

---

*Dr. Hector García founded the American G.I. Forum in 1949. The Forum, composed of World War II Mexican American veterans, has been an educational and civil rights advocacy organization.

Ruben Salazar was killed
by Los Angeles County sheriffs
after the disruption of the Chicano Moratorium
on August 29, 1970.

Index

Compositor: G&S Typesetters, Inc.
Text: 10/13 Galliard
Display: Gill Sans Book
Printer: BookCrafters, Inc.
Binder: BookCrafters, Inc.